A CENTURY-LONG JOURNEY TO THE DAY OF REDEMPTION

The 2016 World Baseball Champion Chicago Cubs

Kent Kloepping
and
Gene Shippy

Dusty Lane Memories   Tucson, Arizona

Copyright 2017 by Kent Kloepping and Gene Shippy

All rights reserved. No part of this book may be reproduced or transmitted in any form or by any means, electronic or mechanical, including photocopying, recording, or by any information storage and retrieval system, without permission in writing from the author.

Contact the publisher at:
Kent B. Kloepping
7660 E. Adams Dr.
Tucson, AZ 85715
phone: 520-885-7253
E-mail: kuntakenty@aol.com

This edition was prepared for publication by
Ghost River Images
5350 East Fourth Street
Tucson, Arizona 85711
www.ghostriverimages.com

Cover photos are from Wikimedia Commons
Front cover photo
File:The Cubs celebrate after winning the 2016 World Series. (30658637601) (2).jpg
Arturo Pardavila III from Hoboken, NJ, USA
Back cover photo
File: 1908 Chicago Cubs.JPG
George R Lawrence

ISBN 978-0-692-85903-2

Library of Congress Control Number: 2017904037

Printed in the United States of America
April 2017

Contents

To the Reader 5
Dedication 6
Introduction 7
Prologue – Summer – 2016 9
The 2016 Season – Games 1–179 15
Epilogue 297
A Final Thought 299
Baseball Wisdom – Contributors – 300

To the Reader

I am not a best-selling author, nor do I ever expect to receive a Pulitzer Prize. In fact I really don't want a Pulitzer Prize. Given the opening sentence above, I wanted to alert the reader that what follows; the text, the grammar, punctuation, sentence structure the proofreading, and the final product are solely my responsibility. This note to the reader is not intended to make excuses for any of the shortcomings of this effort as it is what I have to offer. As an unknown author of modest writing skills (if that) I do not have the luxury of a cadre of support personnel like editors, grammarians, proofreaders or even a ghost writer to "clean up" after me.

So if you find mistakes in punctuation, sentence structure, spelling, or obscure things like dangling participles (whatever they are) just take a deep breath, but don't tell me. Ha! If the mistakes offend you, you have my permission to change them in the book you have. However, if they are really very egregious I suggest you may want to just burn that page!

As Benny Hill, the rascally British comedian used to whimper when one of his skits went awry, "it's not my fault, it's not my fault." I can't escape responsibility because I did do it! I'm at peace or at least satisfied with this literary (maybe just a journal) endeavor. You also will be happy if you accept the philosophy of my friend named Howie, who says simply, but eloquently "it is what it is."

KBK

Dedication

To all the truly faithful Chicago Cubs fans,
Present and past, and all those who still love
America's great national pastime.

Introduction

Tinkers, to Evers, to Chance, a link to the past, oh so sublime.
For faithful Cub fans it rekindles memories of a golden time.
And now, exuberant youth are dancing and shouting with glee, while others quite old just smiled and simply cried.
For this day it was written in the book of life for all to see, that the curse of the billy goat had finally died
No longer are we followers feeling aghast,
We can now forget that hurtful past.
Thanks to the baseball gods who have vanquished the book
Of defeat and gloom; its pages are torn, ravaged and curled.
For the Chicago Cubs are the 2016 champions of the baseball world.

Kent Kloepping

Prologue
Summer – 2016

I know this guy who lives in Illinois. We've been friends since 1954, our first year in high school. Since we are both still alive that means our friendship has spanned 63 years.

It's relatively easy to lose track of classmates from years ago, but in the case of Gene, of whom I just alluded to, I hear from the guy all the time; sometimes by e-mail but also by telephone. In fact at this writing, May 8, 2016, I've spoken to him 24 times out of the last 30 days since April 4 via the old Alexander Graham Bell instrument. The reason is that Gene is a Chicago Cub baseball fan, a devout follower of the Cubs whose home is the ivy – covered outfield walls of Wrigley Field.

In truth, he's much more than just a fan, he is in my view a "Cubnatic." While he's mostly a normal, rather nice guy, when it comes to the boys from Sheffield and Waveland Avenue he's kind of in the ecclesiastical realm of adoration for these boys of summer.

Maybe it's just simpler to say that he loves the Cubs.

I recall back in high school days (the 50s) he was already a rabid Cub fan, even with all their years of losing, once he adopted them as his team he became completely loyal to those "lovable losers," as they were called back in those days. He was loyal with a capital L. Maybe that's his middle name, loyal, could be. Odd, it just occurred to me that after 63 years I don't know his middle name. I'll ask him the next time he calls.

While he suffered all those years with those north side Chicago guys, by contrast I followed the New York Yankees. I got interested in Major League baseball in 1948 listening to the World Series that featured the Cleveland

Indians and the old Boston Braves. I was three years post-polio using a wheelchair and although I couldn't play the game I was fiercely competitive in activities I could participate in; like card games, croquet (yes croquet), who could read the most books, who could stay under water the longest, or catch the most fish. Thus I chose "the winners", a team that most Midwesterners referred to as the "damn Yankees." My all-time hero, and probably still today, was a powerful switch hitter by the name of Mickey Mantle. Gene's guy was a fellow he liked referred to as, EBMVP, that is Ernie Banks most valuable player. Ernie won back-to-back MVPs as the National League's best in 1958 and 1959.

Yes, "Mr. Cub," really a great player and even a better human being. I remember the day the Cubs signed him, giving him a whopping $10,000 contract. At the time, he was playing for the Kansas City Monarchs of the old Negro professional baseball league. What a bargain!

Gene and I often argued the question of their individual greatness, that is Mantle versus Banks, ie, who's really the better player. We never really solved the question, and I guess today we both might still hold to our initial views of 60 years past.

But I have strayed from the central purpose of this narrative, that Gene has seen the need to call me 24 times in the past 30 days. It's because every time the Cubs win he calls me. I mean every time, without fail! Today their record is 24 – 6, so 24 calls. I don't even have to watch TV to know if they won or lost; if he doesn't call I know they lost. I'm not sure when or why the calls initially began – maybe two or three years ago – but now it's almost automatic – not only myself, but my wife who is a loyal Diamondbacks fan and also my son expect to hear from Gene. My son will sometimes count the seconds after the game ends (if we are watching it or following it on game cast) and generally Gene's call arrives within 30 seconds!

When I answer the call, the conversation goes something like this:
Gene: "Well they did it again."
Kent: "Yes I saw most of this one."
Gene: "What do you think of that play Baez made? (before I could answer his question he continued)
What a spectacular stop and the throw was even better."
Kent: "Yes it sure was, what a good win. But what's wrong with Soler, he couldn't hit a bull in the butt with a banjo. What, three strikeouts?"
Gene: "Oh relax, it's early he'll come around."
Kent: " Gene, my God he's only hitting .200"
Gene: "So what, recall last year you were always ragging about Fowler – holy cow he was on base all the time."

Kent: "Well yes, but below .200 is awful."

Then we usually break into an extended BS session, then more BS, and even extended BS re: the pitching, hitting, fielding, umpiring, the weather, and other mundane topics that come to mind. The conversation usually ends with Gene signing off optimistically stating "I hope I can call you tomorrow bud." (That is if the Cubs win.)

Kent: "Take it easy."

He also sends a short e-mail summary the morning after the game.

So what's the purpose of this endeavor? I suppose we could simply call it keeping a daily journal of the 2016 Chicago Cubs baseball season.

Having never kept a daily or game by game Journal, I wasn't sure what format would be best. After a bit of experimenting I ended up with a sort of "boiler-plate" for the basic daily information: as Game #, Teams, Date, Final (game score) and Record (Cubs cumulative wins and losses.)

Then the main body, the really important stuff of the daily summary includes: Gene's daily e-mail, the game Recap, a category titled Extra Innings, then Today's Baseball Wisdom, and finally Baseball History this Date.

There are a number of issues that weighed in on our decision to keep the journal/narrative on this year's Chicago Cubs season. Several years back Gene and I had talked about keeping track of each game for a season, but we didn't follow through. But with all the hype surrounding the prospects of 2016 I called Gene about the idea he said "well it sounds like an idea but I'm no writer."

"Don't worry about the writing Gene, I'll take care of most of that, but what I need from you is input on such areas as game analysis, bitching about umpiring, what you would've done as a manager, second guessing, anecdotes, history, positive thinking (keep me from being negative) and of course any other relevant BS that you have tucked away." He paused for a short period and then readily agreed to sign on. Shortly I knew he liked the idea because he immediately launched into one of his pet peeves, ("irritations" he calls them).

"Okay," he jumped in, "why the devil can't Lester throw to first base; he's a disaster." (It's well-known that Lester has terrible problems fielding a ground ball and making a simple throw to first base). Gene continued his rant, "he's 34 years old and pitched for years and can't make a simple throw to first base. What's the hangup? He needs a psychiatrist!"

I had to chuckle, Gene was hooked.

I think deep down in the hearts of all real Cub fans is the hope and expectation that the summer and fall of 2016 could be a truly special year for the very talented Cub team. Lending hope to my enthusiasm is that I believe the curse of the Billy goat is gone. My fantasy is that the rasty bugger has ended up on the table as a feast for wandering Bedouins somewhere among the dunes of Saudi Arabia.

In reality it's somewhat difficult for me to fully understand my motivations, why I feel the need or want to document what transpires with the Cubs this season, every game, Gene's telephone calls, all of it.

Besides accumulating a whole bunch of material, I'm not sure what we're going to end up with. The narrative will have an abundance of facts and statistics (game day data, and anything you might want or not want to hear about the Cubs.) Hopefully the commentary will also be somewhat entertaining. But also importantly this treatise is intended to be educational. For I am one who subscribes to the concept of "life – long learning" not only formally as in grade, high school or in a university setting but also daily in our every day world of experience. Thus, in addition to each day's Recap of the game there is another category of relevant information (at least we think so) for the reader who might find the daily statistical and analytical discussions (dare I say mundane or even boring), included under the heading "Extra Innings." This information is mostly related to the game or other baseball matters, but not necessarily always.

Then, building on the idea that this document is hopefully not only factual and entertaining but also educational/informative, Gene and I have discovered through our extensive research into the culture of American baseball that in fact there are seemingly endless "pearls of wisdom" that have been uttered mostly by the primary actors in the drama of baseball, namely the players. The reader will recognize names like Yogi Berra, Dizzy Dean, Bob Uecker, Joe Garagiola, Casey Stengel, Babe Ruth and other notables. Interspersed the reader will also find comments from other folks in or related to the "sports world." The dialogue may be from a manager, a writer or another individual of note who's sharpness of perception was deemed worthy of inclusion. Recognizing the invaluable contributions these gems can have for one's self edification and enrichment to our daily lives we have for each game included a prize thought-provoking comment under the heading, "Today's Baseball Wisdom."

As some of you may know I believe humor and especially laughter are literally therapeutic for both body and soul, however if these snippets of wisdom fail to enlighten your day, bring a smile or a chuckle, or broaden your horizons, our defense is simply "we didn't say, it they did."

In keeping with a general theme of education, it has become apparent, (at least in my opinion) that a final category of information should be included for the benefit of the reader. As important in our lives as contemporary information is for us, so too is one's grasp and knowledge of the past, that is history, especially noteworthy historical events, and even more specifically happenings we can equate to a given day in history. And as this work has focused on baseball, it follows that notable daily events in the annals of baseball should be included. Thus we have such happenings included under the heading, "Baseball History This Date."

With no intention of committing a blaspheme, in the eyes of those who ascribe to the importance of daily Bible reading, I humbly suggest that reading daily baseball trivia could also be "good for the soul."

Before I end this already too long prologue there's one final housekeeping item of explanation to dispense with. The reader will recall that e-mails from Gene are part of the daily write up of the games. But did you note that his messages are labeled V-mails, not e-mails? E-mails changed to the V-mails on May 13, game number 34 which the Cubs won 9 – 4. The phone rang, (of course) and Matthew said, "well, I'd guess that's the Voice of Victory." (AKA Gene). It was, and henceforth his e-mails became V-Mails.

Finally, whatever the fundamental reason or reasons why the decision to embark on this project, they may remain mostly unknown. Maybe I was just looking for an excuse to resume writing again on a regular basis. The last couple of years I have started two novels and have ended up with what some label as "writers block." Maybe it's just a summer project for myself and Gene. However the more I thought about the matter, it occurred to me that in fact there was an underlying phenomenon that seem to be prompting me to move ahead with this effort. I think it's about friendship. Gene and I have been "buds" (as he likes to say) for six decades. Friends do things together, like fishing, hiking, movies, chase women, take a trip together, get drunk or whatever. A good number of things we used to do together wouldn't work anymore as we're getting too old. Ha!

Essentially I think this endeavor is a kind of acknowledgment and validation of our relationship that has endured for so many years. A bond that has been one of openness, honesty, and candor. But even more fundamental I might suggest it has to do with the lynch pin of our relationship; a characteristic of humans that today I believe is in mighty short supply. It's called loyalty. And Gene has been for me, for all these many years, a most loyal friend. It's kind of odd when I do a sort of personal inventory of what kind of guy is Gene. He's kind of a liberal (maybe more than just a kind of a liberal) and I've become a staunch conservative. He's a true fan always looking for the positive, but I always want to win, I'm a "sore loser," and frequently I can get negative about my team and the players. Gene is a "Catlik" (Ala Archie Bunker), and I'm a Lutheran. He always claims he's poor (financially) and he thinks "I'm loaded" (neither is accurate). He doesn't like basketball, while almost my favorite sport is college basketball. A mutual friend of ours once said about Gene "he doesn't have a mean bone in his body," while my wife sometimes accuses me of having a "vicious" streak." I love baking in the Arizona sunshine, but old Gene abhors hot weather.

It doesn't sound like we'd be very good friends does it? To the contrary we are good "buds" and I think I know the answer, it's loyalty, that engenders trust and that trumps all the differences.

So since we are still good friends and can't do a lot of things we would have done in our younger years we decided to spend the summer 2016 traveling with the Cubbies, hopefully on a journey of destiny.

The 2016 Season
Games 1–179

Game: #1

Teams: Cubs @ LA Angels
Date: Monday, April 4
Final: Cubs win 9-0
Record: 1 – 0

V – mail: "Wow, what a way to start the season. Everything went like us Cubs fans would like it to for the rest of the year. Boy I hate these late nights."

Recap:

Angel Stadium had thousands of Cubs fans in attendance and the boys from the north side of "Chi-town" didn't disappoint with Arrieta yielding only two hits over seven innings.

Montero homered with three RBIs, Rizzo and Soler drove in early runs. Fowler had three hits and Zobrist two singles. The Cubs scored in the first, fourth, six, and seventh. Szczur added a three run double in the ninth. All the highlights were Cubs. Grimm and Wood finished with "nothing across" as they say.

Extra innings:

Gene stayed up and watched the entire game! He said "I'm exhausted and will have to do this again tomorrow night. (Note have to, it's not an option not to watch for him. Ha!)

Gene has been "chomping at the bit" to get this season going. One day he is optimistic, but the next day expresses doubts, recalling the 1969 catastrophe of the Cubs under Leo Durocher. They had a nine-game lead on August 16 but collapsed and lost to the Mets. Many speculated that Durocher had worn out his pitching staff. Well who knows, could have been though as in those years they didn't have all of the specialized relief pitchers that they have today. So this is 2016 and hope springs eternal.

Today's baseball wisdom:

"A good win; you know you have to win the first one if you want to win them all"

Gene Shippy

Baseball history this date:

April 4, 1974 Hank Aaron ties Babe Ruth's home run record by hitting number 714.*

* (Yes a notable event, but also notable is the fact that the Chicago Cubs win game number one in their quest for a World Series title after 108 years!)

Game: #2

Teams: Cubs @ LA Angels
Date: Tuesday April 5
Final: Cubs win 6-1
Record: 2-0

V – mail: "Well I could get use to this. It's really great to see two of their top-notch pitchers get off so well in the first two games. Also nice to see the hitting."

Recap:

Lester had a great outing, backed by homers from Rizzo, Fowler and Matt Szczur. Lester went seven innings with four hits and one earned run, no walks and seven strikeouts. Lester, the six-year $155 million contract holder, in his second year with the Cubs said, "physically and mentally I'm light years ahead of where I was last year at this point."

This is the first time the Cubs have started 2 – 0 since 1995. They have won there last 11 regular-season road games. As a side note, Szczur made his first start of the season in left field one day after his alma mater Villanova won the NCAA men's basketball championship on a buzzer beating three-pointer by Kris Jenkins.

Extra innings:

Another night game and Gene watched the entire game. He called after the game and it must have been close to midnight back in Illinois. He really did sound tired but now they leave California for Arizona so it won't be quite as late.

Today's baseball wisdom:

"In 1962 I was named minor league player of the year, however it was my second season in the "big's."
Bob Uecker

Baseball history this date:

1972 -Baseball season was delayed due to a players strike. The strike was from April 1 to April 13. 86 total games were never played as the league refused to pay the players while on strike. Houston and San Diego only played 153 games, 9 fewer than normal. They lost $5,000,000.

Game: #3

Teams: Cubs @ Diamondbacks
Date: Thursday, April 7
Final: Cubs win 14-6
Record: 3 – 0

V – mail: "Well I'm not sure what to say; it was great to see the Cubs win their third in a row, but that injury to Schwarber is really terrible. I understand he has a torn ACL and is probably gone for the year. That is really too bad as I think he was going to have a really good year."

Recap:
John Lackey pitched for the Cubs. He was with St. Louis last year along with Jason Heyward, so I guess the Cubs raided the Cardinals roster. Ha!

Holy cow, pitch number one by Lackey went out of the ballpark as Jean Segura really blasted it out. Crap, my negative thinking immediately set in (as Gene says) as I'm wondering if we signed a loser in Lackey. Well he settled down and the Cubs won 14 – 6. Rizzo had six RBIs in the game and obviously they had plenty of other hits to go around.

Extra innings:
But what terrible news as second-year man Kyle Schwarber and Dexter Fowler collided in right-center chasing a high fly ball and Schwarber was carried off the field on a stretcher. A later MRI confirmed that he had torn his ACL. He's gone for the year.

Did anyone see a damn goat anywhere in the stadium?

Gene didn't call, so I called him the next day. He said he didn't want to aggravate Marlys as she's a Diamondback fan. Marlys told him that he could call her anytime his Cubs won, but be ready to get a phone call when her Diamondbacks beat the Cubs.

Still can't get over Schwarber going down. I think it's really a big loss the Cubs. Negative me is thinking, is this an omen?

Today's baseball wisdom:
"It's pitching, hitting, and defense that wins. Any two can win. All three make you unbeatable."
Joe Garagiola

Baseball history this date:
1971 – The dismissal of Curt Flood's suit against major-league baseball is upheld.

Game: #4

Teams: Cubs @ Diamondbacks
Date: Friday, April 8
Final: Cubs Lose 3-2
Record: 3-1

V – mail: "The Cubs wasted a good job by Jason Hammel. He allowed one run and four hits with three bases on balls and six strikeouts. The Cubs scored early but didn't add on."

Recap:

Yes, the Cubs engaged in one of their past behaviors, score early, 2 in the third inning and never score again after a 14 – 6 win in their last game. Really frustrating to watch, which unfortunately I did.

What really got me "bent" was allowing Strop to pitch to Goldschmidt in the eighth inning with the Cubs ahead 2 – 1. For God sakes walk the guy, as he's known to be a great clutch hitter. There are two outs, and a runner on third, which means there are two bases open; even if you walk him and the next guy you get to face a guy struggling with a .188 batting average (Castillo). I'm yelling my head off, telling Maddon to walk him, but he didn't listen to me. Geez! Of course we all know what happened, Goldschmidt got a hit and tied the game. Then Arizona scored again in the ninth and game over.

Extra innings:

Well, Marlys was happy for her Diamondbacks after the shellacking they took last night. She didn't call Gene as she had threatened to do.

The Diamondbacks pulled off a really strange double play in the game. Heyward was on first for the Cubs and Fowler on third. Rizzo hit a sharp grounder to Goldschmidt at first who throws to the catcher Castillo, who catches Fowler in a rundown, Fowler is tagged out by the shortstop Nick Ahmed, covering third, who throws to the right fielder covering first, who tags out Rizzo. If you were keeping score the play would look like this on your score sheet: 3 – 2 – 6 – 9.

I know Gene will give me "some crap" about saying "unfortunately watching the game." He'll blister me with something like, "and you call yourself a Cub fan?" Maybe I can use my disability as an excuse. How about, "well you know us people with 'post-polio syndrome' can easily get nervous."

Think that will work?

Today's baseball wisdom:

"I got a charge out of seeing Ted Williams hit; once in a while they let me try and field some of them, which sort of dimmed my enthusiasm."
Rocky Bridges.

Baseball history this date:

1968 – Baseballs opening day is postponed because of Martin Luther Kings' assassination.

Game: #5

Teams: Cubs @ Arizona
Date: Saturday, April 9
Final: Cubs win 4-2
Record: 4 – 1

V – mail: "I was afraid they were going to do it again; scored three early runs (first-inning) and then do not add on. Thankfully Hendricks pitched really well and held them in check."

Recap:

Rizzo, Bryant, and Montero all had RBIs in the first inning off Greinke, the $205 million man and actually that was enough to win the game. They get another run in the fourth which held up for the win. Greinke is now 0 – 2 in his first two starts. Last year with the Dodger he was 19-3 with an ERA of 1.66 Today he gave up seven hits and four earned runs. However after the first inning he only gave up four more hits and the last run was scored on a sacrifice fly. He really is a tough pitcher and will eventually get a lot of wins.

Hendricks was also very good, pitching 6 2/3 innings giving up four hits, two earned runs, one walk and five strikeouts.

Extra innings:

The Cub players were talking among themselves before the game about how best to attack Greinke, something they've been doing since the middle of spring training games. Maddon said he loved to see the discussions as "when our guys go up to hit, it's contagious and they talk."

"It's beautiful," Maddon said.

"I think that's a great sign of solidarity among the players, a critical key to the concept of a "team."

Kyle Schwarber will return to Chicago to meet with the team doctors when the Cubs leave on Sunday. He's finished for the season after tearing two ligaments in his left knee after colliding with Dexter Fowler in the outfield.

Today's baseball wisdom:

"Airplanes may kill you, but they won't hurt you."
Satchel Paige

Baseball history this date:

1974 – San Diego Padres owner Ray Kroc (McDonald's entrepreneur) addresses fans, "ladies and gentlemen I suffer with you. I've never seen such stupid baseball playing in my life."

Game: #6

Teams: Cubs @ Arizona
Date: Sunday, April 10
Final: Cubs win 7-3
Record: 5 – 1

V – mail: "Jake was the show today going seven innings allowing three runs on eight hits and striking out six. He is now 2 – 0 for the year. He also had a two-run homer off Shelby Miller."

Recap:

Not a very exciting game, as maybe I was trying to be "low key" as today was Marlys' birthday; wow she turned 77, but I was careful not to dwell on that number.

Arrieta was tough and he looks like the same guy that he was last year when he was so dominating. He got help today from three guys who aren't the superstars; Soler had a two-run homer, which made me feel good as he will now need to play more with the injury to Schwarber. Montero had two doubles and Tommy la Stella had three hits.

I guess I wasn't very involved in baseball today as I thought about the dinner Matthew cooked for his mother on her birthday today. He made chicken satay, a peanut sauce, wonderful cucumber salad, and rice pudding – everything really terrific!

Oh, Marlys was really a good sport about the loss; maybe it was because Matt made such a splendid dinner for her. Of course I was also the beneficiary of his extensive culinary arts, just another way to say "great chow."

Extra innings:

Mark Grace, who is the D-backs assistant hitting coach delivered a video message to Cubs catcher David Ross who is retiring at the end of this year. Grace relived the night he gave up Ross's first major league home run in 2002. Grace was pitching as its team was being blown out and Ross hit a home run off of him. Ross doffed his hat toward the Diamondbacks dugout in gratitude.

Today's baseball wisdom:

"Cobb is a prick, but he sure can hit. God Almighty that man can hit."
Babe Ruth

Baseball history this date:

1947 – Happy Chandler, baseball Commissioner, suspends Leo Durocher

A Century-Long Journey to the Day of Redemption

for the 1947 season for "Association with known gamblers."*

*(Before he was suspended Durocher played a note worthy role in erasing baseball's color barrier. He let it be known that he would not tolerate the dissent of those players who opposed Jackie Robinson joining the team. He said "I do not care if the guy is yellow, or black, or if he has stripes like a "freakin"(Leo used the big "F" word) zebra, I'm the manager of this team and I say he plays."

Game: #7

Teams: Cubs/Cincinnati
Date: Monday, April 11
Final: Cubs Win 5 -3
Record: 6 – 1

V – mail: "Terrible weather for baseball as it was 34° in Chicago when the game started, but the Cubs hung in there and won again."

Recap:

Really a tough game as young Brandon Finnigen of Cincinnati took a no-hitter into the seventh inning. Cincinnati got him from Kansas City in a trade for Johnny Cueto last year. He is really a good one for the years to come. The Cubs were behind 3 – 0, but got 2 in the seventh inning. Then in the eighth Addison Russell cracked a three-run home run to win the game 5 – 3. The Cubs only had three hits the entire game and Cincinnati had seven, but the Cubs got two hits in the seventh and then Russell's home run was the third hit.

This was the Cubs home opener for the 2016 season

Extra innings:

Wow, 34° is terrible! As my friend Bob would have said, "boy that's colder than a witches tit in the Klondike." Bob, now gone, was really a great guy and told me a story once about being on guard duty in Anchorage Alaska (outside) with the temperature 30 – 40° below zero and the wind blowing. They forgot that he was out in the weather and he said he really thought for a while he would freeze to death. Well they remembered him and he did survive, although he said it was unbearably cold. Chicago wasn't quite that cold, but I've become a real Arizona "wuss"and anything below 40° as I see it is potentially life-threatening!

Even though the Cubs fans are great beer drinkers I wonder how many ice cold brews they sold that night?

Today's baseball wisdom:

"Baseball is 90% mental, the other half is physical."
Yogi Berra

Baseball history this date:

1907 – New York Giant Roger Bresnahan becomes the first catcher to wear shin guards.

Also:

1899 – The National League announced that next year baseball would have two umpires.

Game: #8

Teams: Cubs/Cincinnati
Date: Wednesday, April 13
Final: Cubs win 9-2
Record: 7 – 1

V – mail: "Another nice win for the Cubs. Good pitching by Lackey and some timely hitting for a nine– two win."

Recap:
The Cubs jumped on starter Alfredo Simon for five runs in the first inning. Five different Cubs each drove in a run in the inning including Lackey. They added two more in the third inning, and essentially the game was over. Kind of a slow, not very exciting game as the Cubs were issued 10 walks.

Kris Bryant hit his first home run of the season. Lackey pitched 6 2/3 innings allowing two runs and six hits. Cahill, Richards, and Ramirez finished the game, as they say, "nothing across."

Extra innings:
It's nice to start the season 7 – 1. Marlys' old Minnesota "Twinkies" are 0 – 8 as are the Atlanta Braves. Boy that's really miserable, and I can think back when the team might have been the Cubs. I haven't talked with Marge Vogt as she is a real big Twins fan. Hopefully they will get their act together and start winning.

Today's baseball wisdom:
"There is no defense against bases on balls."
Joe Garagiola

Baseball history this date:
1946 – Eddie Kleep, a white pitcher was signed by defending Negro league champions the Cleveland Buckeyes. During warm-up before a game he was barred from the field in Birmingham, Alabama. The police came and said "we have no mixing here." *

*(There is conflicting information on the date as another source said the day he was barred was March 24 instead of April 13; As after March 24 he is never again mentioned in Buckeye press coverage. Isn't it ironic that one league was trying to keep a black player out and a black league had to kick out their only white guy!)

Game: #9

Teams: Cubs/Cincinnati
Date: Thursday, April 14
Final: Cubs win 8-1
Record: 8 – 1

V – mail: "Jason Hammel was the story today, pitching six scoreless innings and also driving in a run. Cubs win 8 – 1 and their record is 8 – 1."

Recap:
The game was close through seven innings with the Cubs ahead 3 – 0. They got five runs in the eighth inning to put the game away. Jason Hammel pitched six scoreless inning's, as the "voice" noted in his V-mail. Plenty of timely hitting to support Hammel as Fowler and Russell each had three hits. Bryant also hit his second home run in two days. This is the best start for the Cubs in the last 47 years. It's much too early to worry, but hardcore Cubs fans remember 1969 when they started 11 –1 and then collapsed in August/September and lost to the Mets. I don't think it will happen this year. Justin Grimm came on in relief in the ninth and gave up a run.

Extra innings:
Joe Maddon said on winning "this is all about the players. I have nothing to do with this. Our players and coaches have done a great job of prepping. One of our goals is to get off to a good start. The guys took it to heart."

Today's baseball wisdom:

" I can't very well tell my batters don't hit it to him. Whenever they hit it he's there anyway."
Gil Hodges on Willie Mays.

Baseball history this date:

1925 – First regular-season Cubs game to be broadcast on the radio (WGN)

Game: #10

Teams: Cubs/Colorado
Date: Friday, April 15
Final: Cubs lose 6-1
Record: 8 – 2

V – mail: "The young guy for Colorado really threw a good game. Tough to win when you only get one run."

Recap:
So a guy named Chad Bettis goes six innings allows no runs and only three hits. Never heard of this dude before. The Cubs did get one run off another guy named Chad, the former Diamondback Chad Qualls.

Colorado got only three earned runs as the Cubs made four errors; Bryant had two, and Russell and Rizzo each had one. Bettis had good defense behind him including a runner thrown out at the plate as Soler tried to score on a safety squeeze in the fifth inning. Also Parra and Gonzalez made diving catches in the outfield and second baseman DJ LeMahieu (former Cub) made a really nice over the shoulder catch. Oh well, tomorrow is another game.

Extra innings:
Each player, for both teams, wore jersey #42 on the 69th anniversary of Jackie Robinson becoming the first black major leaguer.

Also, Javier Baez, who had been out with a thumb injury, drove all night from Iowa after he was told that his triple A rehab assignment was over. Baez arrived after 6 AM and was activated off the disabled list before the game. Then he didn't play!

Today's baseball wisdom:

"There is no room in baseball for discrimination. It is our national pastime and a game for all."*
Lou Gehrig

*(As Gehrig died in 1941, his expression was made long before Jackie Robinson entered baseball in 1947)

Baseball history this date:

1997 – baseball honored Jackie Robinson by retiring #42 for all major league teams.

Game: #11

Teams: Cubs/Colorado
Date: Saturday, April 16
Final: Cubs win 6 – 2
Record: 9 – 2

V – mail: "Jake was spectacular today, as he threw eight innings of shutout baseball. He's off to a terrific start, continuing his pitching from last year."

Recap:
Yes, I have to agree with the "voice" that Arrieta was spectacular. He now has a string of 48 2/3 scoreless innings at Wrigley Field dating back to July 2015. Maddon lifted Arrieta after the Cubs had scored six runs. Rizzo and Soler hit back-to-back home runs in the fourth inning and Fowler added a three-run shot the seventh. Travis Wood came in to finish the game and proceeded to give up a two-run homer to González. Old Joe Maddon doesn't waste any time and he immediately jerked Wood. Pedro Strop came in and got the final two outs.

As a side note, it was a nice day in Chicago the temperature 77°.

Extra innings:
A key aspect of Arrieta's success has been his slider. Not only is it fast, it's very deceptive. His slider moves horizontally over the plate at a faster rate than any other qualified pitcher, at 9.9 ft./s. The past three years opponents are hitting only .181 against his slider. The major league average over three years is .217.

Today's baseball wisdom:

"It ain't braggin if you can back it up."
Dizzy Dean

Baseball history this date:

1929 – The Yankees become the first team in the major leagues to wear numbers on their uniforms.

Game: #12

Teams: Cubs/Colorado
Date: Sunday, April 17
Final: Cubs lose 2-0
Record: 9 – 3

V – mail: "I never heard of this guy before, did you? Pitched one heck of a game as the Cubs just couldn't do anything with him."

Recap:

The Cubs only got two hits in seven innings off a guy named Tyler Chatwood, who missed all of 2015 and most of 2014 because of elbow surgery, known as "Tommy John surgery." Jon Lester actually pitched a great game for the Cubs going 7 1/3 innings allowing four hits only one earned run and had 10 strikeouts. Boy that's a tough one to lose.

For the Rockies, Nolan Arenado, 25-year-old third sacker had two solo home runs. He's a great young hitter. When I wrote this on May 22 I checked his totals and he already had 14 home runs in 42 games and was batting .307. This is only his third year in the major leagues.

Extra innings:

I was thinking about Tommy John surgery. Medically, the surgery is Ulnar Collateral ligament (UCL) reconstruction. The ligament in the elbow is replaced with a tendon from elsewhere in the body. The surgery was first performed in 1974 by Dr. Frank Jobe, LA Dodgers team physician on a pitcher named Tommy John who had won 28 major-league games. He won 164 more games after the surgery. His 10 – 10 record in 1976 after the surgery was considered "miraculous." Today many pitchers have the surgery and go on with their careers. Truly amazing.

Today's baseball wisdom:

"Good pitching will always stop good hitting and vice – versa."
Casey Stengel

Baseball history this date:

(1) 1953 – Mickey Mantle hits a 565 foot home run in Washington DC's Griffith Stadium.

(2) 1960 – Cleveland Indians trade Rocky Colavito to Detroit for Harvey Kuenn.*

(3) 1947 – Jackie Robinson bunts for his first major-league hit.

*(Many Cleveland Indian fans never forgave the tribe for trading Colavito.)

Game: #13

Teams: Cubs @ St. Louis
Date: Monday, April 18
Final: Cubs win 5 – 0
Record: 10 – 3

V – mail: "What a great job by John Lackey. Seven innings four hits and no runs and 11 strikeouts."

Recap:
John Lackey returned to Busch Stadium for the first time and as the reporter said "he had a little extra in the tank." Per above, Lackey went seven innings no runs and four hits with 11 strikeouts. He struck out Moss three times and fanned Matt Carpenter and Stephen Piscotty twice. There really isn't much to say about the game as Lackey was in complete control from the beginning. Travis Wood, Pedro Strop, and Cahill pitched the last two innings without allowing any runs.

For the first 13 games of the year every Cubs starter has gone at least six innings. For this day and age that's really amazing.

Dexter Fowler had a double and a home run, Zobrist a two bagger, and Bryant, Russell, and Lackey each had an RBI.

Extra innings:
The Cubs starters going at least six innings in every game this year is the longest streak in the majors since 1988 when the Astros had a 22 game streak and the Indians went 17 games.

Today's baseball wisdom:

"I was in the top 10% of my law school class, I am a doctor of jurisprudence; I have an honorary Dr. of laws, so would somebody please tell me why I spent four mortal hours today conversing with a person named Dizzy Dean?"
Branch Rickey

Baseball history this date:

1981– This date the longest game in professional baseball was played; the Pawtucket Red Sox tie the Rochester Red Wings 2 – 2 in 32 innings. The game was resumed the next June 23 and Pawtucket won the game 3 – 2 in the 33rd inning.

Game: #14

Teams: Cubs @ St. Louis
Date: Tuesday, April 19
Final: Cubs win 2 – 1
Record: 11 – 3

V – mail: "Terrific game by Jason Hammel; he threw six innings, allowed only one run, no walks and six strikeouts. Also drove in both runs for the Cubs."

Recap:

Jason Hammel did pitch six strong innings and had the only two RBIs. Hammel a career .136 hitter is 2 for 6 with a double and a 1.00 ERA for the season. Four Cub relievers, Warren, Wood, Strop, and Rondon finished the game with Rondon getting the save.

Ex-Cardinal Jason Heyward is hitting only .170 but he threw out Matt Holliday at the plate to end the fourth inning. His stellar defense has made a big difference in the series with the Cardinals. Let's hope he begins to hit.

Extra innings:

Kyle Schwarber, out for the season, underwent successful surgery to his left knee to repair torn ligaments. Really a shame as I think he's going to be a great hitter and the Cubs will miss him and his bat.

Today's baseball wisdom:

"Roberto Clemente could field the ball in New York and throw out a guy in Pennsylvania."
Vin Scully

Baseball history this date:

1960 – Baseball uniforms began displaying players names on their backs.

Game: #15

Teams: Cubs @ St. Louis
Date: Wednesday, April 20
Final: Cubs lose 5-3
Record: 11 – 4

V – mail: "Tough loss especially to those Cardinals."

Recap:
Gosh, sure would have been nice to have swept those dastardly Cardinals. It didn't look good right off as Grichuck robbed Rizzo of a home run with an over the wall catch. The play would seem to help Carlos Martinez settle into seven strong innings. Hendricks had a rough start, giving up two runs each in the first and second innings. He only lasted 5 1/3 innings giving up seven hits, four runs and he also had two walks. He did strike out five.

The game was delayed three hours and 21 minutes due to rain in the seventh inning. Grichuck, who made a great catch off of Rizzo, joked that he watched the replay of his catch 72 times during the rain delay!

Extra innings:
Up next is Jake Arrieta who is 3 – 0 with a .133 ERA who will open a four-game series at Cincinnati. Cincinnati will throw Bryan Finnigen, 1 – 0, with a .204 ERA. Cincinnati got him in the trade with Kansas City for Johnny Cueto. He's a promising young prospect.

Today's baseball wisdom:

"You wouldn't have won, if we would have beat you."
Yogi Berra

Baseball history this date:

1946 – The first TV broadcast in Chicago, Cubs versus Cardinals (WBKB). But it didn't work, only the TV station saw the broadcast. Later, on July 13 the telecast was successful, but the Cubs lost 4 – 3 to the Dodgers.

Game: #16

Teams: Cubs @ Cincinnati
Date: Thursday, April 21
Final: Cubs win 16 – 0
Record: 12 – 4

V – mail: "Well Arrieta is at it again; the second no-hitter in two years. What more can you say about the guy, he's just phenomenal. If he continues pitching this way he may wind up winning the Cy Young again."

Recap:
　Holy cow, holy cow a complete rout, but the story was all Jake Arrieta. The guy not only had a nine inning shutout, it was another no-hitter! He gave up no hits, walked four and struck out six. The Cubs had home runs by Bryant, Zobrist, and Rizzo and they scored early and often with a total of 18 hits. Arrieta added to his club record of 24 consecutive quality starts since June 21 of 2015 with a record of 20 – 1. He is 15 – 0 in 16 starts since last August 1, allowing a total of only seven earned runs. His fortunes have changed dramatically with the Cubs since the July 2013 trade from the Baltimore Orioles. Arrieta has gone 40 – 13 with a 2.17 ERA including 22 – 6 and a 1.77 ERA in his 2015 Cy Young season. In four seasons with the Orioles he was 20 – 25 with a 5.46 ERA. How do you figure that?

Extra innings:
　Gene called and raved on and on as did the baseball analysts on ESPN, and the Cincinnati players. So did the Catholics, Lutherans, Presbyterians, gays, illegals, street people, "bad guys," in and out of prison and other "ne'er-do-wells," all who were singing his praises.. Oh, I forgot the Mormons, I'm guessing they are already looking at his genealogy.
　I've included a short piece from ESPN about his performance: *
　* A Bittersweet Anniversary.
　"Three years ago Thursday night, in his fourth start of 2013 with the Orioles, Arrieta took the loss as the O's fell to the Dodgers 7 – 4. He allowed five runs on two hits and five walks over four innings, earning him a demotion to the minors the next day. He would make just one more start for Baltimore, a June 17 loss to Detroit in which he allowed five runs and 10 hits over 4 2/3 innings pitched, pushing his ERA for the season to 7.23. Less than a month later on July 2 he was traded to the Cubs along with Pedro Strop for catcher Steve Clevenger and pitcher Scott Feldman."
　Wow, what a trade for the Cubs !

Today's baseball wisdom:

The Athletics pounded pitcher Bobo Newsom, taking an 8 – 0 in the fifth inning. Newsom entered his clubhouse slammed his glove against the wall. "What's eating you a teammate asked?"

"How the hell can a guy win when you don't get any runs," Newsom answered.

Baseball history this date:

1977 – Billy Martin (manager for the fourth time) pulls his Yankee starting lineup literally out of a hat. The Yankees won the game from the Blue Jays 8 – 6. *

*(The Yankees had started 2 – 8, so Martin pulled the lineup from a hat. He did it six times, all wins, before they lost.)

Game: #17

Teams: Cubs @ Cincinnati
Date: Friday, April 22
Final: Cubs win 8 – 1
Record: 13 – 4

V – mail: "Another terrific performance by Jon Lester. He pitched seven innings allowing only one run, five hits, one walk and four strikeouts. Really in complete control the entire game."

Recap:
The Cubs have scored 24 runs in the last two games. I think the Reds aren't too thrilled with the boys from Wrigley. Gene called, very upbeat, not only about the hitting, but especially Lester's pitching. "Another quality start" he chirped and proceeded to run through his performance. He did give up a home run to Cozart in the sixth, but that was it.

The Cubs had seven different guys who drove in the eight runs; Rizzo and Baez each hit a home run and Bryant and Fowler each had doubles. The score was 4 – 0 until the eighth inning when the Cubs put it away with four more runs.

Extra innings:
The following is an excerpt from ESPN entitled Selling Fast:
"Cubs fans bristled that their "Try Not to Suck" T – shirts weren't allowed at Busch Stadium this week because of the Cardinals long-standing policy prohibiting shirts with the word. (I guess they didn't like the word suck). Cubs manager Joe Maddon came up with the slogan and designed the shirt to raise money for his foundation. The dust – up resulted in a spike of sales of the $30 shirts, with $56,000 raised the last two days. That puts the season total over $500,000 from shirt sales.

Today's baseball wisdom:

"I set records that will never be equaled. In fact, I hope 90% of them don't even get printed."
Bob Uecker

Baseball history this date:

1959 – Whitey Ford strikes out 15, beating the Senators 1 – 0 in 14 innings.

Also

1957 – All of the National League teams are now integrated as John Erwin Kennedy is the first black player on the Philadelphia Phillies.

Game: #18

Teams: Cubs @ Cincinnati
Date: Saturday, April 23
Final: Cubs lose 13-5
Record: 13 – 5

V – mail: "This is the kind of game that you might as well forget about and wait for tomorrow. Cincinnati's hitters just exploded."

Recap:

I guess the Reds had enough runs scored against them. (24 runs the last two games). Today they scored 11 times in the last three innings. Seven runs in the sixth inning and two each in the seventh and eighth, winning convincingly 13 – 5. They had 15 hits including four home runs. John Lackey went 5 2/3 with seven hits and six runs. Cahill, Ramirez, and Richard each gave up 3 – 2 – 2 runs, each in an inning or less. The win ended the Cubs eight straight wins against the Reds. They were 5 – 0 this year, outscoring Cincinnati 46 – 7! The Reds hit three home runs in the seventh inning; two three-run shots and a solo.

Extra innings:

I got to thinking that baseball is fundamentally a game of statistics and streaks; "it never happened before, or I never heard of that before, or it's the first time in 50 years that it happened." There are seemingly endless kinds of statistics. Games do not simply report scores and things like hits and runs. We also, for example, have for pitchers things like IP, H, BB, S0, HR, PC, ERA's, WHIP, GS, GC, SHO, P/GS, BA. (You'll have to look them up if you really want to know). Therefore I thought it noteworthy to point out that with today's 13 – 5 Cubs loss, the Cubs record for the year is also 13 – 5.

But we also have to keep track of what the hitter's are doing. To wit: their statistics include AB, H, W, R, RBI, 2b, 3b, HR, S0, GP, SB, CS, OBP, SLG, and OPS. Once again I'm going to leave it to the reader to check out these initials. The process will not only make you an expert in baseball trivia you will become a much more informed fan!

Oh no, I left out the single most important statistic, that is W – L. That's simply wins and losses. Maybe the game is just a matter of who has the most "W's."

Today's baseball wisdom:

When a reporter was told to get the reaction from Dominican players of the San Francisco Giants concerning the assassination of Generalissimo

Trujillo he came back from the clubhouse and approached his editor. "They said they didn't do it!"

Baseball history this date:

1999 – Fernando Tatis, of the St. Louis Cardinals, hit two grand slams in the third inning, both off Chan Ho Park. His eight RBIs in one inning is still unmatched.

Game: #19

Teams: Cubs @ Cincinnati
Date: Sunday, April 24
Final: Cubs win 9 – 0
Record: 14 – 5

V – mail: "It's hard to believe that the Cubs pitching staff has been so dominant beginning the year. With five starters all pitching really well it sure looks good even though it's very early in the season."

Recap:

Payback for yesterday! The Cubs jumped out to an 8 to 0 lead and never looked back. Rizzo hit two 2 run home runs, one in the first and one in the third. Hammel was really tough, going six innings allowing no runs, three hits, two walks and seven strikeouts. Warren, Wood, and Rondon all went 1 – 2 – 3 in the seventh, eighth and ninth innings. The game was really kind of "ho – hum" after three innings. The Cubs added a run in the sixth, but with the pitching, there was little excitement after the early outburst.

Extra innings:

Gene, who takes every game, and pitch seriously, didn't see it as boring or ho-hum. He'll often say to me, if I stopped watching, "what kind of fan are you anyway? If they lose you can find something you didn't like; if they win you still can find something that ticks you off." Then he did laugh a little.

Marlys says much the same; she won't watch a game with me as her favorite line is "why are you so negative?" My response is "I'm not negative, I'm just doing my analysis of the game." I think she said, "oh bullshit!"

On another note, do you like instant replay? Rizzo's second home run took 2 minutes and 17 seconds to determine if there was no fan interference. Now that's irritating; I'm not being negative, but it is a pain in the "tush."

Today's baseball wisdom:

"So when you come to a fork in the road, take it."
Yogi Berra

Baseball history this date:

1957 – Chicago Cubs pitcher's walk a record nine Reds in the fifth inning.

Game: #20

Teams: Cubs/Milwaukee
Date: Tuesday, April 26
Final: Cubs win 4 – 3
Record: 15 – 5

V – mail: "Well as is usually the case Hendricks pitched well enough to win, but gets no run support as they get him one run in five innings; of course he doesn't get the decision."

Recap:

Well I can't say he is a poor sport but he was irritated that Maddon jerked Hendricks after five innings giving up only two hits and one run with the game tied 1 – 1. It was kind of odd that he did as Kyle had only thrown 69 pitches through the five innings. Maddon is a funny guy and he really has a quick trigger when it comes to his pitchers. It seems that if he sees anything he doesn't like "banggo" the pitcher is gone. I told Gene he should e-mail Joe and ask him what the devil's going on. He replied "Ha, like I'd get an answer."

The Cubs scored two in the sixth and one the seventh for a 4 – 1 lead. The "druggie," that is Ryan Braun, got a pinch-hit two-run double in the eighth, but the Cubs held on for a 4 – 3 win. Now they are 15 – 5 for the year. What a start!

Extra innings:

It occurred to me that I never saw a baseball game in Milwaukee. The Boston Braves moved there in 1953 into their new ballpark, Milwaukee County Stadium. They went 92 – 62 and finished second to the Dodgers that year. Their big hitter was Eddie Mathews the third baseman who hit 47 home runs that year. It wasn't until 1954 that they had to insert a young unproven outfielder into the lineup after Bobby Thomson broke his ankle in spring training. That young man was named Henry Aaron. They won the World Series in 1957 with Lew Burdette winning three games in the series. Oh my God he fidgeted so much when he was pitching it was impossible to watch him. Oh, in 1963 old Warren Spahn at age 42 won 23 games; then he was only 6 – 13 in 1964 his last year. In 1965 they moved to Atlanta.

Today's baseball wisdom:

"Now there's three things that can happen in a baseball game; you can win, you can lose, or it can rain."
Casey Stengel

Baseball history this date:

1990 – Nolan Ryan ties Bob Feller's record of pitching 12 one hitters.*
*(Wow, he also had 7 no-hitters, one at age 43 and one at age 44.)

Game: #21

Teams: Cubs/Milwaukee
Date: Thursday, April 28
Final: Cubs win 7 – 2
Record: 16 – 5

V – mail: "Another win for the Cubs, but it would have been nice if Arrieta had gone six innings to keep his streak of quality starts going."

Recap:
Arrieta's scoreless streak ended at Wrigley Field after 52 2/3 innings. A fifth inning double ended his streak. He gave up a run and three hits and four walks in five innings. The temperature was 45°, cloudy with a 12 mph wind at his back that seemed to bother him. So after five innings Maddon lifted him. Arrieta initially protested, then agreed with the decision that he had had enough. The Cubs were ahead 6 – 1 and after throwing 119 pitches against Cincinnati on April 21 Arrieta then had six days of rest. He acknowledged he was not accustomed to extra days off. He has a very precise training regimen, and maybe the six days lull in pitching threw him off.

Extra innings:
Arrieta's streak of 24 consecutive quality starts also ended at 24, two shy of Bob Gibson's record in 1967 – 68. "I saw 92 pitches, I saw the Cubs trying to win a World Series, I saw the next five years of his career," Cubs manager Joe Maddon said, "all that stuff mattered much more than breaking Gibson's record."
I think Maddon is really a good manager; he's absolutely got his priorities for the team correct. Way to go Joe.

Today's baseball wisdom:

"Sporting goods companies pay me not to endorse their products."
Bob Uecker

Baseball history this date:

1988 – The Baltimore Orioles lost their American League record 21st game in a row.

Game: #22

Teams: Cubs/Atlanta
Date: Friday, April 29
Final: Cubs win 6 – 1
Record: 17 – 5

V – mail: "Terrific job by Jon Lester; he pitched seven innings and gave up one run and two walks with 10 strikeouts. Szczur hit a grand slam in the eighth to win the game."

Recap:

The final score doesn't look like it was much of a game, but hold on – the score was 1 – 1 going into the eighth inning. Lester was outstanding for the Cubs per Gene's comments above. The Cubs just couldn't get anything off the young guy named Aaron Blair. The guy went six innings and gave up one run, three bases on balls and had three strikeouts.

Then old Joe (Maddon that is) replaced Soler with Matt Szczur in the top of the eight, for defense. In the bottom of the eighth Rizzo singled in a run and then Matt hit a grand slam for the 6-1 win. Strop had pitched the eighth so he got the win and Rondon closed.

Extra innings:

Earlier this year the Diamondbacks and Atlanta made a big trade. I learned today that this guy Blair was one of the Diamondbacks top minor-league pitchers. Two seasons at the AAA he was 10 – 2 with an ERA of 2.43. He along with Ender Inciarte and Dansby Swanson (the number one pick in the 2015 major league draft) were traded to Atlanta for Shelby Miller. Miller, a "hard luck" pitcher with Atlanta had a very low ERA but a terrible record. So the Diamondbacks thought they were getting a really quality guy. But whoops, as of May 29 Miller was 1 – 6 with an ERA of 7.09! If the guys that the Diamondbacks gave to Atlanta do anything, this could be another infamous trade like the Brock for Broglio fiasco! I have to add that, as a Cub fan, it almost makes me ill writing that last sentence.

Today's baseball wisdom:

After Pete Rose's remarkable hitting streak of 44 games was halted he was ambushed by the press. One reporter asked Pete if he was relieved. Pete snapped back, "well I am pissed off."*

*(His streak which began June 14, 1978 and ended against Atlanta on August 1 of the same year, just 12 games short of Joe DiMaggio's still standing record of 56 games.

Baseball history this date:

1988 – The Baltimore Orioles beat the Chicago White Sox 9 – 0 for their first win of the season after 21 losses. (A major league record).

Game: #23

Teams: Cubs/Atlanta
Date: Sunday, May 1
Final: Cubs lose 4 – 3 (ten innings)
Record: 17 – 6

V – mail: "A game that might have been won, but the reliever, Rondon let it get away."

Recap:
Julio Teheran went seven innings, allowed only two hits, one walk and he had nine strikeouts.

He was simply outstanding and left in the eighth inning leading 3 – 0. He is really a talented young pitcher.

The Braves bullpen gave up two runs in the eighth and one in the ninth to tie the score. But Rondon gave up two hits and a walk which gave Atlanta a 4 – 3 lead. The Cubs didn't score in the bottom of the tenth and lost.

Gene called, a bit upset with Russell, even though he singled in the tying run in the ninth. Gene was not happy with him because he booted a ground ball that led to 2 runs. (It would have been a double play).

Extra innings:
Joe Maddon likes to do zany things for the team to "keep them loose," like last year's "pajama flight" when they all wore their Pjs on the airplane. Today, Jason Heyward sported pink shorts and a matching sports coat as part of Maddons minimalist "zany suit" theme for the trip to Pittsburgh. David Ross was asked where he got American flag jacket with stars down one side and stripes on the other, "the trash" he replied.

Today's baseball wisdom:

"When ole Diz (Dean) was out there pitching it was more than just another game. It was a regular three ring circus and everybody was wide awake and enjoying being alive."
Pepper Martin

Baseball history this date:

1968 – Phillies pitcher J. Boozer is ejected for throwing spitballs during warm-up!

Game: #24

Teams: Cubs @ Pittsburgh
Date: Monday, May 2
Final: Cubs win 7 – 2
Record: 18 – 6

V – mail: "Jason Hammel is now 4 and 0; he went five strong innings today giving up only two runs."

Recap:
   Yes Hammel had another really good outing. Five innings giving up only two runs, five hits, one base on balls and three strikeouts. Warren, Grimm, Wood and Strop finished the game and allowed no runs.
   Fowler, Rizzo and Baez each had two hits with Rizzo having two RBIs. Ross also had two RBIs.
   There was "bad blood" during the game and home plate umpire Laz Diaz warned both teams after each pitcher hit an opposing player. There is apparently still bad feelings from last October's bru-ha-ha when both benches cleared during the one-game playoff. Sean Rodriguez, of the Pirates, was ejected from that game and he went ballistic again during this game.

Extra innings:
   As the players were being introduced along with the coaches and managers I took note that the Pirate "skipper" was Clint Hurdle. He was the manager of the Rockies at one time and did well, reaching the playoffs. Once you see Hurdle you won't easily forget him, that is his face. He has a very pleasant demeanor, but notably he has huge bulging chipmunk – like cheeks, that appeared to be packed full, at least on one side. Well, his mouth is full of gum! I watched him on previous occasions and as the game progresses, especially in a close one, he begins shoving sticks of gum into his mouth. I had an image of a fireman on an old-fashioned steam locomotive feeding wood into the firebox. He chews ferociously, as if his jaws were being driven by a human locomotive drive rod. Like the locomotive, the more pressure (steam) the faster go the wheels as does his chewing. He's a real beauty!

Today's baseball wisdom:

   "When I began playing the game, baseball was about as gentlemanly as a kick in the crotch."
   Ty Cobb

Baseball history this date:

1920 – The first game of the national Negro baseball league was played in Indianapolis. The Indianapolis ABCs beat the Chicago American Giants.

Game: #25

Teams: Cubs @ Pittsburgh
Date: Tuesday, May 3
Final: Cubs win 7 – 1
Record: 19 – 6

V – mail: "What more do you say about Jake? His ERA is now 0.84. He gets a lot of press coverage, but he deserves it."

Recap:
Arrieta was terrific again, going seven innings and allowing only two singles, two walks and five strikeouts. A real key to Arrieta's pitching and success is that (as Gene pointed out) he doesn't get upset or frustrated if things don't go his way at some point. For example, in the first inning he issued consecutive walks – no problem – he followed with a strikeout, a fielders choice, and a grounder back to him and that was the end of the inning.

The Cubs scored two in the second and that was actually all they needed to win the game. Bryant had three hits and six Cubs each had an RBI including Arrieta. The Cubs have won seven of their last eight games.

Extra innings:
Pirates manager, Clint Hurdle, (old chipmunk cheeks) tried an unorthodox lineup that included Matt Joyce (.317 BA) in right field thanks to his .500 batting average (7-14) against Arrieta. However the last time Joyce faced Arrieta was in 2013 when Arrieta was struggling with Baltimore. But that's not true today and Joyce went 0 – 3; he never got the ball out of the infield.

Today's baseball wisdom:
"I ain't ever had a job, I just always played baseball."
Satchel Paige

Baseball history this date:
1936 – Joe DiMaggio made his major league debut this date and got three hits.

Game: #26

Teams: Cubs @ Pittsburgh
Date: Wednesday, May 4
Final: Cubs win 6 – 2
Record: 20 – 6

V – mail: "Another nice performance by Lester, going 5 2/3 scattering eight hits with two walks and five strikeouts. Three relievers finished the game giving up two runs."

Recap:

The Cubs swept the Pirates at their home ballpark. Zobrist had a three run home run and Rizzo had a solo shot. Lester got the win, but he had to pitch himself out of a couple of tight spots. Pittsburgh loaded the bases in the fourth inning and had runners on first and second in the fifth but didn't score. After two singles and a walk in the fifth Lester struck out the next two and got a fly ball to right to end the inning. Not really much else to say about the game, Baez did have an RBI also.

Extra innings:

I really like Anthony Rizzo as he does so many things well, hitting, fielding and he's a smart ballplayer. He still very young only 26 years old. But sometimes I can't figure him out as a hitter. He can really get "hot" and also really go into the "deep freeze." For example, in his last 12 games he's hitting .362 (17 – 47) with 16 RBIs; that's after hitting .163 in his first 14 games. He has a good eye and nice swing, but he really can go into a deep slump. Manager Maddon says it's just "bad luck" as his batting average when he hits balls in play was "just atrociously low." Maybe that is the case.

Today's baseball wisdom:

"Slump? I ain't in no slump, I just ain't hitting."
Yogi Berra

Baseball history this date:

1982 – Minnesota Twins rookie outfielder Jim Eisenreich, who suffers from Tourette's syndrome, removed himself from the game, due to taunts from the Boston Red Sox bleacher fans.

Game: #27

Teams: Cubs/Washington
Date: Thursday, May 5
Final Cubs win: 5 – 2
Record: 21 – 6

V – mail: "Kyle Hendricks was really sharp today, throwing six scoreless innings. Great to see the Cubs get him enough runs to win."

Recap:
Along with a really nice pitching performance by Hendricks the Cubs did give him run support, which is not always the case. Ben Zobrist drove in four runs in the opener of a four-game series, between two of baseball's hottest teams. Travis Wood couldn't finish the ninth, giving up a two-run homer to Jason Werth. Rondon came in to get the last out.

The Cubs are now 21 – 6, their best start since 1907 when they were 23 – 4. Tomorrow they get "mad Max" Scherzer who is 3 – 1. He is 1 – 0 with a 1.42 ERA in his last three starts at Wrigley Field. So they have their work cut out for them. Jon Lackey goes for the Cubs.

Good win, but again kind of "ho – hum." Sorry Gene but I didn't get very excited.

Extra innings:
"The worst game we've played in a while but we were still in the ballgame," said manager Dusty Baker. Well, my comment on that is, "what's that you say Dusty, you're down 5 – 0 in the ninth and you're still in the game?" Baloney!

On an unrelated game note, I recently read an article (April 2016) about the sale of baseball rules written in 1857 by a Daniel Adams. They sold at auction for 3.26 million! The rules established 90 – foot base paths, nine innings to a game, and nine men on a side. He referred to batters as "strikers," balks as "baulks" and runs as "aces."

Wow, Gene and I could have bought them in 1999 for only $12,650. With the recent price tag of $3.26 million we would have had a tidy profit. Gene, you should have dug some of that moldy money out of your mattress instead of spending it on cheeseburgers!

Today's baseball wisdom:

"If we're going to win the pennant, we've got to start thinking we're not as good as we think we are."
Casey Stengel

Baseball history this date:

1952 – Ron Necciai of the Pittsburgh Pirates Bristol Twins class D Farm team strikes out 27 as he no –hits the Welch miners; four miners did reach base.*

*(I was 14 years old and just beginning to follow baseball, and I remember reading the story about the 27 strikeouts. Amazing!)

Game: #28

Teams: Cubs/Washington
Date: Friday, May 6
Final: Cubs win 8 – 6
Record: 22 – 6

V – mail: "The Cub hitters got to Scherzer this time; he had really been tough on the Cubs at Wrigley before this game. Lackey pitched well, but the relievers Richards and Grimm each gave up two runs."

Recap:
The boys from Wrigley really got to "mad Max" today. The Cubs scored seven runs off of him, the most he has given up since he joined the Nationals a year ago. They scored seven runs in five innings. They get two in the second two more in the third and three in the fifth for a 7 – 2 lead. They had four home runs by La Stella, Rizzo and Zobrist had two. Zobrist has three home runs in his last two games. (See Gene, trading Castro wasn't such a bad idea, was it?)

As Gene stated above, Richards and Grimm each gave up two runs in the eighth inning and Rondon came in and shut Washington down.

Extra innings:
Before the game the broadcasters were "singing the praises" and rightly so about Scherzer. To wit: last year in one stretch he pitched a one-hitter with 16 strikeouts; next game he retired 26 in a row (I was watching the game) then the 27th batter leaned in on the pitch and got hit. (The guy was a real "horses a--" in my opinion). He retired the next guy so he had a no-hitter; but he should have had a perfect game if that batter hadn't leaned in over the plate. The next game he pitched five innings before someone got a hit. That's 23 innings allowing only one hit. The announcers compared this streak to Johnny Vander Meer's consecutive no-hitters in 1938 (his first full year in the majors) with the Cincinnati Reds. They concluded that Scherzer's accomplishment was more impressive. I really think so also. Vander Meer was wild, walked three in his first no-hitter and eight in the second one, including filling the bases in the ninth inning. Old Leo Durocher popped out to end that game. Some exceptional defense also helped preserve the second no-hitter.

Today's baseball wisdom:

"Stan Hack has as many friends in baseball as Leo Durocher has enemies."
Gabby Hartnett

Baseball history this date:

1998– Kerry Wood of the Chicago Cubs struck out 20 Houston Astros to tie the major league record held by Roger Clemens. He threw a one-hitter and did not walk a batter in only his fifth career start.

Game: #29

Teams: Cubs/Washington
Date: Saturday, May 7
Final: Cubs win 8 – 5
Record: 23 – 6

V – mail: "A back-and-forth game, the Cubs pulled out the win 8 – 5."

Recap:
Gene called after the game, twice he said. "You're line was busy both times, who the devil were you talking to?" He actually sounded a bit put off with me. Ha! I told him that Marlys and Sue were gabbing, so that was okay with him.

The teams exchanged leads and then in the seventh-inning Russell hit a two-run double to break the tie. "Hot shot" Harper, Washington right fielder, apparently didn't go full out after the ball and it kicked off his glove."I didn't want to hit the wall and get hurt and be out for the year." My thought was, "no you just loafed and missed it."

Russell is an interesting hitter, not a high average guy, but today with his three RBIs he's 10 – 32 (.313) with 16 RBIs with men in scoring position. That's pretty clutch hitting.

Warren (3 – 0) got the win with one scoreless inning. Again I reminded Gene that Warren came in the Castro trade, but she still isn't completely happy about that deal.

Extra innings:
This is not a relevant bit of baseball data, but I just heard the news and will note the incident here.

Ann Day, sister of former Supreme Court Justice Sandra Day O'Connor was killed today in Tucson. She was an Arizona State Senator For 10 years and a Pima County supervisor from 2000 – 2012. A 24-year-old under the influence of marijuana, evidently driving at a high rate of speed, jumped a median and hit her head on and killed her. He was not seriously injured. God that's awful.

Today's baseball wisdom:

"I'm no Joe Morgan, but I'm pretty good for a white guy!"
Pete Rose (on his speed)

Baseball history this date:

1959 – Roy Campanella night. The largest baseball crowd in baseball history (93,103 in LA Coliseum) see the Dodgers Sandy Koufax beat the Yankees 6 – 2 in an exhibition game.*

*(The game was a tribute to "Campy" who became a quadriplegic on 1/28/58 in a car crash at age 36. Campanella began playing baseball at age 15 and was signed by the Negro leagues' Washington Elite Giants. He was a star in the Negro leagues during the 40s and signed with the Dodgers in 1946.)

Game: #30

Teams: Cubs/Washington
Date: Sunday, May 8
Final: Cubs win 4 – 3
Record: 24 – 6

V – mail: "I really never expected the Cubs to sweep the Nationals, even though they were at home. They are sure playing great baseball."

Recap:
Arrieta is going for #7 today he's 6 – 0. Gene had said "I suppose Arrieta will lose, as he has to lose some time."

I started watching the game, but when things don't go well I "bail out" and don't watch the game on television. Sure enough a hard smash off Bryant's glove led to a run and eventually the Cubs were down 3 – 1. I'm such a poor sport I turned it off. After a while I go to the computer and "watch" a game cast of the action. It's a simulated version of the playing field, pictures of the hitter and pitcher, reporting of hits, walks and balls in play. Balls are green, strikes are red and balls in play are blue. For some reason I can watch the simulcast, even if the Cubs are losing, but not the live action on television. I finally got my courage up and checked the computer and I'll be damned the game was in the 13th inning tied 3 – 3. Washington did not score in the 13th and in the bottom of the 13th with one out Javier Baez smacked a 415 foot home run to win the game 4 – 3. Arrieta only went five innings so he didn't get the win. The Cubs record is now 24 – 6, that's an .800 winning percentage. Harry Caray would have exclaimed "Holy Cow!"

Extra innings:
Gene called after the game, he had been to Chicago attending the visitation for his son's father-in-law who passed away in his sleep at the age of 64. I had met him at Beth's visitation and he was quite a character. He was a big Sox fan and we exchanged our thoughts and expressions of loyalty to our individual teams. One of his daughters is married to Paul, Gene's son, and the other daughters were also very pretty girls.

Earlier, Gene and I had discussed the importance of this series; he said "I do hope the Cubs could win three out of four. The "Nats" are a tough team with really good pitching like Zimmerman, Strasburg, Scherzer and others. The baseball analysts were suggesting this series might show us how the Cubs really stack up against a really good club. Well the Cubs swept the series.

Today's baseball wisdom:

As the Cubs are playing .800 ball, today's baseball wisdom seems appropriate.

"According to the sporting news, over the last four years Wade Boggs has hit .800 with women in scoring position."

David Letterman

Baseball history this date:

1973 – Ernie Banks filled in for Cubs manager Whitey Lockman who was ejected during the game. So technically he became baseball's (major leagues) first African-American manager.

A Century-Long Journey to the Day of Redemption

Game: #31

Teams: Cubs/San Diego
Date: Tuesday, May 10
Final: Cubs win 8 – 7
Record: 25 – 6

V – mail: "Two big left-handers that can't seem to bunt; a grand slam on an 0 – 2 pitch, ouch! Rondon still perfect."

Recap:
Gene called after the game and was quite nervous that the Cubs almost blew the game. He's really taking his part seriously in the narrative of the games. He said, "here's my beef for today. We have those two multi-million dollar outfielders both left-handers who won't or can't bunt. San Diego does an extreme shift of infielders to the right side with the third baseman at the shortstop position. For Christ sakes they make all that money and can't lay down a bunt to third which would be a sure hit. What the hell's wrong with them?" I had to laugh as he was really fired up about this game. He ended his comments with "if they can't lay down a simple bunt how do they expect to be seen as complete ballplayers?" He's right of course.

The Cubs jumped out to an 8 – 3 after seven innings. Jon Lester went five innings and allowed three runs. After that a parade of pitchers followed him, six in total, with Rondon finally shutting the door. The grand grand slam that Gene mentioned above came off Warren in the eighth inning with two out and an 0 – 2 count on the hitter. Well maybe Warren isn't such a hot deal after all. (from the Yankees in the Castro trade).

Extra innings:
Pursuant to Gene's complaints about left-handers who won't bunt and also Jon Lester who won't throw to first base I think I have a solution. Gene had said maybe Lester needs a psychiatrist. Well I was once a licensed psychologist. In fact I still remember my number, #549. Maybe I could renew my license, hang out a shingle, contact the Cubs during spring training in Mesa, and offer my services in behalf of Lester and those left-handers. I'm about 99% sure that I could "cure" Lester of his inability to throw to first and also convince the lefties to bunt. Lets see, therapy four times a week at $250 an hour for eight weeks that's only eight grand, a drop in the bucket for those "million dollar men." I would have to have an attendant to help me in Mesa so Gene could drop down to be my assistant. Of course we'd have to attend all the spring-training games in Mesa. Front row, box seats to closely monitor Lester's every move and make sure the lefties bunt when

appropriate. I think I'll drop the Cubs an e-mail today concerning my offer. They surely won't refuse, would they?

Today's baseball wisdom:

Asked if Joe DiMaggio could bunt, manager Joe McCarthy replied, "I don't know, nor have I any intention of ever finding out."

Baseball history this date:

1967 – Henry Aaron hit the only inside the park home run of his career against Jim Bunning.

Game: #32

Teams: Cubs/San Diego
Date: Wednesday, May 4
Final: Cubs lose 7 – 4
Record: 25 – 7

V – mail: "Foggy and chilly in Chicago. The Cubs played like their heads were in the clouds. A very sloppy game. Kyle Hendricks pitched great today with a quality start. He was charged with two earned runs and really should have only been one. The game was lost because they left a lot of men on base."

Recap:
I had seen on game cast that the Cubs were leading 4 – 2. Then San Diego got four runs, three off Pedro Strop. There was no phone call when I got home later, so I knew the Cubs had lost. The loss ended their eight-game winning streak.

Gene is big on "quality" starts. I think that means at least six innings of "good pitching." I'm not sure what good means. I guess the term quality start is written in the baseball gods handbook. Somehow in my mind if you lose a game, who gives a damn if it was a quality start or a "p – – – poor start." I'll have to remember to talk to Gene about the details of quality starts, who came up with the idea, and how do you define "good."

Extra innings:
As this was written quite some time ago I now see that I had nothing in this category. I had noted in the margin that the temperature today in Tucson was 94°. The forecast for tomorrow is 100°! Holy smokes that's hot for this time of year. Tucson and Chicago should have traded some temperatures.

Today's baseball wisdom:

"It's a great day for a baseball game; let's play two."*
Ernie Banks
*(Well today the Cubs are playing two, to make up for a rain out.)

Baseball history this date:

1980 – Pete Rose, 39 years old, steals second, third, and home all in one inning for the Phillies.

Game: #33

Teams: Cubs/San Diego
Date: Wednesday, May 11 (second game of doubleheader)
Final: Cubs lose 1 – 0
Record: 25 – 8

V – mail: "Great pitching for both teams; Lackey threw a gem, giving up only three hits, but lost 1 – 0."

Recap:

Oh no, as old Al McCoy (announcer for the Phoenix Suns basketball team) used to say "heartbreak hotel." John Lackey was terrific giving up one run on three hits and still lost the game. San Diego used four different pitchers, and while they gave up four hits they allowed no runs. The Cubs struck out 14 times. Tough to lose this kind of game. An article on ESPN said that the last team to go 33 games before losing two in a row were the 1929 A's. Coincidentally, they beat the Cubs four games to one in the 1929 World Series.

Here's my negative for the day; it's Soler, as he struck out four straight times, and is now hitting .175. Already Schwarber's loss has hurt the Cubs. While he played, he demonstrated that he was a much better hitter than Soler. If he hadn't gotten injured, he would be the starting left fielder.

Extra innings:

Today "mad Max" Scherzer struck out 20, yes 20, Tigers; the most since Kerry Wood (Cubs) fanned 20 in 1998. Interestingly an article on ESPN several days ago discussed the likelihood of a 20 strikeout game. They concluded that it wasn't very likely. Ha! Wrong again you "experts."

Today's baseball wisdom:

"Always go to other people's funerals, otherwise they won't come to yours." Yogi Berra

Baseball history this date:

1959 – Yankee catcher Yogi Berra's errorless streak ended at 148 games.

Game: #34

Teams: Cubs/Pittsburgh
Date: Friday, May 13
Final: Cubs win 9 – 4
Record: 26 – 8

V – mail: "Back on track after losing two to San Diego."

Recap:
The game was on MLB network, but Marlys and I were running errands so I didn't see any of the action. I did check on game cast on the computer and saw that the score was 8 – 2, but I didn't turn on the TV. Hammel had another good game as he pitched 6 2/3 innings giving up eight hits and two runs. Cahill gave up a two-run homer in the ninth inning to McCutchen. The Cubs had three home runs today by Russell, Bryant, and Ross. Russell and Ross hit three-run homers and Bryant's was a two-run shot. They drove in eight of the nine runs for the Cubs. They scored three in the fourth and five the fifth, and added a run in the eighth.

Extra innings:
Gene called and after the usual "BS" concerning the game we got into an extended discussion on how a seemingly innocent call on a strike or a ball (or a play) can completely change the outcome of the game. Gene said the home plate umpire called ball three on what was obviously strike three on Addison Russell. He promptly hit the next pitch out of the park for a three run homer. Likewise two games ago, against San Diego, Baez made an error which led to three runs and ostensibly a loss for the Cubs. Gene and I both have a real problem with the often "outrageous strike zones" of the umpires. I think they should get rid of the home plate umpire and call the game electronically. Maybe because we have replays of the pitches one can see how badly some umpires missed the call; then again, maybe the umpires are just lousy.

Today's baseball wisdom:

This was the date that Matt, my son, made the crack about Gene being "the voice of victory." He said, very soberly, "yes, Gene Shippy, the voice of victory!"*

Matthew Kloepping

*(so I had to change all the e-mails to v-mails)

Baseball history this date:

1955 – Mickey Mantle hit three consecutive home runs at Yankee stadium, all over 463 feet; one was over 500 feet

Game: #35

Teams: Cubs/Pittsburgh
Date: Saturday, May 14
Final: Cubs win 8 – 2
Record: 27 – 8

V – mail: "Well, maybe Arrieta won't lose a game the entire year. Ha! He will eventually but he sure is tough so far this year."

Recap:
Arrieta went eight innings, struck out 11 and gave up two earned runs. For a while it didn't look good as he gave up four hits and two runs in the third inning. Then Rizzo hit home run #11 and that seemed to give Arrieta a real lift, as after the third inning he gave up nothing. Addison Russell also had a home run.

Gene called after the game and left a message. I called back and we got into a discussion about Arrieta's "no discount" contract remarks. In essence, he said that other top-flight pitchers were getting long-term, multi-million dollar contracts, and when it came time to renegotiate his contract he wasn't thinking about giving the Cubs a discount. I told Gene that kind of worries me. Gene, of course, always optimistic said, "oh BS" they all talk that way, don't worry he'll sign."

I sure hope so, if he decided to play hardball with the negotiation, the Cubs could be looking at a contract in the 150 – 200 million dollar range.

Extra innings:
Matt and I went to the University of Arizona women's softball game. Truly a great game to watch: a lot faster than a baseball game, and a lot of the gals are really good looking. Ha! Seriously, next to college basketball, I think it's my favorite sport to attend. The gals of Arizona won 11 – 2 and hit four home runs. It was senior day, and we were all pulling for the only senior, Loren Young to hit one out. Her last at-bat she hit one to dead center and the other teams' centerfielder caught it with her back to the wall. What a Hollywood ending if the ball had gone out.

Today's baseball wisdom:

(With Arrieta pitching so well again this year, I found a comment that I think fits the situation.)

"If Satchel Paige and I were pitching for the same team we would clinch the pennant by the Fourth of July and go fishing until World Series time."
Dizzy Dean

Baseball history this date:

1989 – For the first time since 1948, a player, Kirby Puckett, of the Minnesota Twins, hits four consecutive doubles.

Game: #36

Teams: Cubs/Pittsburgh
Date: Sunday, May 15
Final: Cubs lose 2 – 1
Record: 27 – 9

V – mail: "Another great pitching performance by the Cubs Lester; he gave up one run and two hits in six innings plus, but Cole was better as we lost 2 – 1. We had our chances."

Recap:
I don't think I like Koreans, especially Jung Ho Kang, as he got a double for an RBI and then hit a home run off Rondon to give Pittsburgh a 2 – 0 lead. In the bottom of the ninth Fowler walked and Heyward singled putting runners on first and third with no outs. Bryant flied to center, Rizzo flied to right, and a run scored making it to 2-1; but Zobrist grounded out to end the game. Gee, what if Rondon hadn't thrown the gopher ball, the game is tied 1 – 1. I know, it's like saying what if an elephant had wings! As Gene said, Cole was really tough, throwing seven innings, no runs, three hits, and seven strikeouts. Melancon, a former University of Arizona pitcher, got the save.

Extra innings:
I couldn't think of anything more to add to the game today so I tossed in this little tidbit.

We have a problem with squirrels in our neighborhood. They don't climb trees, they just run around on the ground, dig holes, or live under piles of debris and generally are a nuisance. They get in my garden and eat the tomatoes, egg plant and anything else that they think is edible. Well, Matt finally trapped a big dude (they're called rock squirrels), and hauled his butt (that is the squirrel) off to Fort Lowell Park to release him. It must be rock squirrel "heaven" as there is lots of grass, water, pecan trees, and probably lots of lady squirrels. This guy will know what to do, as he had a really big pair of "huevos." Lucky guy!

Today's baseball wisdom:

Maybe Cole, the Pittsburgh pitcher, took the advice of a wily, crafty old-timer who said: "My pitching philosophy is simple – keep the ball away from the bat."
Satchel Paige

Baseball history this date:

1941 – Joe DiMaggio starts his 56 game hitting streak. The Yankees lost the game 13 – 1

also

1912- Ty Cobb assaults a fan in the stadium. (See May 19 write-up.)

A Century-Long Journey to the Day of Redemption

Game: #37

Teams: Cubs @ Milwaukee
Date: Tuesday, May 17
Final: Cubs lose 4-2
Record: 27 – 10

V – mail: "Maybe it's because the Cubs are doing so well, that opposing teams, especially the pitchers, really get up for the games."

Recap:
Some dude named Anderson held the Cubs hitless for seven innings. His ERA before this game was above 5.00, but today one would think he was a Cy Young winner.

Kyle Hendricks didn't have his best game as he went 5.1 innings giving up five hits and allowing four runs.

Zobrist got a single in the eighth and then in the ninth Heyward and Bryant hit back-to-back home runs. The Cubs have scored a total of three runs in the last two games. What in the world is going on?

This game was so disappointing I really have nothing more to say other than, "crap we lost again."

Extra innings:
Gene called around 3:30 PM. "What," I said, "I thought the game was at night." Well, it was an evening game but he called with a news flash. The Cubs signed old Joe Nathan, a 41-year-old guy coming off Tommy John surgery. He was a great reliever for the "Twinkies" as he had 260 saves from 2004-2011 with an ERA of 2.16. This game made me think of Vernelle Kohn, Marlys' sister who "loved" Joe Nathan when he was a great reliever for the Minnesota Twins from 2004 – 2011. Vernelle passed away in 2009. The Twins had many good years back then (unlike this year) and Vernelle was a very knowledgeable fan. We had many extended discussions about baseball strategy, managers' decisions, skills of individual players and especially "our teams."

Vernelle was 100% loyal to her Minnesota "Twinkies" and Nathan was her guy. Somehow I'm sure she is celebrating today.

Today's baseball wisdom:
"Nobody ever had too many of them (pitchers)."
Casey Stengel

Baseball history this date:

1915 – Cubs pitcher George" zip" Zabel relieved with two outs in the first inning and winds up with a 4 – 3 win in 19 innings over Brooklyn in the longest relief job ever.

Game: #38

Teams: Cubs @ Milwaukee
Date: Wednesday, May 18
Final: Cubs win 2 – 1
Record: 28 – 10

V – mail: "What a game; a case of I don't want it you take it. Lots of good pitching and defense. David Ross, the catcher, accounted for four outs in eight innings. He threw out two trying to steal and picked off two guys from second base."

Recap:
I recalled an old rural Midwestern expression from my childhood that appropriately described the Cubs inability to get any hits in this game. The saying was, "they or he couldn't hit a bull in the ass with a broomstick." They were very fortunate to win this game.

Joe Maddon, the manager of the Cubs, did his magic in the bottom of the 12th with the bases loaded and no outs for Milwaukee. He made a number of defensive moves and brought in Travis Wood to pitch. Wood has to be the hero of the game as he got all three outs and Milwaukee didn't score. Then in the 13th with a bases-loaded for the Cubs, he walked for the winning run. The Cubs used their entire team except for several starting pitchers for the game.

Extra innings:
Gene is really a fan of the highest caliber; or someone being less charitable might call him a fanatic!

Whatever the case, I called him the next day because I had gone to bed not knowing who won after seeing them tie the score at 1 – 1 in the ninth inning. Beginning with the fourth inning he proceeded to recount the entire sequence of plays all the way through the 13th inning. Now I can remember a lot of plays that happen, but he had the whole damn game memorized in addition to remembering all the defensive moves that Maddon had made. Gene used to say that he was a poor student and not as smart as a lot of other guys; that's a lot of "BS," as anyone who can follow a game that closely and remember it has something up there more than just rocks!

Today's baseball wisdom:

"One thing you learned as a Cub fan, when you bought a ticket you could bank on seeing the bottom of the ninth."
Joe Garagiola

Baseball history this date:

1912 – The Philadelphia Athletics routed the Detroit Tigers 24 – 2, as the Tigers were using amateur players in protest to Ty Cobb's suspension.

A Century-Long Journey to the Day of Redemption

Game: #39

Teams: Cubs @ Milwaukee
Date: Thursday, May 19
Final: Cubs lose 5 - 3
Record: 28 – 11

V – mail: "Well I don't know where the Brewers are coming up with all these pitchers; wherever they came from they are sure giving the Cub hitters fits."

Recap:
What in the world is wrong with the Cubs? They have lost five of their last eight games and have scored just eight runs in losing three of their last four. They had only six hits and 11 strikeouts today. The Brewer pitcher Guerra, gave up a lead-off home run to Fowler, but only two runs after, with one scoring on a wild pitch. Gene says I'm a pessimist, but I'm still worrying about losing Schwarber as a hitter. Soler is hitting only .187, Montero has gone 0 – 20 before getting a triple, and Heyward is hitting .225. Also, Rizzo has been slumping lately. Zobrist is about the only guy who's doing well at this point, hitting .328 and he has reached base safely in 26 straight games. My oh my oh my!

Extra innings:
Milwaukee currently has a record of 18 – 23. They had a better record than I realized, but with Guerra, a guy named Nelson (I think he's the top guy) and Anderson who beat the Cubs two days earlier they will win more than a few more games.

On a side note, old Morley Safer (as my father used to say) "kicked the bucket today." I always liked him, especially on 60 minutes and all kinds of other gigs that he did.

Today's baseball wisdom:

"I had slumps that lasted all winter."
Bob Uecker

Baseball history this date:

1912 – American league president Ban Johnson tells the Detroit Tigers that if they continue the protest over Ty Cobb's suspension they will be banned from baseball."*

*(Cobb had jumped into the stands and assaulted a fan who was heckling him. The fan had called Cobb (an avowed racist) "a half N – – – – R." The fan had lost his hands in accident, and when the crowd yelled at Cobb to

stop the assault because the guy had no hands, Cobb said "I don't care if he has no feet." Cobb returned to playing after serving a 10 game suspension during which his teammates and team owner had supported him.)

Game: #40

Teams: Cubs @ San Francisco
Date: Friday, May 20
Final: Cubs win 8 – 1
Record: 29 – 11

V – mail: "Thanks to Jake Peavy for letting the Cubs find their bats. A great night for our Jake as he gave up only one run in seven innings. Kris drove in four runs and Ben and Jorge went back-to-back. Ben's found water (San Francisco Bay). The bullpens lefties closed out the game for the Cubs."

Recap:
Before I do the recap here, I wanted the reader to note how strongly Gene has identified with this group at this point. He doesn't use last names, everything is on a first name basis, i.e. Kris, Ben, Jorge, and so on. He is a fan with a capital F!

Arrieta won again and is now 8 – 0. The Cubs have won his last 22 starts dating to last season and he is 19 – 0 during that stretch. Heyward crashed into the fence making a great catch off Denard Spahn (the first batter of the game for the Giants) and had to leave the game. An MRI later will tell how much damage there is, if any.

Extra innings:
Gene said, "Arrieta is amazing; I watched the entire game and didn't get to bed till after midnight."

Zobrist homered into "McCovey Cove" (the Bay) for his sixth homer, becoming just the 38th opposing player and the second Cub (Corey Patterson) to reach San Francisco's Bay waters with a "splash hit."

Today's baseball wisdom:

"Bob Gibson is the luckiest pitcher I have ever seen. That's because he picks the night to pitch when the other team doesn't score any runs."
Tim McCarver

Baseball history this date:

1920 – Policemen raid the Cub's bleachers and arrest 24 for gambling.

Game: #41

Teams: Cubs @ San Francisco
Date: Saturday, May 21
Final: Cubs lose 5 – 3
Record: 29 – 12

V – mail: "The first time a starting pitcher did not make it through five innings. That's the story of the game as the Cubs were unable to catch up." (Sent at 7:05 AM, 5/22)

Recap:
Per Gene's comment above, it's an amazing statistic that 41 games into this season and counting the last seven games of the previous year, Cub pitchers have gone 48 straight games with at least five innings pitched. (Just another bit of baseball trivia that soon will be forever swept into the dustbin of history).

The Cubs have now lost six of their last 10 games. A baseball analyst said, "the Cubs now learn what can happen when Rizzo and Lester struggle." Rizzo was 0 – 5 and Lester went 2.2 innings giving up six hits, five runs and three walks. I watched it only through the second inning when Cain, the pitcher wacked a two-out two-run double. I did see Bryant hit a home run in the third inning, but then I left; when I came back it was 5 – 1, as Buster Posey had hit a three run homer.

Extra innings:
Pitching seems to kill the Cubs these days. Cain, the Giants pitcher, who is now 1 – 5, won for the first time in 15 consecutive starts. In previous years he had really been tough, but he had surgery in
2014 for chips in his elbow and had several stints on the disabled list in 2015. With his reemergence the Giants could be a tough team to beat. Their pitching staff is potentially really a good one, with Cain, Bumgarner, Peavy, Cueto, and Jeff Samardzja.

Today's baseball wisdom:

Johnny Blanchard sat in the Yankees clubhouse crying after he learned he had been traded to Kansas City. Concerned for his teammate, Mickey Mantle sat down and tried to console Blanchard. "Don't take it so hard John, just think in Kansas City you are going to get a chance to play." "Hell, I can't play Mick, that's why I'm crying."

Baseball history this date:

1969 – After 9015 at-bats Hank Aaron is lifted for a pinch-hitter named Mike Lum, who promptly doubled in a 15 – 3 win over the Mets.

Game: #42

Teams: Cubs @ San Francisco
Date: Sunday, May 22
Final: Cubs lose 1 – 0
Record: 29 – 13

V – mail: "Another great pitching match up. Typical run support for Kyle Hendricks."

Recap:
What in the world is going on? Hendricks pitches another gem and loses 1 – 0. He's among the top four or five pitchers in the major leagues who gets little or no run support. Obviously the offense is struggling; for example, Rizzo is 1 – 22 on this road trip. He is really an enigma as a hitter, as he can get really hot and then boom, colder than an ice cube. Russell is also struggling terribly as he struck out four times today against Bumgarner. He has struck out 12 times in the last 6 games Hendricks allowed only the one run on a double by Bumgarner. He gave up only three hits, and three walks in 5 1/3 innings of work. Unfortunately Bumgarner was terrific as he went 7 2/3 innings, allowing no runs, three hits, and seven strikeouts.

Extra innings:
Jason Heyward who injured himself making a diving catch in Friday's 8 – 1 win over San Francisco suffered a contusion on his right side near his ribs. He had "robbed" Denard Spahn of extra bases leading off for the Giants in the first inning. Gene said it was the best outfield catch he had ever seen.

Today's baseball wisdom:

"There are a number of factors that contribute to the outcome of a game, but when you get right down to it, the key to winning the game is to score more runs than the other team."
Kent Kloepping

Baseball history this date:

1990 – Andre Dawson of the Chicago Cubs, received a record five intentional walks in a game.

Game: #43

Teams: Cubs @ St. Louis
Date: Monday, May 23
Final: Cubs lose 3 – 4
Record: 29 – 14

V – mail: "It's always tough to lose a well pitched and played game to the Cardinals. That one hurt, but we are still 15 games over .500."

Recap:
The Cubs were leading 3 – 1 after six innings with Lackey breezing along. Then he gave up a pinch-hit two-run homer to Matt Adams. St. Louis leads the majors with nine pinch-hit homers. Grichuk then won the game in the ninth with a home run off Warren.

I hope the Cubs don't start their old ways, that is scoring early, but never adding on any runs and eventually losing the game. I really do dislike those Cardinals. I think they are a bunch of lucky "SOB's."

I called Gene and told him he needed to e-mail Maddon and get the Cubs back on track. Gene was a bit, "sober" as I don't think he appreciated my attempt at humor. Ha!

Extra innings:
The Cubs did dodge a bullet as Jason Heyward may return in 2 to 3 days after running into the wall three days ago in San Francisco. They really need his defense in the outfield.

Today's baseball wisdom:

Alan Bannister talking about Rod Carew said, "He's the only guy I know who can go 4 for 3!"

Baseball history this date:

1883 – Today there was a game between one-armed and one – legged players.*

*Before radio broadcasts, novelty games were organized to get fans in the stands while their team was traveling. (For example, fat versus skinny guys, black guys versus Chinese dudes, and clowns versus women). Obviously this was many years before the idea of "political correctness" came into being. Such games make me think of the historical "sideshows" that were always a part of traveling circuses, supposedly exhibiting all kinds of "human and animal freaks."

I thought maybe the guys who had lost her limbs came from the Civil

War, but the article said that most of the men had lost their limbs in railroad accidents. Jeepers tough job back then.

Game: #44

Teams: Cubs @ St. Louis
Date: Tuesday, May 24
Final: Cubs win 12 – 3
Record: 30 – 14

V – mail: "I don't get it, why leave Hammel in the game after seven scoreless innings? He's leading 8 – 0 so take him out and turn it over to the bullpen."

Recap:

We heard from the "voice of victory" even before the game was over. In fact he called with one out in the ninth and the Cubs leading 12 – 1. "Hey, it's not over I remarked." Gene said kind of matter-of-factly, "well, with an 11 run lead in the ninth I'm not too worried."

The game was on ESPN, and I was outside when Marlys yelled at me, "hey the Cubs are on TV." I replied, "okay, but are they behind?"

"No, she said, it's the second inning and the Cubs are up 6 – 0." They didn't score again until the fifth inning and again I started worrying about them not adding any more runs. Then Soler hit a two-run shot (good to see him hit one) and they scored four in the ninth to put it away. St. Louis scored one in the eighth and two in the ninth. The Cubs beat Michael Wacha who gave up eight earned runs, his career worst eight runs in four innings. He is usually really a tough pitcher.

Extra innings:

Jason Heyward returned to the lineup for the first time since last Friday. Lucky he wasn't hurt more. Gene has definite ideas about what is a hit and what is an error. ESPN gave a Cardinal a hit in the ninth that La Stella had bobbled. I told Gene later that the announcer had called it a hit. "Bull, it was an error, he snorted." I checked the box score later and sure enough it was an error." Okay, touché Gene.

Today's baseball wisdom:

"Charlie Gehringer is in a rut. He hits .350 on opening day and stays there all year."
Lefty Gomez

Baseball history this date:

1935 – The first major league night baseball game was played in Cincinnati. The Reds beat the Phillies 2 – 1.

A Century-Long Journey to the Day of Redemption

Game: #45

Teams: Cubs @ St. Louis
Date: Wednesday, May 25
Final: Cubs win 9 – 8
Record: 31 – 14

V – mail: "I'm too old for this kind of stuff. Just when you think the game is in the bag those Cardinals come roaring back. They sure can ruin the day."

Recap:
So the Cubs break out early and score 6 runs in the second inning for a 6 – 2 lead with Arrieta pitching. I think no problem Arrieta will handle these guys. Whoops, he gives up two more in the fourth and now the score is 6 – 4. Maddeon lifts Arrieta in the sixth for Warren, and in the same inning Bryant smacks a three run homer. So now the score is 9 to 4, but Warren promptly gets nailed by Halliday for a three run homer and the score is 9 – 7. Then Adams blasts one off Wood in the bottom of the seventh and now it's 9 – 8. Oh no, I can't watch, and I don't, I go get a haircut. Grimm and Strop shut them out in the seventh and eighth (Wood only pitched to Adams as Maddon doesn't fool around and jerked him immediately). Rondon, the Cubs closer, came on in the ninth. I didn't see it, but the "voice of victory" called and left a message; he sounded a bit stressed. Well, why not, the first guy gets a single, the next guy gets a single; now there are two on and no out and up comes Yadier Molina, a great clutch hitter. Holy cow, Rondon stuck him out. Then he KO'd Grichuk and got Gyroko to ground out. Gene sounded almost giddy with relief. Ha!

Extra innings:
Arrieta became the first club to win his first nine decisions since Kenny Holtzman in 1967. (The year the Cubs blew an eight game lead in August to the Mets). Arrieta's start is the best to start a season since Jim McCormick went 16 – 0 in (get this) 1886!

Today's baseball wisdom:

"Even Napoleon had his Watergate."
Yogi Berra

Baseball history this date:

1919 – Casey Stengel releases a sparrow from under his baseball hat.*
*(Stengel, playing for the Pirates in center field, had a ground ball go through the legs and the fans "hooted" at him. On the way back to the dugout

he found a sparrow and put it under his hat. When he came to back later he lifted his hat, releasing the sparrow. In effect, "giving the fans the bird.")

Game: #46

Teams: Cubs/Philadelphia
Date: Friday, May 27
Final: Cubs with 6 – 2
Record: 32 – 14

V – mail: "Another quality start for Jon Lester as he went 6 1/3 strong innings allowing only one earned run, six hits, two bases on balls and seven strikeouts. Also the Cubs hit three home runs to support his pitching."

Recap:
Yes, Lester was really good again today, and three long home runs by Ross, Soler, and Bryant gave them all the runs they needed. Bryant has hit four home runs in his last seven games, Ross (a.k.a. "grandpa") now has 100 homers for his career. Known principally for his great defensive and savvy skills behind the plate, he has been a surprise offensively, with four home runs and 17 RBIs. Speaking of surprises, Zobrist had two more hits and is now hitting .350! The game had two rain delays, 56 minutes in the seventh-inning, and 37 minutes in the ninth.

The game was on Comcast and I left the computer with rain beginning again in the ninth. When I got back, the "voice of victory" had called. He missed the ninth also, so I went to Comcast and gave him a rundown.

Extra innings:
I decided to add a note of humor for this section today. Tommy Lasorda, the colorful manager of the Los Angeles Dodgers, was asked the age of his two elderly pinch hitters, Manny Mota, and Vic Davalillo. Lasorda shrugged, and said "I don't know, but somebody told me they were waiters at the Last Supper."

Today's baseball wisdom:

From another classic Casey Stengel quip. Sitting in the dugout with Bob Cerv, several minutes passed before Stengel spoke. He said, "nobody knows this but one of us has been traded to Kansas City." That was 1956.*

*(Some say the comment was pure fiction but it really did sound like a classic "Stengelism". It was a terrible trade for the Yankees as Cerv almost won the Triple Crown in 1958.)

Baseball history this date:

1987 – Phil Niekro, of the Yankees, became the third pitcher in major league history to make his 700th start. The other two were Cy Young, but the other was a surprise, as it was a modern day guy named Don Sutton.

Game: #47

Teams: Cubs/Philadelphia
Date: Saturday, May 28
Final: Cubs win 4 – 1
Record: 33 – 14

V – mail: "Well, they finally got Hendricks some runs, 4, and he pitched a fabulous game."

Recap:

Gene wasn't totally happy as the defense blew Hendrick's shutout in the ninth. Uncharacteristically, Fowler and Zobrist both watched a pop foul drop between them. So now there's a man on second and he gets to third on a groundout. Howard is batting and the Cubs shift their infield way to the right. Howard strikes out, but Montero has to throw to first, and does record the out. However because of the shift, the guy on third had a huge lead and when Montero threw to first the guy came home. Hendricks really was good, a complete game, one run, five hits, no walks, and seven strike-outs. In contrast to Hendrick's great performance, the Chicago Bears wide receiver Alshon Jeffrey singing, "take me out to the ballgame" in the seventh inning, had, to say the least, a rendition that was memorable. It, or he, was simply terrible. Ha!

Extra innings:

Here's a bit of women's softball information. The University of Arizona softball gals beat Auburn today 5 – 3 in the first of a three-game series in the super regionals at Auburn. The crowd (99% Auburn) was shocked as University of Arizona was unranked and Auburn was ranked as the number 4 team in America with a 52 – 9 record. I'd love to see them knock Auburn out and go on to the World Series, especially since Auburn's coach is an old fart named Clint Myers. He was the former coach for Arizona State women's team, and as such, I find it very difficult to pull for anyone associated with Arizona State University (or as we like to say at the University of Arizona), that school up the road known as, "Tempe Normal State Teachers College." In addition to his previous affiliation with "Tempe Normal" he is an obnoxious old buffoon, at least in my opinion.

Today's baseball wisdom:

"I walk into the clubhouse today and it's like walking into the Mayo Clinic. We have four doctors, three therapists, and five trainers. Back when I broke in, we had one trainer who carried a bottle of rubbing alcohol and

by the seventh-inning he'd already drank it."
Tommy Lasorda

Baseball history this date:

1995 – The Chicago White Sox (5) and the Detroit Tigers (7) combine for a record 12 home runs at Tiger Stadium.

Game: #48

Teams: Cubs/Philadelphia
Date: Sunday, May 29
Final: Cubs win 7 – 2
Record: 34 – 14

V – mail: "Well, the Cubs have won five in a row and they are now 20 games over .500. Remember in previous years when we worried about them getting to the .500 mark. Let's hope it continues."

Recap:

Another good win for the Cubs and everybody seems to chip in. Bryant, Rizzo, Montero, and Zobrist all had RBIs. Zobrist had a three run homer and is now hitting .351 – wow who would have guessed that he would come on this strong. But again it's the pitching as Lackey went seven strong innings, giving up four hits and one run and now has a good ERA of 3.16. However, he is fifth among Cub starters in ERA as Arrieta is 1.72, Hammel is 2.17, Lester is 2.48, and Hendricks is 2.93. All I can say is that's pretty damn good!

Extra innings:

Joe Maddon expressed his appreciation for the Cubs not easing up on "sweep day." That is having a series won and then letting down on the potential sweep day. "These guys are not letting down," he said. The Cubs have already swept the Angels, Reds, Brewers, Pirates, and the Nationals. They are 11 – 4 – 1 in 16 series.

Today's baseball wisdom:

"Look at him, he knows he's going to hit me, and I know he's going to hit me, so I'm going to walk him."
Harvey Haddix*
*(to his catcher with Willie Mays at bat)

Baseball history this date:

1990 – Rickey Henderson steals a record 893rd base, breaking Ty Cobb's record.

A Century-Long Journey to the Day of Redemption

Game: #49

Teams: Cubs/Los Angeles Dodgers
Date: Monday, May 30 (Memorial Day)
Final: Cubs win 2 – 0
Record: 35 – 14

V – mail: I must have failed to record Gene's mail as I don't have it. Instead I'll report his call after the Cubs won. I was following the game on game cast, and Gene called about 10 seconds before the game ended on my computer. Evidently there is a slight delay on the computer compared to the television broadcast.

Recap:
Jason Hammel only pitched two innings and then left with a leg cramp. He had given up only a single in the second inning. Enter the Cub relievers, and Wood, Grimm, Strop, and Hector Rondon proceeded to pitch seven perfect innings. That's 21 up and 21 down! Wood went four innings and the other three guys one inning each.

Zobrist and Rizzo each drove in a run and that was all there was to the game. Cubs pitching has been amazing. Gene chuckled throughout our entire 10 – 12 minute discussion, totally delighted with his beloved Cubbies.

Extra innings:
My gosh baseball has changed in the last 50 to 60 years. (Since I started paying attention about 1948 – 1950). It's the pitching, I mean, or maybe it's a change in strategy, as today the Cubs used five pitchers. In today's game, it is very common to see a starter go six or seven innings and then see 1, 2, or 3 more relievers come in to finish the game. Pitching a complete game these days is a rarity. But back in the 50s, a guy named Robin Roberts, who pitched for the Phillies (1948 – 1961) once pitched 28 straight complete games during the 1952 – 1953 season! Unbelievable! Warren Spahn of the old Boston Braves and then Milwaukee Braves from 1949 to 1954 had complete-game totals of, 25, 26, 25, 19, 24, and 23.

Another "workhorse" of the late sixties and early seventies was Canadian born Ferguson Jenkins of the Chicago Cubs. From 1967-1972 he had complete game totals of 20,20,23,24,30, and 23. Traded to Texas, he had additional complete game totals of 29 and 33.

(Here's a short piece from Wikipedia):
"In the early 20th century it was common for most good major league pitchers to pitch a complete game almost every start, barring injury or ejection. Pitchers were expected to complete games they started. Over the course

of the 20th century, complete games became less common, to the point where a good modern pitcher typically achieves only one or two complete games per season. In the 1904 MLB season, 87.6 % of starts were complete games. In 1944 45.2%, but in 2014 only 2.4% of all starts were completed To put this in perspective, as recently as the 1980s 10 – 15 complete games a year by a star pitcher was the typical "standard."

The trend over the past 110 years clearly demonstrates how fundamentally the role of the starting pitchers has changed.

There is one startling exception to this trend that transpired in 1980. Rick Langford of the Oakland Athletics pitched twenty-two straight complete games from May 23 to September 12. The manager, Billy Martin, removed him the 23rd start after 8 and 2/3 innings, much to Langford's relief. Crafty old Charlie O. Finley was the owner and I wondered if he had supplied Langford with some kind of "joy juice." Now I'm just kidding, so don't run for your lawyer!

Today's baseball wisdom:

"Once Musial timed your fastball, you're infielders were in jeopardy."
Warren Spahn

Baseball history this date:

1956 – Mickey Mantle misses by 18 inches of hitting a home run clear out of Yankee Stadium.

Game: #50

Teams: Cubs/Dodgers
Date: Tuesday, May 31
Final: Cubs lose 0 – 2
Record: 35 – 15

V – mail: "It was pitching again in this game as Jake and the opposing hurler threw shutout baseball for seven innings. The bullpen gave it up in this one. The final score was 5 – 0 LA."

Recap:

I got no call from the "voice" as the Cubs lost. Just the rather terse v-mail from my friend, see above.

The analysts said,"the Los Angeles Dodgers found a way to win when facing Jake Arrieta, throw a one-hitter." That's what Kazmir and two relievers did. Arrieta didn't lose but it broke a 23 game streak of games that the Cubs had won when Arrieta started. Arrieta gave up two hits, four walks, and eight strikeouts, and lowered his ERA to 1.56.

Extra innings:

There's really not much to report on the game with the Cubs only getting one hit. The Cubs catcher Miguel Montero made two errors in a span of five pitches; he bobbled a grounder and then threw wild to second base. Also, Neil Ramirez was put on assignment by the Cubs and I think maybe he was claimed by the Brewers. I thought he was pretty good, and Maddon said "if he's healthy he's got a wipe – out slider." I wonder why they are letting him go? Speaking of getting only one hit, it reminded me of what Bob Uecker once said live on the radio (see below,"wisdom").

Today's baseball wisdom:

"That's all we got, one God damn hit." Another guy in the booth responded, " you can't say God damn on the air." To which Uecker replied, "don't worry nobody's listening anyway."
Bob Uecker

Baseball history this date:

1937 – The Brooklyn Dodgers snap New York Giants pitcher Carl Hubbell's 24 game winning streak.

Game: #51

Teams: Cubs/Dodgers
Date: Wednesday, June 1
Final: Cubs win 2 – 1
Record: 36 – 15

V – mail: "Pitching, pitching, pitching – that's the name of the game, and so far at game 51 the Cubs pitching has been lights out."

Recap:

Lester really did pitch a masterful game; but I'm a coward and I guess the best way to describe me is I'm a "chicken" kind of fan. Pessimistic says my wife and also Gene. I turned on the game (ESPN) and the second pitch that Lester threw, a guy named Kiki Hernandez (I never heard of him) hit the pitch out of the park! Oh crap! I stopped watching for a while and then checked the score on the computer and saw that Bryant had hit a monster home run in the third and the Cubs led 2 – 1. I just couldn't watch waiting for the Dodgers to hit one out with a guy on base and win the game 3-2 as the Cubs couldn't hit the dodger pitcher Bolsinger and two other relievers. Well, the Dodgers didn't score and we get to the ninth inning. I gritted my teeth, turned on the television and watched Lester, still in the game. He got two easy groundouts and then a strikeout. Hooray, Cubs win 2 – 1.

Extra innings:

Lester had 10 strikeouts and no walks; he threw 113 pitches and retired the last 15 Dodgers he faced. I'm not a fan of the pitch count mania, that is setting a limit on how many pitches the guy can throw and when he reaches that point he gets jerked, ridiculous. Stop worrying about wearing the guy out. Lester makes 20 million a year and he wouldn't have to pitch another game and he's still set for life. Hell, he could go fishing every day with Dizzy Dean and old Satchel Paige! (see Baseball Wisdom, game #35)

Today's baseball wisdom

"I don't like the pitch count. How are you gonna develop your arm? If you're a track man you say, hey you can't run too much! Or if you're a boxer you say, hey you can only box 3 rounds. It's not right."
Tommy Lasorda

Baseball history this date:

1975 – Nolan Ryan, of the California Angels throws his fourth no-hitter and beats the Baltimore Orioles 1 – 0.

Game: #52

Teams: Cubs/Dodgers
Date Thursday, June 2
Final: Cubs win 7 – 2
Record: 37 – 15

V – mail: "Hendricks was terrific again, but he should have had a shutout."

Recap:
The Cubs coasted to an easy victory with four home runs – Heyward, Bryant, Rizzo, and Baez. Baez also made a fantastic catch at second, lunging to snag a liner. The game, however once again really belonged to the pitching staff, that is Kyle Hendricks. He threw a complete game his last start and went eight strong innings today, with Maddon electing to lift him for a pinch-hitter in the eighth. Not only did Maddon have praise for Hendricks, he now knows that he can go beyond five or six innings, and that's really important. Hendricks is really an interesting pitcher; no blazing fastball, or wicked curve, or slider, but he gets guys out with his great control. He must be a smart guy and the Cubs do call him the "Professor."

Extra innings:
The "voice" called, really pleased with the win but p'od, because in his view the two runs the Dodgers got were "not deserved." Gene, you have to understand is a huge fan of Hendricks. He has often said that Hendricks style of pitching reminds him of the Hall of Famer Greg Maddux. I can also see the similarities.

Anyway, here's Gene's complaint:

#1) The first dodger run came on a home run, however Hendricks threw three straight pitches in the same spot, the umpire called two strikes and then pitch #3 he called a ball. On the next pitch the guy hit the ball out of the park. He should've been out.

#2) There was a dodger on second base. The Cub catcher had a passed ball so the guy goes to third. Then a sacrifice fly scores the second run. The next batter makes an out. They count the run as an earned run; "Baloney," said Gene, "it wasn't Hendricks fault!" Ha!

You see, it's part of Gene's character. He's a very loyal guy and fan and I tend to agree with him. Last game, a 4 – 1 complete game for Hendricks against the Phillies, the Cubs defense blew Hendricks shut out in the ninth. Gene was "really ticked off" about that one as it should have been a shutout. Well, I guess that's right.

Today's baseball wisdom:

"Once he hit a line drive past my right ear. I turned around and saw the ball hit his ass as he was sliding into second."
Satchel Paige (on cool Papa Bell's speed)

Baseball history this date:

1942 – Boston Red Sox star Ted Williams enlists in World War II as a US naval pilot.

Game: #53

Teams: Cubs/Diamondbacks
Date: Friday, June 3
Final: Cubs win 6 – 0
Record: 38 – 15

V – mail: "Unbelievable how well not only the starting pitchers and the relievers are going these days. What a pleasure to watch them play."

Recap:
The same old story – great pitching, first by John Lackey who went 6 2/3 innings, allowing no runs, five hits, two walks and nine strikeouts. Warren, Strop and Grimm finished the shut out. For the Diamondbacks, 23 year old Archie Bradley went six innings, four hits, 10 strikeouts and the only run he gave up came when Owings (who's not used to playing centerfield) misjudged the flyball hit by Rizzo. D – back relievers then gave up five runs in the eighth when two intentional walks backfired and Russell and Baez both hit two out two-run doubles. Of course, the "voice" called and we chatted Re: the game. He said the weather was gorgeous, in the 80s, no humidity, sunny and a slight breeze.

Extra innings:
As Gene was talking about the weather I suddenly flashed back to a game at Wrigley that I attended some time in the early 1960s when I was home for the summer from college. I had a precocious young cousin named Rick Earlywine who lived over in the next farm place. He was an extremely bright young man, nice kid and a great baseball fan. One beautiful summer day, in early June, Gene, a.k.a. "the voice," two other friends and I took Rick to a baseball game at Wrigley Field. The four of us were about 20 years old and Rick was probably 12 to 14. He loved the game but I don't remember who won the game. No matter we all had a good time and it was a lifetime highlight for Rick.

Tragically a number of years after he was killed on Thanksgiving day when the tractor he was driving rolled over on him.

For some unknown reason when Gene began describing the weather in Chicago for today's game it brought back poignant memories of that day at Wrigley, years past.

Today's baseball wisdom:
Babe Ruth was dying on April 27, 1948 when he went to Yankee Stadium

a last time. He made a famous speech in a voice once full of joy, but now in a melancholy croak. "The only real game in the world, I think is baseball," and the Babe also said the game was for the kids- six and seven year old. "It was for them to grow up and dream on."

(unknown author)

Baseball history this date:

1932 – Lou Gehrig is the first major leaguer to hit four consecutive home runs in a game. The Yankees beat the A's 20 – 13.

Game: #54

Teams: Cubs/Diamondbacks
Date: Saturday, June 4
Final: Cubs win 5 – 3
Record: 39 – 15

V – mail: "Pitching again! Hammel gave up a two-run homer in the first inning and that was it. He went seven innings, two runs, one hit, and six strikeouts."

Recap:

It's unbelievable how their pitching continues to be so strong. Fowler and Rizzo each hit home runs and Rondon pitched a perfect ninth inning. Tomas (Yasmani) hit a home run off Pedro Strop in the eighth inning for the Diamondbacks only other run. After giving up a home run, Hammel pitched the next six innings giving up only one more hit. Very impressive. All five Cub starting pitchers have ERA's under 3.

Before the game the Cubs held a moment of silence for Mohammed Ali, who passed away yesterday at the age of 74.

Extra innings:

In addition to watching baseball I have been following and watching the University of Arizona's women's softball team. They did miss the World Series by one game. It's a good game at their level, fast, and pitching again a key. It's different than baseball, in that the field is smaller, the bases shorter, it's a seven inning game, uses a large ball, but essentially the same idea with three outs, strikes, balls, and who gets the most runs.

There is however, a clear difference in the games. Why I wondered? Then I had a revelation, yes a sudden epiphany! I know, it's the jockstrap. In baseball the boys wear one to protect their huevos. But in softball, women's that is, there is no need. In men's baseball, that's why the guys often have to grab, shift, hike, scratch, and "jiggle their jewels." The ball grabbing behavior is really an integral part of baseball; and it fundamentally sets it apart from women's softball. As Lily Tomlin would have said, "and that's the truth."

Today's baseball wisdom:

"He hits from both sides of the plate, he's amphibious."
Yogi Berra

Baseball history this date:

1953 – Pittsburgh trades outfielder Ralph Kiner and Joe Garagiola to

the Chicago Cubs.*
   *(Called by some the second worst trade ever by the Pirates)

Game #55

Teams: Cubs/Diamondbacks
Date: Sunday, June 5
Final: Cubs lose 3 – 2
Record: 39 – 16

V – mail: "A really strange game today. Arizona put 10 balls in play for the five innings that Jake pitched and got nine hits and one groundout. They struck out 12 times and were thrown out on the base path for the other two outs."

Recap:
Arrieta's franchise record of 20 straight wins ended today. The loss can only be described as weird. He pitched five innings struck out 12 of the 15 guys he faced but gave up nine hits. As Gene said, of the 10 balls put in play nine were hits. I wonder what the percentage would be that 90% of the balls put in play would be safe hits. I'd wager that happens very rarely. (Well, here's another statistic that the baseball gurus need to research and catalog.) Jake did give up three runs and that was the ballgame as Cub relievers shut out Arizona for the rest of the way. Jake's last regular-season loss was July 25, 2015 when Cole Hamels no-hit the Cubs at Wrigley.

Extra innings:
I have noticed, with increasing regularity, that when Gene is Speaking about the Cub players, he often refers to them by their first name. He doesn't say Arrieta or Rizzo or Fowler did such and such, he says Jake, Anthony or Dexter. While that isn't typical in conversation about baseball, that the players are referred to by their first names, my take is that Gene's language reflects the spirit of a "true fan." It's like the Cubs are really a part of his family. That's loyalty, and again I think that's his middle name.

Today's baseball wisdom:

"If God helped you hit that home run the last time up, who struck you out the time before?"
Sparky Anderson

Baseball history this date:

1974 – the Oakland A's Reggie Jackson and Bill North engaged in a fight in their clubhouse at Detroit.*

*(They were teammates, and after other players broke up the fight, a few minutes later they started again!)

Game: #56

Teams: Cubs/Philadelphia
Date: Monday, June 6
Final: Cubs win 6 – 4
Record: 40 – 16

V – mail: **"Jon Lester was on his game again. Eight innings of shutout baseball. Bullpen not so good as they gave up four in the ninth. Good thing Cubs had six."**

Recap:

Lester was really tough again. On June 1 he had a complete game beating the Dodgers 2 – 1. I was kind of surprised that Maddon lifted him today after eight really strong innings. Also he only had 95 pitches and still looked fresh. Lester said, "I told him I was fine but I also told him he's the manager." Lester added " I've tried before with him and I think I have won maybe one in the last two years."

Grimm gave up a three-run homer in the ninth and the next guy for the Phillies whacked one off Rondon. Then a bloop single and up comes Howard. If he hits one out the game is tied at 6 – 6. But he didn't.

Bryant, Rizzo, and Fowler each had three hits.

Extra innings:

Philadelphia really must hate Lester; he's 6 – 0 in eight career starts against them. He lowered his ERA against them to 1.46 Today, he struck out nine with no walks and only four hits. I can imagine any game they play against the Cubs they hope that Lester doesn't show up. Ha!

Today's baseball wisdom:

"You know what they do when the game gets rained out? They go to the airport and boo landings."*

Bob Uecker

*(Philadelphia fans had a terrible reputation for booing anything and everything; so Uecker made the crack about them)

Baseball history this date:

1938 – Future Cub fan Kent Kloepping was born on this date.

(This was just a test to check and see that in fact you're really reading every word!)

Game: #57

Teams: Cubs/Philadelphia
Date: Tuesday, June 7
Final: Cubs lose 3 – 2
Record: 40 – 17

V – mail: "A good game, however Kyle had another earned run that should not have been. He went five innings and was charged with two runs. Final Phillies 3 – 2."

Recap:
Why in the devil won't the Cubs score runs when Kyle Hendricks pitches? Again today they got him two lousy runs. Two Philly pitchers, Eickhoff went seven innings, one run, two hits and Gomez the reliever got out of a bases-loaded jam with no outs in the eighth inning allowing only one run. Another Cub went on the disabled list today, Soler, for 15 days so the Cubs called up Albert Almora Jr. from their AAA farm club in Iowa. He grounded out in his first at-bat as a pinch-hitter. Maybe as Gene and Marlys say, I'm too pessimistic, but I really think the Schwarber injury (tore his ACL the second or third game of the year against the Diamondbacks) may come back to haunt them.

Extra innings:
Last Friday I made some comments about differences in baseball, a man's game, and softball that both sexes play, but today is mostly associated with women at the college level. Well aside from the jockstrap issue it must be pointed out that there was once a women's professional baseball league, created by the Cubs P.K. Wrigley. It was called the all American Girls Professional Baseball League. "AAGPBL."

Founded in 1943, it flourished during the war (II) years, but with the return of men from the conflict interest declined and the league folded in 1954. In fact I had said that my first interest in baseball originated when I listened to the 1948 World Series between the Cleveland Indians and the Boston Braves. Well, that's really not true. I first got interested in and listened to the Rockford Peaches, while I was in a 1947's version of a rehabilitation center in Rockford, Illinois. It was located at 407 Kent St. just across the street from the Booker T Washington Center. When the nurses turned out the lights, I think at 7 PM, I had a small radio that I turned on just loud enough to hear and listen to the Peaches game. Besides the Peaches, some of the other teams were: the Battle Creek Bells, the Grand Rapids Chicks, the Peoria Red Wings, Muskegon Lassies, and the South Bend Blue Socks.

I had a favorite player on the Peaches. Maybe it was her name that made me decide she was my favorite. I never saw her play or in person but I never forgot her name. She was Rose Gacioch, and she was my first baseball hero. I often thought of her in later years and wished I had met her.

In 1992 Hollywood released a film,"A League of Their Own," about the league. However, Rose Gacioch was not a name listed in the cast of players, so I boycotted the film. Ha!

Today's baseball wisdom:

"The trouble with women umpires is that I couldn't be angry with one. I'd put my arms around her and give her a little kiss."
Casey Stengel

Baseball history this date:

1906 – The Chicago Cubs score 11 runs in the first inning beating the New York Giants 19 – 0.*

*(Also see baseball history this date for June 8)

Game: #58

Teams: Cubs @ Philadelphia
Date: Wednesday, June 8
Final: Cubs win 8 – 1
Record: 41 – 17

V – mail: "It's hard to believe that the pitching continues to be so dominant. John Lackey goes seven innings, allows no runs, three hits and has eight strikeouts."

Recap:
Gene called and said he couldn't recall any past teams of the Cubs when the pitching had been so dominant. He also said that he hoped no one got hurt and the level of pitching could continue. I got to thinking about Kyle Hendricks, and wondering why the Cubs can't at least get him five or six runs when they get seven, eight and even more runs for the other guys.

The Cubs had brought up Albert Almora Jr. as Soler has been put on the disabled list. He got a single driving in a run in the eighth inning and earlier in the game he threw a runner out at the plate in the first inning.

I had called Gene back and we started talking about the 1969 Cubs (who blew the pennant to the Mets) as their pitching was also very good. I said I liked the current five starting pitchers for the Cubs better than the 1969 group. All five have ERA's under 3. That is: Arrieta 1.80, Hammel 2.14, Lester 2.06, Lackey 2.63 and Hendricks 2.90. The 69 cub starters ERA's were: Jenkins 3.21, Hands 2.49 Holtzman 3.58 and Selma 3.63. Maybe it was a different era, and hard to compare. Also we are just over one third of the way into the season.

Extra innings:
"Looking sharp"
Inspired by Jon Lester's suggestion, Cub players coaches and staff all wore blue and white NBA – like track suits to the ballpark throughout the series and will continue on this way to Atlanta. Themed Road trips have become a part of the teams identity under Joel Maddon. (One trip, they all flew in their pajamas).

Today's baseball wisdom:

"With the A's, we depended upon pitching and speed to win. With the Giants we depended on pitching and power to win. With the Indians we depended on an act of God."
Alvin Dark*

*(Alvin Dark comparing teams he managed over the years)

Baseball history this date:

1989 – The Pittsburgh Pirates scored 10 runs in the first inning (the best inning since 1942) which prompted the Pirate broadcaster, Jim Rooker to say he would walk from Pittsburgh to Philadelphia if the Pirates lost. The Phillies did beat them 15 – 11 and Rooker walked the distance at the end of the season.*

*(He strolled the 308 miles in 13 days, raising $80,000 for charity in the process.)

Game: #59

Teams: Cubs @ Atlanta
Date: Friday, June 10
Final: Cubs lose 5 – 1
Record: 41 – 18

V – mail: "The so-called worst team in baseball had the best pitching Friday night as the Cubs lost 5 – 1."

Recap:
Yes, that was my sentiments also. Bud Norris, who just returned to the Atlanta rotation, pitched seven strong innings, allowed one run, four hits, no walks and six strikeouts. I'm beginning to think the Cubs are a little schizophrenic when it comes to hitting. They scored eight runs this past Wednesday, hit two home runs and got 13 hits and today they get "zip," "nada." They end up with four measly hits. Once again, my paranoia about losing Schwarber begins to rattle around in my head.(maybe it happens because there's nothing else up there). As of today, Soler and LaStella are on the DL and Rizzo is day to day with back tightness. What in the world is going on?

A bright spot at least for two games has been the young guy Albert Almora just up from AAA. He made two fine defensive plays today, threw out a guy at the plate and made a nice running catch. He drove in a run his first game and today doubled in the Cubs only run.

Extra innings:
Arrieta goes tomorrow, and of course Cubs fans have high hopes. I read an article today that speculated on just "how good the Cubs really are." Unfortunately it essentially echoed my paranoia with the statement, ".... it's perplexing they have lost that many, 12 times to cellar dwellers."

Today's baseball wisdom:

"During my 18 years I came to bat almost 10,000 times. I struck out about 1700 times and walked maybe 1800 times. You figure a ballplayer will average about 500 bats a season. That means I played seven years without ever hitting a ball"
Mickey Mantle

Baseball history this date:

1944 – Joe Nuxhall, age 15, of the Cincinnati Reds, becomes the youngest player in the major leagues.

Game: #60

Teams: Cubs @ Atlanta
Date: Saturday, June 11
Final: Cubs win 8 – 2
Record: 42 – 18

V – mail: "Wow, four home runs. Jake never had it so good. He pitched seven solid innings and gave up two runs. Final 8 – 2."

Recap:
Gene's v – mail originally said that the final score was 8 – 1. I suppose he was in a hurry and hit 1 instead of 2. I did correct his v-mail but as I am noting the matter today, he will eventually see it, and likely say "no I didn't do that." Ha!

Heyward, Rizzo, Montero, and Bryant all had home runs. The ESPN game recap stated that Arrieta armed with an early lead looked almost unhittable to the Braves. The Braves manager, Brian Snitker (what a name) remarked "It kind of got away from us a little bit and a little bit is a whole lot with him." (Arrieta that is)

Extra innings:
Arrieta, who had two hits, said he wanted to be in the All-Star home run Derby, joining Madison Bumgarner of San Francisco. "Bumgarner is a pitcher" Arrieta continued, "if he's in it I honestly think that would probably be the most adrenaline I would ever have." I wonder why Bumgarner is going to be in the Derby? I'll have to ask Gene or my neighbor Dave Clark, who is a Giant fan.

Today's baseball wisdom:
"Cool Papa Bell was so fast that he could get out of bed, turn off the lights across the room, and be back in bed under the covers before the lights went out."
Josh Gibson*
*(Gibson and Bell both were stars in the old Negro Baseball League)

Baseball history this date:
1938 – Cincinnati's Johnny Vander Meer no hits the Boston Braves 3 – 0.

Game: #61

Teams: Cubs @ Atlanta
Date: Sunday, June 12
Final: Cubs 13 – 2
Record: 43 – 12

V – mail: "Lester was exceptional in this one. He went seven innings and allowed no earned runs. Lots of offense in this one as the Cubs scored often and won 13 – 2."

Recap:

The "voice" is correct in that Lester has really been pitching extremely really well, especially his last three starts. Today he gave up no runs. His last start he had eight shutout innings, and the start before that he beat the Dodgers 2 – 1, giving up only 1 run. He's won his last four starts and his ERA is now a sparkling 1.89.

The Cubs also had a "field day" hitting. They had 16 hits, with Heyward and Rizzo each getting three. Ross, Baez, and Zobrist each had two with Baez getting a three run homer. I hope we didn't use up all our runs today as tomorrow it's the Nationals and "mad Max Scherzer" who is really tough when he is on his game. He can be almost unbeatable.

Extra innings:

I continue to worry a lot about the bullpen as Warren (from the Yankees for Castro) gave up another run in one inning. He started out very strong, but his ERA is now 4.24, which I think is too high for a reliever if you are going to have any confidence in him. He also has 14 walks in 23 innings, which again is too high for a relief pitcher (of course all of this discourse is simply my opinion). However, confirming my doubts a bit about the relief pitching is the fact that the Cubs have signed "old" Joe Nathan (available in July) the former great stopper for the Twins. Also, today they claimed a guy off waivers from Oakland who has a 7.39 ERA. He's recovering from surgery as he had bone chips in his elbow. Cagey old Joe Maddon isn't "resting on his laurels."

Today's baseball wisdom:

"He'd give you the shirt off his back. Of course he'd call a press conference to announce it."
Catfish Hunter*
*(speaking about Reggie Jackson)

Baseball history this date:

1997 – The first ever baseball interleague game was played between the San Francisco Giants and the Texas Rangers. The Giants beat the Rangers 4 – 3.

A Century-Long Journey to the Day of Redemption

Game: #62

Teams: Cubs @ Washington
Date: Monday, June 13
Final: Cubs lose 4 – 1
Record: 43 – 19

V – mail: "Scherzer was on his game as he was perfect through five innings. Hendricks stayed with him for that long but gave up three runs in the sixth. Final 4 – 1 Washington."

Recap:
Gene sends his v-mails the next morning after the game.

I started to watch the game, but after Scherzer retired the first 16 Cubs he faced, I thought, the heck with this, I'm not going to watch "this flame –thrower" wipe out the Cubs. If you think I'm a poor sport, you're damn right I am, I hate watching "my team lose." I can always check the computer later and find out if they won or lost. It's a lot less painful that way. What was really tough was that 10 of the first 11 Cub batters struck out. "Holy cow, Harry would have exclaimed." The Cubs tied the score 1 – 1 in the sixth and bango Hendricks gives up three in the bottom of the six. Oh well, as Scarlett O'Hara said rather poignantly, "tomorrow is another day."

Extra innings:
I'm not the smartest baseball fan in the world, but a number of years ago when the Diamondbacks traded a young "fireballer" for a guy named Edwin Jackson, I about had a stroke. Jackson was just so – so at the time and Scherzer, (to anyone who bothered to look at him) surely had to recognize his potential. Not as bad as the Lou Brock trade for Ernie Broglio (maybe), but it really was an asinine trade and the Diamondbacks should've known it. I suppose on paper the trade looked okay as the Diamondbacks did get two starting pitchers, Jackson and a guy named Ian Kennedy. Kennedy was okay for a while, but never really reached the level that they thought he would. I really didn't like the trade, and I suppose now I would be accused of having 100% hindsight. Whatever, I was right on this one.

Today's baseball wisdom:

"Most ball games are lost, not won."
Casey Stengel

Baseball history this date:

1948 – This was Babe Ruth's final farewell at Yankee Stadium. He died August 16th.

Game: #63

Teams: Cubs @ Washington
Date: Tuesday, June 14
Final: Cubs win 4 – 3
Record: 44 – 19

V – mail:" A nail-biter, but the Cubs held on after giving up a run on a walk and then they did the same thing to the Nationals. Rondon shut them down, 1, 2, 3 in the ninth."

Recap:
The "voice" called within 30 seconds of the final out. My first words were "I'm too old for this crap." I didn't know the game was on TV, but happened to look at the MLB network and there it was. The seventh-inning and the Cubs leading 3 – 2. Washington scored a run in the seventh (sacrifice fly) to come within one run of the Cubs. Strop had come on in the seventh and got a strikeout but gave up the sac fly. Travis Wood comes on in the eighth and promptly walks the leadoff guy. That's never good news. Of course he ends up scoring and the game is tied 3 – 3. Now, I'm about ready to change my shorts. Now the top of the ninth, aha the Nat's walk our leadoff guy. Ross sacrificed him to second and (wouldn't you know it, I told you so) Almora the rookie just up from AAA one week ago doubles in the runner and the Cubs lead 4-3. Hector (we used to call our dog Harry, "Hector The Protector") Rondon shut the Nat's down in order. Maybe I'll call him "Hector The Protector," from now on.

Extra innings:
Here's a bit of trivia for all those hard-core baseball enthusiasts who like statistics. This is about the "400 club." That is, today John Lackey started his 400th major league baseball game; he now joins two other active pitchers who have 400 or more starts in the majors. One is CC Sabathia of the Yankees with 462 starts, and the other is Bartolo Colon with 479 starts for the Mets. But wait, there's more for you trivia buffs. How about Colon, at age 43, with 18 years in the major leagues hitting his first home run this year. A two-run shot on May seventh against the Padres. Baseball fans everywhere went berserk, tweeting such things as:

#1) "Whoever called the Kentucky Derby the greatest 2 minutes in sports haven't seen Bartolo Colon's home run trot and bow."

and #2) "After centuries of debate we finally have an answer. Bartolo Colón hitting a home run proves that God exists and he loves us all very much!"

Today's baseball wisdom:

After his playing days, his broadcast trademark was worrying about pitchers walking batters. He would say, "oh those bases on balls."
Frankie Frisch*
*(Gene and I are with you on this one Frankie)

Baseball history this date:

1952 – Boston Braves pitcher Warren Spahn strikes out 18 Cubs in 15 innings.*
*(The Cubs won the game in the 15th inning 3 – 1)

Game: #64

Teams: Cubs @ Washington
Date: Wednesday, June 15
Final: Cubs lose 4 – 3 (12 innings)
Record: 44 – 20

V – mail: "The pitching was terrific through seven innings in this game. However, due to two bad calls the Cubs were done in in the ninth inning."

Recap:

Heartbreak Hotel! Wow, Hammel outpitched Strasburg (who is 10 – 0). Strop gives up a home run in the eighth and Washington leads 2 – 1. Rizzo hits a two-run homer in the ninth and the Cubs lead 3 – 2. Rondon walks the first guy in the ninth (here we go again) and he scores with two outs. Ramos got the single that drove in the run. I was yelling my head off "don't pitch to him" as first base was open and the guy is hitting .333. The next guy is hitting .230. But Maddon won't listen to me. Then in the 12th inning Cahill hits a guy with one out: he steals second and a .200 hitter drives him in. I had stopped following the game on the computer, but I knew they brought in Warren who gave up a hit; game over. I know I'm a worry wart but I'm really concerned that the Cubs may have an Achilles heel with their relief pitching. Their relievers aren't terrible but their combined ERA is not all that good.

Extra innings:

Gene called after the game he was not a happy camper either. He said that Harper walked leading off the ninth and eventually scored the tying run with two outs. He said that Harper should have been called out on strikes on two different pitches. The announcers were flabbergasted that the umpire had called both of the pitches balls.

Well, I'm one for allowing a team to challenge a call by a home plate umpire, maybe only once a game. If either one of those pitches had been reviewed, Harper is out and the Cubs win. Again, only in my opinion, I think a number of home plate umpires are really arrogant SOB's.

Today's baseball wisdom:

"Never trust a base runner with a limp. Comes a base hit and you'll think he just got back from Lourdes."
Joe Garagiola

A Century-Long Journey to the Day of Redemption

Baseball history this date:

1930 – The first night game at Ebbets Field (Cincinnati Reds and Brooklyn Dodgers). Cincinnati Reds Johnny Vander Meer hurls unprecedented second consecutive no-hitter.

Game: #65

Teams: Cubs/Pittsburgh
Date: Friday, June 17
Final: Cubs win 6 – 0
Record: 45 – 20

V – mail: "Jake Arrieta pitched two-hit ball over six innings striking out 11, three walks and no runs. He really is amazing."

Recap:

Arrieta was again simply terrific. He gave up back-to-back singles in the third inning then proceeded to strike out the next three guys. In the sixth he walked the bases loaded then followed with two strikeouts to end the inning. Maddon lifted him after six innings as his pitch count was at 112. Matt Szczur had a two-run homer and Almora, the rookie, had three hits. In nine games Almora is hitting .429. The Cubs called up their 2015 minor league player of the year, 24-year-old Willson Contreras, a catcher.

Extra innings:

Pitching is the key to winning at the major-league level, maybe at any level. So far the Cubs pitching has really been terrific, especially the starting five. In 1954 when the Cleveland Indians won 111 games (lost 43) they had great pitching. Lemon and Wynn both won 23 games, Mike Garcia won 19, Art Houtteman 15, and Bob Feller, then a 36-year-old went 13 – 3. Three of the guys ERA's were under three and two at 3.09 and 3.35. Their top relievers, Narleski, Mossi and Newhouser had ERA's of 2.22, 1.94, and 2.51. Astonishingly, the New York Giants beat them four straight in the World Series. Lemon, Wynn, Garcia and Lemon again lost the four games.

I just hope the Cubs relievers hold up. (Geez, maybe I need therapy, I worry all the time.)

Today's baseball wisdom:

"Winning isn't everything, it's the only thing."
Vince Lombardi

Baseball history this date:

1953 – This date the most runs were scored in one inning, 17, by the Boston Red Sox.*

*(This is a modern-day record, as the all-time record was set September 6, 1883 by the Chicago White Stockings (now the Chicago Cubs) who scored 18 runs in one inning against the Detroit Wolverines.)

Game: #66

Teams: Cubs/Pittsburgh
Date: Saturday, June 18
Final: Cubs win 4 – 3
Record: 46 – 20

V – mail: "Lester hung in there and some great defense behind him helped the Cubs win."

Recap:

Jon Lester went six innings and allowed three runs, seven hits and had three walks. He was a bit "shaky" but three home runs by Rizzo, Bryant, and Ross, all solo, scored the first three runs. They got their fourth run on a great bunt by Ross. Russell and Baez both made spectacular plays in the third and sixth innings that snuffed out potential rallies. They are both outstanding defensively, and even though Baez is only hitting .254 and Russell .231 they will win games with their defense. "Grandpa Ross", as they call him, is also a great defensive catcher and surprisingly playing only part-time has contributed a good deal offensively.

Extra innings:

The Cub game today was good, my day was bad ! Today, at Walmart, I decided to drive off a 6 to 8 inch curb in my wheelchair and dive headfirst onto the pavement. I skinned my elbows and knees, did a job on my face, bruises, contusions and five stitches. Also broke my glasses. Matt said "you look like you had been in a brawl."

Well, as this project is about baseball his remark made me think of the Jimmy Piersall – Billy Martin scrap way back on May 25, 1952. Martin had a hair trigger temper and Piersall had some apparently fairly serious mental health issues.

At Fenway Park Piersall was needling Martin (who had broken his ankle in spring training) while they both were warming up before the game started. Piersall, mockingly asked Martin "how did you break your ankle, did you trip on your garter belt?" Then he added, "or did your freaking bloomers get in the way?" That did it, Martin allegedly fired back "you're crazier than a shit-house rat, shut up or I'll shut you the F- - K up." With that they both raced to the Red Sox tunnel, and although Piersall was taller and 25 pounds heavier Martin flattened him with two quick punches. Coaches broke it up, but I wonder if Piersall's face was in as much disarray as his mind.

Today's baseball wisdom:

"Some people have a chip on their shoulder, Billy Martin had a lumber yard."
Jim Murray*
*(Sports writer LA Times)

Baseball history this date:

1972 – The US Supreme Court, in a 5 to 3 decision, confirms the lower court ruling on Curt flood's case, upholding baseball's exemption from antitrust laws.*
*(See baseball reserve clause)

Game: #67

Teams: Cubs/Pittsburgh
Date: Sunday, June 19
Final: Cubs win 10 – 5
Record: 47 – 20

V – mail: "Cubs win 10 – 5. Hendricks 12 strikeouts in six innings. The Cubs had five home runs all by players under 26 years old. Yes the young guys really socked the ball today. Baez is 23, Rizzo 26, Contreras 24, Bryant 24 and Russell 22."

Recap:
Contreras, the rookie catcher just up from AAA, hit the first major league pitch he saw for an estimated 415 foot home run to center field. A fan returned the ball to Contreras. The Cubs now have a 12 ½ game lead in their division with the Cardinals coming to town. Boy, you can never write off those blasted redbirds as they have a long tradition and history of winning. I hope the series goes well. It was really great to see the run support for Hendricks ("the Professor") as the Cubs call him. He had a terrific outing, six innings, one earned run, no walks and 12 strikeouts. Once again two relievers Warren and Richard each gave up two runs. Maybe Gene is right about the Cubs not getting much for Castro in the Yankee trade, as Warren continues to struggle.

Extra innings:
Jacob Stallings, the son of the new University of Pittsburgh basketball coach, Kevin Stallings, started today and went 0 for 4 including two strikeouts against Hendricks. Kevin was the coach at Vanderbilt for 17 years (1999 – 2016) and had a number of really good years.

Today's baseball wisdom:

"The biggest thrill a baseball player can have is when your son takes after you. That happened when my Bobby was in his championship Little League game. He really showed me something. He struck out three times, and made an error that lost the game. Parents were throwing things at our car and swearing at us as we drove off. Gosh I was proud."
Bob Uecker

Baseball history this date:

1846 – The first officially recognized baseball game (played by the Cartwright Rules) was played with the New York nines defeating the Knickerbockers 23 – 1 at Hoboken, New Jersey.*

* (Alexander J. Cartwright developed these rules which were adopted on September 23, 1845. They are referred to as the "Knickerbocker Rules" as that is the name the team called themselves the day the rules were ratified. These original twenty eventually evolved (with a number of changes) into the rules of today. I noted that 172 years later, that one rule, #17, has remained unchanged. It stated "All disputes and differences relative to the game, to be decided by the umpire, from which there is no appeal.")

Game: #68

Teams: Cubs/Cardinals
Date: Monday, June 20
Final: Cubs lose 3 – 2
Record: 47 – 21

V – mail: "A great game that was decided by a base running error; a rookie mistake cost the Cubs." Final score 3 – 2

Recap:
Yadier Molina made a perfect throw to third base in the last of the ninth to cut down Albert Almora trying to take third-base on a ball in the dirt to Zobrist. Then Zobrist singled which would have tied the game. No runs were scored after the third inning as Lackey went six innings, seven hits and three runs. Garcia of St. Louis went six innings six hits and two runs. Tough way to lose to those despicable Cardinals who had lost five straight.

Extra innings:
It really is a "small world."
Every time the Cubs and Cardinals get together I seem to reminisce about past games that I attended between these two teams. Here's another reminisce.
54 years ago, July 18, 1962 when I was a student at Southern Illinois University, Marlys (we weren't married then) and another couple drove to St. Louis to watch the Cubs and Cardinals at old Sportsman's Park. The other couple were Ron "stix" Ballatore, a really great backstroker on SIU's swin team and his girlfriend whose name I can't remember. The Cardinals pitched Bob Gibson, a tough, ferocious competitor (he struck out 12 Cubs and they lost 2 – 1). Billy Williams had a home run for the Cubs but that was it as they only got two other hits. Ballatore was a "wild and crazy guy" known on campus for his unconventional antics.
Now fast-forward to the year 2002. I'm at the University of Arizona one day and John Perrin, the senior associate athletic director, was taking me on a tour of new athletic facilities, including a new weight room and a facility they called the "Hall of Honor." We happened to bump into our new baseball coach a guy, named Andy Lopez. In the course of our conversation I mentioned the Cubs/Cardinals rivalry and also told him about my only visit to Sportsman's Park. I told him we went with another couple and the guy's name was Ron Ballatore. Lopez raised his eyebrows and asked "Do you mean stix?" I was really surprised and said "why yes, do you know him?" "Know him, I sure do he is one of my best friends."
Lopez had played shortstop at UCLA (unknown to me) and "stix" was

UCLA's swim coach. UCLA (swimming) won the NCAA title in 1982.

Today's baseball wisdom:

"When I knocked a guy down there was no second part of the story." Bob Gibson

Baseball history this date:

1956 – At Detroit's Briggs Stadium, Mickey Mantle hit two Billy Hoeft pitches into the right centerfield bleachers. They were the first two balls hit there since the stadium was built in 1936.

Game: #69

Teams: Cubs/Cardinals
Date: Tuesday, June 21
Final: Cubs lose 4 – 3
Record: 47 – 22

V – mail: "Another great pitching battle as nobody scored after the fourth inning. Cubs lose 4 – 3."

Recap:
All of the runs in the game were scored by the fourth inning making the final score, as above, 4 – 3. The Cubs outhit the Cardinals 7 to 6 but a threat in the seventh was snuffed out with a great stop by the St. Louis first baseman.

Wainwright, the Cardinal pitcher, hasn't been that good this year (4.73 ERA) but he only gave up six hits and three runs in 6 2/3 innings pitched today. Concepcion (a new reliever) Strop, and Travis Wood gave up nothing in 3 1/3 innings but the Cubs didn't score after being down 4 – 3. Crap!

Extra innings:
Gene's v-mail reveals a good bit about him as a baseball fan. He's right that it was an extremely well pitched game that a "real" baseball fan would appreciate. He is not only very knowledgeable about baseball but he has the ability to set aside his bias's and loyalty as a Cub fan and appreciate quality pitching, hitting, defense, and the strategies of the game. Unlike myself, I have difficulty when "my team" loses. I'm more likely to say (concerning the opponent) those lucky slob's, especially when it comes to the Cardinals.

I shouldn't be making these kind of confessions as my son who threatens me with "Dad it's time for the home," and he may decide to take action on the matter. Ha!

Today's baseball wisdom:
"The only way to prove you're a good sport is to lose."
Ernie Banks

Baseball history this date:
1938 – Pinky Higgins gets his 12th straight hit, a major league record until 1952.*

*(In 1952 Walt Dropo, of the Detroit Tigers, got 12 straight hits. He is the record holder as Higgins had two walks mixed in with the 12 hits.

Game: #70

Teams: Cubs/Cardinals
Date: Wednesday, June 22
Final: Cubs lose 7 – 2
Record: 47 – 23

V – mail: "It was all Cardinals as they controlled the whole game, with good pitching and hitting. The final was 7 – 2 Cardinals."

Recap:

This series was really hard for me to swallow, those blasted Cardinals, back of the Cubs by 12 ½ games when the series started, sweep the series and gain three games on the Cubs. This was the first sweep by the Cardinals at Wrigley Field since 1988. It seems that every pitcher who hasn't been doing well (i.e. Wacha hadn't won in two months) is resurrected against the Cubs. He had allowed only two hits until Willson Contreras (rookie) hit a two-run homer in the seventh. Arrieta lost even though he only allowed one earned run. However, he gave up four hits in five innings, walked four and had 106 pitches in five innings. The Cubs also committed several mental and offensive miscues. This three-game skid is the longest of the year. Grimm gave up four runs in relief and Carl Edwards Jr. also gave up a solo home run.

Extra innings:

Tomorrow the Cubs get Miami with Jon Lester pitching. He's been going really well and has won five straight starts. Because I'm getting paranoid about the Cubs resurrecting pitching careers, I think it's unfortunate that the Marlins are pitching a struggling guy named Wei-Yu Chen who has an ERA of 5.22. I hope he doesn't find his "mojo" tomorrow like Wacha today. I'm still disgusted about the loss and need to get over it. I was going to use the Scarlet O'Hara" tomorrow is another day" line again, but decided to use Gene's typical comment to me when I start "crying the blues" as he says very matter-of-factly "hey, that's baseball."

Today's baseball wisdom:

"We're in such a slump that even the ones that are drinking aren't hitting."
Casey Stengel

Baseball history this date:

1889 – The Louisville Colonels set a major league record with their 26th consecutive loss.

Game: #71

Teams: Cubs @ Miami
Date: Thursday, June 23
Final: Cubs lose 4 – 2
Record: 47 – 24

V – mail: "The only thing to say about this game is that we cannot blame Lester."

Recap:
I knew it, I knew it, this guy Chen goes seven innings and is leading 2 – 1 in the eighth. I think the baseball gods are mad at us Cub fans because we've been so gleeful. I mean Wacha and now Chen, both pitching only so-so, but the Cubs arrive and it's Cy Young time! Lester also pitched well going seven innings and allowing two earned runs. David Ross tied the game with a home run at 2 – 2. Then Strop came in for the Cubs. He proceeded to walk the first guy, wild pitch him to second, and then give up a single and now it's 3 – 2 Marlins. But wait there's more, he gives up a double and it's 4 – 2, the final score.

Gene is correct in that you can't blame Lester. The Cubs have scored nine runs in four games and have lost all four games. "Holy cow" as old Harry Caray would say you usually won't win many games scoring that few runs.

Extra innings:
So now the Cubs have lost four in a row. Meanwhile the Diamondbacks, Marly's team, have been on somewhat of a "tear." I believe they have won nine of their last 12 games and have rallied from behind in the last two games to beat Colorado in Colorado. Their pitching has been much better lately with Greinke outstanding and a young guy named Bradley along with Ray Corbin and also Miller doing well.

I'm writing this on June 26th and wouldn't you know it Shelby Miller (the guy from Atlanta for three, young Diamondback prospects) was awful again yesterday giving up seven runs. Wow, I guess it still looks like a terrible trade.

Today's baseball wisdom:
"The Cubs are like Rush Street, a lot of singles but no action."
Joe Garagiola

Baseball history this date:
1963 – New York Mets player Jimmy Piersall hits his 100th home run.

He circles the bases backwards.*
 *(He was really a strange dude See also Piersall and Billy Martin fisticuffs, game # 66)

A Century-Long Journey to the Day of Redemption

Game: #72

Teams: Cubs @ Miami
Date: Friday, June 24
Final: Cubs win 5 – 4
Record: 48 – 24

V – mail: "What looked like an easy victory turned into a nail biter, but the Cubs went on to win 5 – 4."

Recap:

The "voice" called after the game and said "well it's been awhile since I have called isn't it?" Ha!

This was really a strange game, as both teams scored four runs in the first inning. Then the Cubs scored the only other run of the game in the seventh inning to win it. The Cubs new super-sub Willson Contreras was the story for the Cubs. He hit a two-run homer in the first and his single in the seventh won it for the boys. He's hitting .412 with three home runs in nine games and only 23 at-bats. Hello offense, time to wake up!

Extra innings:

Gene and I had the same initial reaction to the game. The Cubs pitching the first three games wasn't that bad but they scored no runs. This game they get 4 in the top of the first (Gene said, "boy we're getting off to a good start") and then wham, the bottom of the first and the error, two walks and a home run and the score is 4 – 4. Miami never scored again and the Cubs won with a run in the seventh. Now we all know his favorite guy is Hendricks, so he blamed shortstop Russell for the error which led to four unearned runs."Gene," I said," Hendricks walked two guys he gave up the home run not Russell. "Well, that's true, but they wouldn't have come to bat if Russell doesn't make the error."

No use arguing this anymore as you can see it's that loyalty thing with Gene. He's forever a friend, has his team, and a player he admires the most. The only downside of that loyalty is his political leanings, as I think he's a liberal. I keep working on him, telling him how lousy I think Obama is and what a disaster Hillary would be, but I don't think that I've made much of a dent. I still have four months, but it's going to be a tough sell. Ha!

Today's baseball wisdom:

"Those who don't know the value of loyalty can never appreciate the cost of betrayal."

Author unknown

Baseball history this date:

1947 – Jackie Robinson steals home for the first of his 19 times in his career.

Game: #73

Teams: Cubs @ Miami
Date: Saturday, June 25
Final: Cubs lose 9 – 6
Record: 48 – 25

V – mail: "Took it on the chin today, lucky we got one the way this series is going."

Recap:
Holy smokes Cubs get out 4 – 1 and then Ichiro Suzuki beat out an infield grounder which started a four-run fifth for the Marlins. A walk, a single, two doubles and it's 7 – 4- game over. Lackey got banged around pretty good today going 4.1 innings allowing seven runs, all earned, seven hits and three walks. Baseball commentators said it was a "rare sort of loss" for the Cubs who were 33 – 0 when scoring six runs and 44 – 3 when scoring four runs. What's happening to the Cubbies? Or am I just worrying about nothing?

Extra innings:
Baseball is really a funny game. The Cubs have now lost five of their last six games and all the starting pitchers have been beaten. I hope this isn't (here's my eternal pessimism) the beginning of an early summer "swoon" so typical of past Cub teams.

On another subject, speaking of being funny or maybe more to the point unpredictable, the University of Arizona's baseball team was picked to finish in ninth place in the Pac 12. In fact, they finished in third place and got into post-season play. Today, they beat Oklahoma State 5 – 1 to go to the College World Series final on Monday. The University of Arizona won six straight elimination games to get to the final.

Today's baseball wisdom:

"Musial's batting stance looks like a small boy looking around a corner to see if the cops are coming."
Ted Lyons

Baseball history this date:

1976 – Texas Ranger Toby Harrah is the only shortstop in major league history to not handle a fielding chance in a doubleheader.

Game: #74

Teams: Cubs @ Miami
Date: Sunday, June 26
Final: Cubs lose 6 – 1
Record: 48 – 26

V – mail: "Hammel did his job, however he was all alone in his performance. The Cubs lose again."

Recap:

Keeping a daily journal is getting to be a bit depressing as the Cubs went 1 – 6 in the won/loss column for the week. They are scoring runs, six yesterday in a loss and five in the win on Friday. Last Friday Gene had voiced concern about today's game. He said "their ace is going today, but I don't know his name." Then he came up with the name and said "he's really tough." Well it was that all right, the guy pitched seven innings with 13 strikeouts. His name is (was) José Fernandez, only 23 years old who's record is 10 – 3 with a 2.28 ERA. At the Marlins Park (home) he is 24 – 1 with a 1.48 ERA. That's hard to beat.*

*I don't know when I originally wrote up this game, probably the next day, June 27 or shortly thereafter. I'm typing this up on December 6, 2016 and I'm adding these comments because Fernandez died tragically on September 25, 2016 in a boating accident at Miami Beach Florida. He and two others died when his speedboat hit rocks close to shore. A later autopsy revealed that Fernandez had alcohol and cocaine in his blood. What a shame that this great young talent lost his life so needlessly. He was to be a free agent at the end of the 2018 season and estimates of his contract asking price were somewhere in the $200 million range.

Hammel only gave up two runs in six innings, but you have to score a few more runs. Rizzo and Heyward had two hits, Hammel had one, but the rest of the team went 0 – 20. You can't win that way. Four Cub relievers each gave up a run.

Extra innings:

I'm trying to stay optimistic but having trouble as the first 30 games the Cubs were 24 – 6. The last 44 games they are 24 – 20 not much over .500 ball. Maybe Arrieta can "right the ship tomorrow."

Today's baseball wisdom:

"Take it with a grin of salt."
Yogi Berra

Baseball history this date:

1916 – The Cleveland Indians experimented with numbers on their jerseys. (Just one game)

Game: #75

Teams: Cubs @ Cincinnati
Date: Monday, June 27
Final: Cubs win 11 – 8
Record: 49 – 26

V – mail: "Not an easy game to watch as the Cubs had a tough time closing it out. Kris Bryant had a great night with three home runs and two doubles. Cubs win 11 – 8."

Recap:

Gene called and groused for 10 minutes about bases on balls. He said it really irritated him. "Why do they walk the only guy they shouldn't?" He was talking about a guy named Hamilton as the dude is faster than a streak of – – – –, or whatever. Gene, a bit uncharacteristic for him, continued "then he steals bases every time; cripes let him hit it and maybe he'll make an out." Arrieta only went five innings with five walks and five runs with a pitch count in the 90s in only five frames. He's struggled the last two games, but still got the win, and now he is 12 - 2.

Extra innings:

Gene and I had a long "BS" session about Bryant's great night. One of the announcers said the record for total bases was 16. No, both Gene and I remembered Joe Adcock of the Milwaukee Braves getting 18 total bases at old Ebbets Field in Brooklyn on July 31, 1954. We thought it was still the record for total bases, so I went to the Internet. Whoops! I didn't remember that Shaun Green of the LA Dodgers in 2002 against the Milwaukee Braves(at Milwaukee) hit four home runs a double and a single for the major league record of 19 total bases. However Green had six at-bats and hit his fourth home run on bat number six. Thus he only had 15 total bases in five at-bats. Adcock had 18 in five at-bats. Also, I had forgotten that Josh Hamilton had four home runs and a double on May 8, 2012 against Baltimore. Guess who the Baltimore pitcher was, none other then one Jake Arrieta. He gave up two home runs to Hamilton and one to Adrian Beltrae; in total he allowed nine hits and six runs and his record was 2 – 3.

Conclusions: Adcock and Hamilton have the record for five at-bats, that is 18 total bases. Green has the game record of 19 total bases. But hold on fans, Kris Bryant is now the first and therefore the only guy with three home runs and two doubles in a game; it's like having a "full-house" in poker. And that's a tough one to beat. So there!

Today's baseball wisdom:

"Every strike brings me closer to the next home run."
Babe Ruth

Baseball history this date:

1988 – The Reds bat out of order against the Padres in the first inning.

Game: #76

Teams: Cubs @ Cincinnati
Date: Tuesday, June 28
Final: Cubs win 7 – 2 (15 innings)
Record: 50 – 26

V – mail: "It started with great pitching and ended with a grand slam. This will always be remembered as the Maddon game. Cubs win 7 – 2."

Recap:

Every Time I turn on the computer to follow the game on gamecast something bad seems to happen. The Cubs were leading 2 – 1 in the bottom of the ninth and Rondon comes on for the save. He gets Votto (a great hitter) hits the next guy, two singles later the score is tied 2 – 2. Lester had pitched great, and after 7 2/3 innings left with the lead.

Extra innings:

As Gene said this will always be known as the "Maddon's game" because of all his wild maneuvering that eventually got them the win. I'll try a brief summary of his antics. Maddon used three different pitchers in the 15th inning; Wood and Patton had alternated pitching in the 14th inning, Wood pitched the 15th and he had Pedro Strop play left field. The Cubs had used 22 of their 25 players on the roster and Maddon had said "after Rondon blew the save in the ninth, it was all hands on deck." Wood played left field in the 13th and 14th innings and then held the Reds in check after the Cubs scored five runs in the top of the 15th. Also in the 15th inning Jason Hammel (starting pitcher) had pinch-hit for Patton, another pitcher.

"We used a pitcher in left field for the last three innings, right?" Wood asked. "You don't get to see that a lot. It made it fun and interesting, and we pulled off the victory." With Strop playing left field in the 15th, Maddon had remarked "a fly ball to Strop would have been a fitting conclusion." Strop essentially brushed aside Maddon's comment as he said he played outfield in winter softball games.

Then, after all of Maddon's shenanigans, it ends with Baez hitting a grand slam.

Today's baseball wisdom:

"I knew my baseball career was over. In 1965 my baseball card came out with no picture."
Bob Uecker

A Century-Long Journey to the Day of Redemption

Baseball history this date:

1907 – The Nationals steal a record 13 bases off catcher Branch Rickey.*

*(Branch Rickey an innovative baseball executive, who created the first baseball "farm system" was best known for bringing Jackie Robinson to the majors.)

Game: #77

Teams: Cubs @ Cincinnati
Date: Wednesday, June 29
Final: Cubs win 9 – 2
Record: 51 – 26

V – mail: "Kyle won number six today; he went into the seventh with 117 pitches. Grimm, and rookie C.J. Edwards finished the game."

Recap:

Gene called after the game and he was elated as Kyle Hendricks won the game today. Rizzo hit a three run inside the park home run in the first inning. Later Russell and Almora had solo shots. All the position players had one hit, and Baez who won the game last night had three hits today. Gene was really feeling good about the team and he almost "cackled"in reminding me that eight of the nine starters today were 26 years old or younger. Zobrist is 35, Bryant 24, Rizzo 26, Contreras 24, Baez 23, Russell 22, Hendricks 26, and Almora 22. That is really a bundle of young talent.

Extra innings:

As I indicated earlier, Gene was really "wired" about the Cubs today. After losing three of four at Miami he's feeling much relieved with the sweep in Cincinnati.

In our "BS" session he remarked how all kinds of "oddities and firsts" seem to happen when the Cubs are in Cincinnati. To wit: Bryant hits three home runs and two doubles (first time ever in the major leagues), Rizzo hitting an inside the park home run, Former Cub Starlin Castro, in his first game hit two home runs and had six RBIs, Baez's home run in the 15th was the latest grand slam for the Cubs in their history. He had several other items, but I didn't get them down.

Concerning last night ("Maddon's Game") our conversation got around to Joey Votto who had a 15 pitch at-bat against Hendricks. Gene said, "he's really a good hitter and knows the strike zone." "Yes," I replied, "but he's really kind of an ass." Gene attempted to defend him saying that he along with many others were fiercely competitive individuals. "Maybe so, but in his case I still think he's an a-hole."

My dislike for Votto stems from some really terribly disparaging remarks he made about the Cubs team, the organization, and the players. It was a time when the Cubs were really struggling and he essentially said, "they're a bunch of losers and always will be." I wonder what he thinks today with he and his team in last place. Maybe I should send him an e-mail and address it to "loser Votto". No, I won't waste my time, and that would make me a "loser" also.

Today's baseball wisdom:

"Ability is the art of getting credit for all the home runs someone else hits." Casey Stengel

Baseball history this date:

1990 – The Oakland A's Dave Stewart no-hits the Blue Jays, and the Dodgers Fernando Valenzuela no-hits St. Louis 6 – 0. This was the first time in major league history that no-hitters occurred on the same day in each league.

Game: #78

Teams: Cubs @ Mets
Date: Thursday, June 30
Final: Cubs lose 4 – 3
Record: 51 – 27

V – mail: "Tough loss. Lackey pitched well enough to win, but I think Joe Maddon made a mistake in strategy. He played the seventh inning like it was the ninth and an error cost them the game. Final score was Mets 4, Cubs 3."

Recap:

I agree with Gene, why take out Lackey with one out and one on and the Cubs ahead 3 – 1. In comes Peralta and he walks a guy, a rookie singles and now the score is 3 – 2 with runners on second and third. Strop comes in and a fielder's choice makes the score 3 – 3. Baez then throws wild to third and it's 4 – 3 Mets. In the Cubs ninth Montero walks, Zobrist doubles, so runners on second and third with no outs. Bryant strikes out, Rizzo is walked intentionally, Contreras strikes out and Baez pops out. Game over! It's always tough when you have the bases loaded and don't score.

Extra innings:

Today was not a good day for me as a fan. First, the Cubs lose and then the University of Arizona men's baseball team loses 4 – 3 the final game of the College World Series. I think they got "screwed" big time as they scored a run in the first inning and the home plate umpire called him out. Everyone and anyone who saw the play knew he was safe. It's terrible to lose a chance to win in extra innings as the score should have been 4 – 4 in the ninth inning. Once again, it's appalling how poorly some umpires perform, especially the home plate guys. I really believe there needs to be a replay option available, maybe only one per game, for plays at the plate, even strikes and balls. I'm going to write to the NCAA rules committee about the matter. (I'm typing this December 9 and I didn't write the committee. I guess I just blew off steam and then forgot it) As my father used to say, "some people are all talk and no go!"

Today's baseball wisdom:

"Turn out the lights, the party's over."
Don Meredith*
*(From Monday night football with Howard Cosell and Frank Gifford)

A Century-Long Journey to the Day of Redemption

Baseball history this date:

1933 – Dizzy Dean of the St. Louis Cardinals strikes out 17 Cubs in a Cardinal 8 – 2 win.

Game: #79

Teams: Cubs @ Mets
Date: Friday, July 1
Final: Cubs lose 10 – 2
Record: 51 – 28

V – mail: "Hard watching this game. Mets 10, Cubs 2."

Recap:

What a disaster as Hammel gave up four runs in four innings. I guess Maddon decided he needed to "save" his pitching corps as he left Hammel in to get bombed with five home runs. A Met rookie named Brandon Nimmo hit his first major league home run. MLB's statcast said the ball traveled 442 feet. That's a major league home run. Bryant, for the Cubs, hit his 23rd home run and he now has 61 runs batted in. The Cubs struck out 12 times. Ouch, what else is there to say about this game.

Extra innings:

I'm not sure what more to add to this debacle. I'm beginning to feel like a "broken record" as I seem to be repeating the same theme over and over again. Maybe the Cubs pitching staff is overwhelmed; Lackey and Hammel are not young kids and maybe their age is contributing to more fatigue. I still think their relief pitching is potentially an Achilles heel. Concerning the 12 strikeouts by the Cubs, one baseball analyst said "the Cubs failure (often) to make contact, that is to put the ball in play is not a good sign." The Cubs do have a number of young guys and strikeouts are to be expected. Hopefully as the season goes along they will begin to make better contact.

Today's baseball wisdom:

The following is a letter (an excerpt) taken from a book titled, "Boise baseball, the first 125 years by Arthur A. Hart. The letter, written by an Idaho local was sent to Joe "Pongo Joe" Cantillow, the Washington Senators manager about Walter Johnson, who then was with the Weiser Idaho Kids.

"You better come out here and get this pitcher. He throws a ball so fast no one he can see it and he strikes out everybody. His control is so good that the catcher just holds up his glove and shuts his eyes, then picks the ball, which comes to him looking like a little white bullet out of the Pocket. He's a big 19-year-old fellow like I told you before, if you don't hurry up someone will sign him and he will be the best pitcher that ever lived. He throws faster than Addio Jones (Joss) or Amos Rusie ever did, and his control is better than Christy Mathewson's. He knows where he's throwing because if he didn't there would be dead bodies all over Idaho."*

*(Walter Johnson pitched from 1907 – 1927 for the Washington Senators. He won 417 games, second only to Cy Young (511). He was a career shutout leader with 110, 20 more and the number two guy. He was for 56 years the only member of the 3000 strikeout club, from 1927 – 1983.)

Baseball history this date:

1948 – Roy Campanella debuts as catcher for the Brooklyn Dodgers.

Game: #80

Teams: Cubs @ Mets
Date: Saturday, July 2
Final: Cubs lose 4 – 3
Record: 51 – 29

V – mail: "Four is always the magic number in baseball. The Mets scored four and the Cubs three."

Recap:

Arrieta lost his first regular-season road game in 14 months. One of his major flaws as a pitcher with Baltimore (before coming to the Cubs) was his control. Well, déjà vu! The first 8 batters he faced he started with a ball and he went to 3 – 2 four times in a 35 pitch first inning. Rizzo's two-run homer tied the score in the fourth, but a two-run single in the bottom of the fourth held up for a Mets win. Baez almost made a great bare-handed catch, but the ball glanced off his hand. Zobrist hit a home run in the seventh to cut the lead to 4 – 3 but that's where it ended. The Cubs still have the best record in baseball, but (worry wart me) I think I see a few "cracks opening in the dike."

Extra innings:

Lester goes tomorrow and hopefully he can stop the slide. If they lose, it's a stinging reminder of last year's season four-game sweep of the Cubs by the Mets. It's hard to figure out what's happening with the Cubs, as the pitching has not been good and the hitting is very sporadic. Lots of strikeouts and lack of contact is not a very good sign.

Today's baseball wisdom:

Mitch "wild thing" Williams is the only pitcher in history with a minimum of 500 innings pitched to have given up more walks than hits. Commenting on their participation in a celebrity baseball game, teammate Andy Van Slyke said: "Patrick Ewing is 7 feet tall and has a 6 foot strike zone and Mitch walked him."

Andy Van Slyke

Baseball history this date:

1963 – Juan Marichal outdueled Warren Spahn in 16 innings, 1 – 0, at Candlestick Park in San Francisco. Marichal, age 25, pitched all 16 innings while Spahn, age 42, pitched 15.1 innings as he lost the game with one out in the bottom of the 16.*

*(What a difference in baseball today; each team would have used five or six or more pitchers in today's game)

Game: #81

Teams: Cubs @ Mets
Date: Sunday, July 3
Final: Cubs lose 14 – 3
Record: 51 – 30

V – mail: "Write this one off. Just be happy with a 51 – 30 ending the first half."

Recap:
Re: Gene's comment of writing this off, yes the Minnesotans would say "you got that right."

My goodness Lester got "bombed" for nine hits and eight runs in 1.1 innings. Relievers gave up 13 more hits and six more runs. Things got so bad, that Miguel Montero, a catcher pitched 1.1 innings and gave up four hits and one run. The Mets hit five home runs and their 22 hits was a season-high for both stats. Lester was 5 – 0 in his previous seven outings with a 2.03 ERA. His one and a third innings pitched was the shortest of his 301 career starts over 11 major league seasons.

Maddon who I'm beginning to think is a bit too blasé about losing, said "it was just a rough weekend. Give the Mets credit they got us this time like they got us last year. This is a really easy game for me to forget about." I thought, "Really Joe, your team is really playing pretty awful these days and you say the game is easy to forget!"

Lester commented, "I feel like they didn't miss a mistake in the whole series."

Extra innings:
As the Cubs have lost four straight, pitching looking a bit shaky, hitting down, relieves not too swift, and I have my "panties in a wad" I decided to call Gene to get his thoughts. Well, he sounded like Maddon, equally blasé about the matter. "What, the Cubs have lost 10 of their last 14 and you are not concerned?"

He said, "are you are you worried?"

"Well, aren't you?"

"Oh baloney, the Cubs just ran into a red-hot Mets team." Well, I didn't pursue the matter, even though he said he wasn't worried, I don't think he sounded 100% sure. Then I read an article on ESPN and it reflected a good bit of my concerns. One, relief pitching has been spotty, the young guys are not hitting very well, (strikeouts and lack of contact) Further the article said if Lester, Arrieta and the rest of the staff continue to have bad outings things could get sticky the second half of the season. I guess my take on the matter is that Joe and Gene are not worried, but I am. I suppose they're right.

Today's baseball wisdom:

"Major League baseball players should not 'mess' with women's soccer players, they're trained to kick balls!"

author unknown

Baseball history this date:

1939 – Lou Gehrig Day at Yankee Stadium; he makes his "luckiest man" speech.

Game: #82

Teams: Cubs/Cincinnati
Date: Monday, July 4
Final: Cubs win 10 – 4
Record: 52 – 30

V – mail: " Bats came alive in this game as the Cubs rolled over the Reds 10 – 4."

Recap:
The "voice" called – a much happier camper than the past several days. The Cubs jumped out 6 – 0 after two innings. Bryant hit number 24 and Contreras another in the second after they got three in the first. Hendricks had a nice game, (but Gene was not sure why Maddon pulled him after 5.1 innings). He had given up no runs and did win for a record of 7 – 6. His ERA is now second to Arrieta as Lackey, Lester and Hammel's ERA's have gone up over there last several starts. I always worry about relief pitchers, but Travis Wood had been good lately. Then he gave up two gopher balls in the seventh.

Extra innings:
Matt and Marlys were both in the house when the phone rang right after out number three of the game. Gene had called and Marlys said, "yes, the voice of victory has returned." Matt, in the next room added "oh my has the voice finally returned." Ha! They are both now very aware of the routine, that is, especially after a Cub win and shortly a phone call, that we all know who's calling. Gee, it's the fourth of July and the Cubs win and I need to celebrate. Let's see, we have hot dogs, chips, apple pie and yes I probably should drink two beers; a blue moon (Belgian white) and a Stella Artois or as we sometimes say, "Stellas twat."

Today's baseball wisdom:

"Baseball is like a poker game, nobody wants to quit when they're losing, nobody wants you to quit when you're winning."
Jackie Robinson

Baseball history this date:

1939 – The New York Yankees retire their first uniform, Lou Gehrig's #4 at their first old-timers game.

Game: #83

Teams: Cubs/Cincinnati
Date: Tuesday, July 5
Final: Cubs lose 9-5
Record: 52 – 31

V – mail: "You know what you get when you don't get pitching? You lose! Reds 9 – Cubs 5."

Recap:

Yes, pitching, pitching, pitching is the name of the game. John Lackey's winless streak is now at five games. He gave up five earned runs, six hits and five walks in six innings; he's 0 – 3 in his last five starts. Maddon got tossed out of the game for the second time this season arguing a called strike on a 3 – 0 count. Meanwhile, the Cubs hit four more home runs; Bryant number 25 now leads the majors, Russell hit two and Baez had one. At that point the game was 6 – 5 Reds. You can guess what happened when the relief pitchers came on.

Extra innings:

Boy this is really getting sickening. I have been concerned (really bitching) about the Cubs relief pitching most of the year. Iglesias (Cincinnati reliever) pitched two hit ball for three scoreless innings. Cub relievers, by contrast gave up three runs and four hits in three innings. If your relievers continue to give up runs, a chance of a comeback is down the drain. It's not just a single reliever, lately all of the Cub relievers are getting hit, and hard. It's bad news I think.

Today's baseball wisdom:

"The difference between relief pitching today and when I did it is simple; there is too much of it. It's one of those cases where more is not necessarily better."
Bob Feller

Baseball history this date:

1935 – The Chicago Cubs are 10 ½ games back in the National League and go on to win the pennant.

Game: #84

Teams: Cubs/Cincinnati
Date: Wednesday, July 6
Final: Cubs lose 5 – 3
Record: 52 – 32

V – mail: "Another bullpen loss. I hope this losing baseball ends soon."

Recap:
Adam Warren pitched five innings, allowed three hits and left the game leading 3-1. Enter Trevor Cahill who got through the sixth, but then two singles and "bang" a three run shot and the game is over. Cincinnati added another run off Carl Edwards, on a wild pitch. As is the case lately, the Cubs didn't have a hit after the fifth inning. They are now 1-5 in their last six home games after starting 25 – 8 at Wrigley. Also, they have lost 12 of their last 17 games and no longer have the best record in baseball which now belongs to the San Francisco Giants. The Reds stole four bases off of Montero, who is hitting only .197. Geez, neither Gene or I really liked the Montero (from the Diamondbacks) trade for Castillo.

Extra innings:
It's kind of amazing to watch the Cubs "fall from grace." Their performance is reminiscent of past Cub "flops" and that's scary. For years the Cubs would play well into July and then "wilt" like spring flowers. However, it's been many years since the Cubs have had such an unbelievable start, at one time 27 games over .500 and a 13 or 14 game lead. Holy cow, has anyone seen a damn goat in the neighborhood?

Today's baseball wisdom:

"We need three kinds of pitching, right-handed, left-handed, and relief."
Whitey Herzog

Baseball history this date:

1932 – Chicago Cubs shortstop Billy Jurges is shot twice in a Chicago hotel room by a spurned girlfriend, Violet Popovich Valli. She entered his room, 509, with a .25 caliber handgun and shot Jurges in the hand and ribs. He recovered and played third base 17 days later, going 2 – 4.

Game: #85

Teams: Cubs/Atlanta
Date: Thursday, July 7
Final: Cubs lose 4-3 (11 innings)
Record: 52 – 33

V – mail: "The Cubs seem to have lost their clutch hitting as they left a lot of runners on base. I did not see the end of this one as it was too late for me. Final score in 11 innings was Braves 4, Cubs 3."

Recap:
Once again the Cubs, (are they still the "lovable losers") found a way to give the game away. They scored three in the eighth to take a 3-2 lead (all three runs scored with two out) and they bring in their "ace" closer Rondon who proceeds to throw a gopher ball to the first guy, Markasis and it's a 3 – 3 game. He had hit a two-run shot earlier in the game off Hammel and that was it for the Braves (a lousy team with a record of 29 – 57, good for last place) until the ninth inning home run. Markasis, a real "slugger" now has four home runs for the year with the two today. Rondon then struck out the side, BFD! Of course Cubs don't score in the ninth, tenth, or eleventh and another retread, Spencer Patton, with an ERA of 5.56 enters and loses the game in the bottom of the 11th. Gene's v-mail is true as the Cubs put the first two on in the 11th and then Maddon had Russell swing away, no bunt, who hit into a double play; then a guy named Candilario (who is he) pops out and the game is over. Jesus Christ this is ridiculous – off to a fantastic start and now falling flat on their face.

Rereading this, I sound like a completely frustrated, unfaithful, disloyal, Cub fan, well I am! I and many others have waited for years for the Cubs to win it. Maybe I have too many expectations and need to simply "go with the flow."

With all my complaining and the Cubs playing so poorly I decided I needed to add something positive. So attached is a nice feature on the 1919 Cubs that appeared in the local Arizona daily Star newspaper (it's so liberal we call it the "Red Star") but it's a nice article by Greg Hansen.

Extra innings:
I'm a bit annoyed with Maddon and his nonchalant attitude. "It happens to everybody he said at his team's woes; for anybody out there who believes it doesn't happen to every team, you're wrong." Yes all teams have slumps, but starting 25 – 6 then going 27 – 27, does that happen to everyone? I suppose he's right, he's a manager, but I want them to win so badly, that I hate it when they lose.

Today's baseball wisdom:

"If you can't accept losing, you can't win."*
Vince Lombardi
*(I guess I need to listen to that advice)

Baseball history this date:

1948 – The Cleveland Indians sign Leroy "Satchel" Paige.

GREG Hansen's 100 best days in Tucson sports history.
Arizona daily Star, July 5, 2016
story #41, rank #61
"April 11, 1919: Chicago Cubs play first spring training game in Tucson history."

Six months after playing the Boston Red Sox in the 1919 World Series the Chicago Cubs sent a telegram to U of A Baseball coach Pop McHale with a most intriguing proposition. Would the Wildcats be available to play the Cubs on April 11 on the U of A campus? Would they? McHale cleared the calendar and pinched himself. It was true.

The '19' Cubs were the only major league team to stage spring training in the West – in Pasadena California and planned to stop in Phoenix, Tucson, Bisbee, Douglas, El Paso, and Dallas on a barnstorming train voyage to opening day April 24 in Chicago. The news was greeted with such enthusiasm that the star included these words on the front page of its April 6, 1919 issue: "the day will probably be more generally observed as a holiday and any other on the calendar for businesses will practically shut down for the afternoon."

Arizona had been a state for just seven years; the idea of a big league club playing a game in Tucson – the defending National League champs at that, was met with unusual anticipation.

"There will be a regular convention of baseball fans on campus Friday afternoon," the Star reported. "Those who intend to go to the game in automobiles are urged to make arrangements as soon as possible for parking space. Parking will be given free to any party of four who present full price tickets."

When the game began at noon on a Friday afternoon, every parking space and grandstand seat was full, and estimated crowd of 2000, thought to be more than quadruple the size of any previous crowd at a baseball game in Tucson.

The Cubs played their starters, including infamous World Series figure Fred Merkle. McKale eschewed the chance to use two cub pitchers, choosing to use his collegians. The Cubs won 7 – 3.

"The varsity boys showed no evidence of stage fright," the Star reported, "finding themselves in World Series company, the boys touched up two pitchers for 10 hits, thrilling the crowd, which completely filled the grandstand, with an overflow audience filling over 100 automobiles parked to either side."

It would be another 10 years before a MLB team, the Detroit Tigers, staged full-time training in Arizona (Phoenix) and it wasn't until 1947 that the Cleveland Indians moved their spring training operation to Tucson. But the 1919 game at wildcat field set the stage for spring training in Tucson.

As far as can be accurately researched, the Pirates, White Sox and Tigers played multiple spring games in Tucson between 1928 – 1941.

Although no major league team was west of St. Louis until 1958, teams had been training West as early as 1903, the Cubs first year in Los Angeles. In 1905 the Cubs moved to Santa Monica. Spring training stops followed in Champaign Illinois, New Orleans Louisiana, Vicksburg Mississippi, Hot Springs Arkansas, and Tampa Florida, before the Cubs settled in Pasadena from 1917 – 1921. Then came Catalina Island off the coast of Los Angeles the Cubs winter home from 1922 – 1951.

Where are they now? U of A pitcher Louis Slonaker, "covered himself with glory," according to the stars game story. "He twirled a heady, cool game throughout, allowing the World Series contenders of 1918 only 9 bingles." Slonaker was a four-year letterman in baseball, basketball and football, an assistant athletic director from 1922 – 1947, and Dean of men from 1947 – 1863.

How they did it: the Cubs train odyssey to and through Tucson continued immediately after their game with the U of A. The management of the El Paso and southwestern railroad company held the scheduled train from Tucson to Bisbee for two hours, from 2:30 to 4:30 PM.

Editorial note: there was a photo of J. F. "Pop" McHale at the top of this article.

The caption read: "J. F. "Pop" McHale and his Arizona Wildcats took on the defending National League champion Cubs in a spring training game in Tucson in 1919. Chicago won 7 – 3."

Game: #86

Teams: Cubs @ Pittsburgh
Date: Friday, July 8
Final: Cubs lose 8-4
Record: 52 – 34

V – mail: "This is getting more like shades of 69. Can't seem to get a win."

Recap:

It is indeed becoming worrisome. The Cubs have now lost eight of nine and Arrieta was leading in the seventh inning, but he gives up a walk and two singles and then the bottom "fell out." The Pirates scored four runs to lead 7 – 4, and won the game 8-4. Arrieta was charged with six runs and nine hits; his ERA has gone to 2.68 and his record is now 12-4. He has lost three of his last four outings. What's happening?

Extra innings:

Dexter Fowler started a rehab assignment today at class A South Bend. Early in the year a baseball analyst called Fowler a "catalyst" for the Cubs offense. He just seemed to be a guy who got good things happening. Pitching has been a real tough issue recently, but I sometimes think that a key guy like Fowler going out can seriously effect the entire teams offense. Furthermore the bad "mojo virus" can spread to the other aspects of the game, namely pitching and defense. For example, how often does Rizzo make a wild throw like he did today?

Today's baseball wisdom:

"If a tie is like kissing your sister, then losing is like kissing your grandmother with her teeth out."
George Brett

Baseball history this date:

1946 – Baseball grants $5000 as a minimum salary.

Game: #87

Teams: Cubs @ Pittsburgh
Date: Saturday, July 9
Final: Cubs lose 6 – 12
Record: 52 – 35

V – mail: "Oh where has our pitching gone? We score 6 runs and we lose."

Recap:
Oh my yes, I'm running out of adjectives to describe my negative, downtrodden, depressing, shocking, stressful, anxiety ridden, "down in the mouth" or down in the dumps, let alone deplorable, lamentable, bemoaning, dispirited, grievous, and downright sorrowful mental state over this state of affairs with the Cubs.

They get six runs and 14 hits and they still lose their ninth of ten games. I really can't think of anything else to say except that manager Joe Maddon is beginning to sound like some "politically correct" liberal who believes that it's possible to pick up a turd by the clean end!

I really don't understand him saying "I feel like we're fortunate to be up 6 ½ games right now. Actually I don't believe it's a negative I think it's a positive." Really Joe? The team started the year 25 – 6 and that really was a positive I think we would all agree. But failing to label a record of 27 – 29 as a negative is difficult to understand.

Extra innings:
The Cubs losing is really depressing, and I was searching for a positive to lighten up today's commentary, and I found one. ESPN has a panel of experts who are at this date compiling an all-time ranking of the 100 best baseball players of all time. I noted in the right-handed pitchers category that the player listed at #9 also had a story related by a guy named Dan Mullen, an ESPN Senior MLB editor. His father had told him the story. The pitcher at the #9 position was none other than Leroy "Satchel" Paige and the anecdote is as follows:

"I don't have a Satchel Paige story but my father does, and it's too good not to share: Satchel Paige spent his off seasons barnstorming through the country pitching for whomever he could – – the kind of games towns hung posters and advertising so that all of the locals came out to see. This particular time he was with the Baltimore Elite Giants facing the Riverhead (N.Y.) Falcons. The game started like many for Satchel with a 1 – 2 – 3 first-inning – – he even retired Carl Yastrzemski's father for one of the outs. But then things took a twist. A player named Jerry McCarthy, who had a cup of coffee with the 1948 St. Louis Browns belted a triple off the center field fence. Satchel stood there shaking his head in disbelief, and then he did exactly what you're heard legend of but had never been sure if it actually happened: He pulled all of his players except the catcher off the field, telling them to sit down and watch. Nine pitches and three strikeouts later McCarthy was left stranded at third !"

Dan Mullen, ESPN senior MLB editor.

Was he, Paige, really the 9th best right-hander of all times? I'm not sure, but he surely is at the top of the list in American baseball folklore. Gene and I saw him pitch at Davis, Illinois one hot sultry day in the 60s with his barnstorming troupe. He only pitched one or two innings, and the most memorable event was he and the first baseman pulling the "hidden ball trick" on one of our locals who was on first base.

As I spent the time researching his career some I'll provide a few stats about him.

Teams:

In the Negro leagues he was with the Pittsburgh Crawfords 1931, 34, 36, and then the Kansas City Monarchs 1935 and 1940 – 47. He signed with the Cleveland Indians in 1948 stayed with them to 1949. Then he was with the St. Louis Browns 1951 – 53 finally to the Kansas City A's in 1965.

Career stats:

These are major league stats: W – L – 28 – 31, shutouts – 4, innings pitched 476, ERA 3.29, strikeouts 288, whip – 1.279.

Honors: Two – time AL All-Star 1952 – 53, Hall of Fame in 1971.

And, just remember folks, that this guy was no "spring chicken." He was born July 7, 1906, which meant he began his brief major league career at the age of 42. I didn't know he played for Kansas City in 1965 which made him 59 at that time. When Gene and I saw him play in the early 60s he was already past 50. He really is a legendary figure.

Today's baseball wisdom:

"Losing streaks are funny. If you lose at the beginning you get off to a bad start. If you lose in the middle of the season, you're in a slump, if you lose at the end you're "choking."

Gene Mauch

Baseball history this date:

1953 – The Philadelphia Phillies Robin Roberts streak of 28 straight complete games ended. *

*(Pitchers today rarely pitch complete games; The 2016 leaders were Chris Sale of the Chicago White Sox – six games and Johnny Cueto for the San Francisco Giants – five games)

Game: #88

Teams: Cubs @ Pittsburgh
Date: Sunday, July 10
Final: Cubs win 6 – 5
Record: 55 – 35

V – mail: "At least we won our last game before the All-Star break, but it was a close one. Cubs win 6-5."

Recap:
The Cubs wasted two leads, but Kris Bryant, who had three hits and was on base four times drove in the lead and eventual winning run in the eighth inning. The win stopped a five-game losing streak and left them with a seven-game lead over those dastardly Cardinals at the All-Star break. Cub rookies made several mistakes which led to a tying run the seventh (5-5).

Jon Lackey had another inconsistent outing allowing four runs in the first three innings. He did shut the Pirates out for the next three innings. Pitching recently, both the starters and the relievers has for some time not been very impressive. But, even though I'm not convinced of their invincibility, I along with all the loyal Cub fans need to hang in there.

Extra innings:
I wrote this after the All-Star game. I'm not very interested in the game itself (the American League won again 4-2) however, I have an editorial comment on the evening. With much flourish Major League baseball Commissioner Manfred announced that "now and for eternity" (or something like that) the batting champion's for each league will now be named. The American League will be the "Rod Carew" batting championship. For the National League the leading hitter will be called, the "Tony Gwynn" batting champion. Of course the crowd (with the game in San Diego) went wild as Tony played his entire career with San Diego. I'm fine with this selection as he had a lifetime batting average of .3382 and tied for #18 with only four or five guys in the National League ahead of him. Rogers Hornsby at .3585 and Bill Terry at .3412 had higher averages.

But it's the Carew selection that I would submit is a blatant "politically correct" selection. He was a really good hitter lifetime batting average of .3278, again good but not great. He ranked #34th all-time among hitters. Additionally there were more than a dozen American League hitters who had higher lifetime averages. Of course, there was Ty Cobb, the all-time leader at .3664. But he has been so maligned as a person, and he was not a very nice guy, therefore he didn't stand a chance. Well, how about "shoeless" Joe Jackson? Oh no, he was part of the infamous "Black Sox" scandal so scratch him, even though he had a lifetime average of .356 and holds the major league rookie season average at .408. Okay for all the faint of hearts who don't like the bad guys, I think I have some candidates; Ted Williams, lifetime .3444, or Lou Gehrig .3401, or the "Babe" at .3421 Did you ever hear of Tris Speaker whose lifetime average was .3447? How about Harry Heilman .3416?

I'd take Ted Williams, a great hitter, with the highest average in the American League and in the modern era second only to Rogers Hornsby in all of baseball.

It's likely no surprise that as a conservative thinker, I ascribe the real definition of "political correctness" to liberal thinking

Political Correctness: It is the doctrine, recently fostered by a delusional, illogical minority, promoted by a sick mainstream media, which holds forth that it is the entirely possible pick up a piece of shit by the clean end.

Get a life Mr. Commissioner; I guess because you're new to the job you wanted to make some kind of splash that people would remember. Well, many shall, they will suggest you fell into a sewer and made a really big smelly splash.

Today's baseball wisdom:

Kris Bryant who had four hits recently reminded me of a remark by Casey Stengel. He said:

"I broke in with four hits and the writers promptly declared they had seen the new Ty Cobb. It took me only a few days to correct that impression."

Casey Stengel

Baseball history this date:

1914 – The Boston Red Sox purchase Babe Ruth from the Baltimore Orioles.

Game: #89

Teams: Cubs/Texas
Date: Friday, July 15
Final: Cubs win 6-0
Record: 54 – 35

V – mail: "A great way to start the remaining games. Good pitching and hitting. Cubs 6, Rangers 0."

Recap:

The "voice" called and sounded really upbeat. He said "wow two in a row, let's go for more." Kyle Hendricks, who recently is pitching better than all of the other four starters, went six innings, no runs and only three hits. Maddon lifted him for a pinch hitter, Szczur, who promptly doubled in two for a 6 – 0 lead. Four relievers, Edwards, the young guy, Woods, Rondon and Strop held the Rangers without any runs the rest of the way. There was nothing to rave about hitting – wise, but Baez and Almora (in center field) each had two sparkling defensive plays. It was good to have the relievers perform so well. I noticed on the Internet that the Yankees may be willing to unload Aroldis Chapman, the 100 mph Cuban "wild man" (my label), and that the Cubs are probably interested. He's a great strikeout pitcher. He had some domestic issues early this year, (I think that he whacked his wife around some) that were serious enough to get him suspended for a period at the beginning of the year.

Extra innings:

I told Gene I thought that Carew having his name attached to the American League batting championship was blatant "political correctness."

He said "well isn't everything?"

"Not really I replied, our next president Trump, isn't politically correct."

With that Gene said," Oh you think I should vote for him?"

"Why yes of course, better to vote for a bombastic, arrogant guy rather than a criminal."

"Do you mean Hillary?"

"Of course, she is simply a crook."

"Well, okay if you really don't want me to vote for her, I'm willing to do that for old Donald, for say $1000."

"Let me think that over," I replied. Marlys who was listening to the conversation, quipped "hey it's worth the $1000, I'll do it." Well, we made no decision today – to be continued. Ha!

Today's baseball wisdom:

"Mickey Mantle was just everything. At my bar mitzvah I had an Oklahoma accent."*

Billy Crystal

*(Crystal was a huge fan of Mickey Mantle)

Baseball history this date:

1876 – The first no-hitter pitched by George Washington Bradley of the St. Louis Brown stockings. He no-hit the Hartford Dark Blues of the National League.*

*(Bradley won 45 games that year as he pitched virtually every game.

Game: #90

Date: Saturday, July 16
Teams: Cubs/Texas
Final: Cubs win 3 – 1.
Record: 55 – 35

V – mail: "Yo ho ho, three in a row. It's always fun when your team wins."

Recap:
Gene called, and was of course very happy. The Cubs only managed four hits and two runs off Yu Darvish (he's Japanese) who missed all of 2015 with Tommy John surgery. He struck out nine Cubs, but they got two runs on a two-run double by Rizzo. The key to the game was Jason Hammel, who after a fast start early in the season, had really faltered. But today he pitched six innings, allowed three hits, only one run, one base on balls and had seven strikeouts. Relievers Rondon, Warren, And Wood "mopped up."

Extra innings:
Hammel has been having trouble with cramps. His doctor, (this is true) prescribed potato chips because of their potassium content. Hammel said, "if you watch me between innings you'll see me eating potato chips." Hammel typically has not done well after the All-Star break, but he changed his diet during the off season preparing for the second half of the season. When the cramping came, it led to hydrating, which led to potato chips! We'll see what happens the second half.

Today's baseball wisdom:

Harry Caray
Marlys was watching the Diamondbacks they were tied with the Dodgers with two outs in the ninth. Unfortunately, Paul Goldschmidt hit a towering foul ball down the third base line that almost hit the indoor roof. The ball was caught, but the announcer remarked, "you know what old Harry Caray used to say about those sky – high foul balls, he said it's like hitting a home run up an elevator shaft."

Baseball history this date:

1941 – Joe DiMaggio goes 3 – 4 hitting in his 56th straight game.*
*(The streak ended with this game)

Game: #91

Teams: Cubs/Texas
Date: Sunday, July 17
Final: Cubs lose 4-1
Record: 55 – 36

V – mail: "Too much Cole Hamel in this one. Rangers win 4 – 1."

Recap:
I turned on gamecast on my computer for the first inning and Cole Hamel, Texas pitcher, struck out Baez, Bryant, and Rizzo to start the game. Then he struck out all three batters in the second inning. Oh, oh I thought, this is the same guy who no-hit the Cubs last year in his final game for the Phillies before being traded to Texas.

Lackey again really didn't have a very good game. He's now winless in his last seven starts. Baez drove in the only run and aside from two singles leading off the seventh and then Heyward hitting into a double play there wasn't much to talk about.

Extra innings:
The Cardinals did lose (yea) and the last time I looked the Pirates And Nationals were tied 1 – 1 in the 17th inning. I checked later and the Pirates scored in the top of the 18th for a 2 – 1 win. I have nothing more to say about these two games, so I'll move along.

Today's baseball wisdom:

The Cubs must've thought Hamel had gotten some advice from ole Diz Dean himself (I guess from heaven, or maybe not) after he struck out six straight batters to start the game. Dean, supremely confident, that's a nice term, once asked, "son what kind of pitch would you like to miss?"

Dizzy Dean

Baseball history this date:

1941 – Joe DiMaggio's 56 game hitting streak ends in Cleveland.*
*(I Think I told you that in yesterday's write up)

Game: #92

Teams: Cubs/Mets
Date: Monday, July 18
Final: Cubs win 5 – 1
Record: 56 – 36

V – mail: "Lester was on his game as the Cubs prevailed behind Rizzo's three-run homer."

Recap:
Pitching, that is the name of the game, and Jon Lester went 7 2/3 innings giving up only one run. He walked three and had three strikeouts. Strop got one out and Edwards started the ninth but Rondon had to "rescue" him and got an inning ending double play. Szczur had three hits and an RBI. As Gene reported Rizzo had a three-run blast. The Cubs broke an eight-game losing streak to the Mets and the "voice" called within 10 seconds after the game ended. He was in great spirits, "all we need is one more win to capture the series, and as long as we keep winning series that's all we need." I suggested that the Cubs go for a sweep.

Extra innings:
Rizzo agreed with the assertion that his third inning at-bat against lefty Stephen Matz might have been the best of his career! He was being modest as after a 2 – 2 count he fouled off five straight pitches and then whacked an 83 mph changeup an estimated 425 feet. Maddon said "that was a fabulous at-bat; that's what we want to be about, the two-strike at bat." Maddon also said that Rizzo along with Joey Votto of the Reds are the best two-strike hitters in the league. ESPN also added that it was the latest in an at-bat that Rizzo had hit the long ball in his career.

Today's baseball wisdom:
"If the guy was hurt, his team might be hurt, but pitching all over the league would improve."
Casey Stengel*
*(Stengel commenting on Harvey Kuenn as a hitter)

Baseball history this date:
1999 – David Cone of the New York Yankees, becomes the 15th pitcher in major league history to throw a perfect game (6 – 0, Montréal)

Game: #93

Teams: Cubs/Mets
Date: Tuesday, July 19
Final: Cubs lose 2 – 1
Record: 56 – 37

V – mail: "I did not see any of the game last night. It sounds like it was well pitched from both sides."

Recap:
The game was on ESPN, but I can't seem to watch them. I'm afraid, especially with close games that they will lose. When the Mets tied the score at 1 – 1 in the seventh inning I turned the game off. Guess what? The Mets got a run in the ninth off Rondon, who's statistics suggest that he tends to "blow" close games 50% of the time. But wait, the Cubs load the bases with no outs in the bottom of the ninth. Szczur then grounds out to third and Kris Bryant hits into a double play. Crap!

The Mets closer Familia saved his 49th straight regular-season game. That's what the Cubs need, a closer who actually "closes." Now there are rumors, hot and heavy, that the Cubs are going to make a move soon. Yesterday Rizzo won the game but today he was 0 – 4 with four strikeouts. Szczur, who had three hits yesterday couldn't get the ball out of the infield; that's what killed them in the ninth.

Extra innings:
After reading Gene's v-mail on the 20th when I'm writing this, I called him. I was really ticked about the loss and started complaining. As always he's philosophical and said "hey that's baseball you can't let games like this get to you, you'll go nuts."

I said, "that's not possible I'm already in 'la la' land much of the time. The bottom line is that I'm a terribly poor loser and want my teams to win all the time." Marlys said, "you really don't like sports, you should hear yourself complaining." Gene's take on the game was that "it was really a great baseball game and if the Cubs had won the Mets fans would be just as unhappy as you are."

I have to admit that Gene and Marlys are probably right. I simply want to win and I forget about the quality of the game. I don't think I can change, so I will just think "bad thoughts" about the other team and not verbalize my hostility in losing. (Maybe I really should delete this section, as both Gene and Marlys will really hammer me with this paragraph). Ha!

Today's baseball wisdom:

"Rollie Fingers has 35 saves. He has a better record than John the Baptist." Lon Simmons

Baseball history this date:

1933 – The first time in major league history that two brothers on opposing teams hit home runs in the same game. Rick Ferrell (Red Sox) and Wes Ferrell (Cleveland Indians)

Game: #94

Teams: Cubs/Mets
Date: Wednesday, July 20
Final: Cubs win 6 – 2
Record: 57 – 37

V – mail: "Kyle Hendricks was very good as he allowed no runs in 6 1/3 innings. Anthony Rizzo hit two homers to help provide offense. Cubs win 6 – 2."

Recap:
Gene called and left a message. "Well this game should make you happier than you were yesterday as the Cubs won. Rizzo had two long home runs, 451 feet and 436 feet. Hendricks pitched into the seventh inning and allowed no runs, one walk and eight strikeouts."

Hendricks is doing well, as I noted that he has the second lowest ERA at home among National League pitchers. He is at 1.36 and Clayton Kershaw of the Dodgers is at 1.31. Hendricks' overall ERA is third best in the majors and he hasn't allowed a run in his last three appearances. He's really turned into a top-flight hurler and he's only 26 years old.

Extra innings:
Next up is a three-game road trip to Milwaukee to take on the " brew crew." Gene said he was going to the game on Friday and was a bit concerned about the weather as it's going to be close to 100° and with the humidity, the heat index could get up to 110°.

On another note, it was 40 years ago today, 1976, that Hank Aaron hit his 755th and final home run. The article said he was second all-time in home runs. I feel rather strongly about the matter and my comment on him being second is simply, "BS." He is first among the non-drug users. Barry Bonds, the "PED King" shouldn't even be listed. Aaron is also the all-time leader in RBIs. He has 2297, Babe Ruth has 2213, and believe it or not Alex Rodriguez is listed at #3. He also should not be listed because of his use of the PED'S. The supreme drug user, Bonds is listed at #4. Any of his records should simply be dumped into the garbage bin.

The real rankings for RBIs are Aaron, Ruth, Gehrig (my second all-time hero along with Mickey Mantle) Stan "the Man" Musial, and Ty Cobb.

As a final note, the single-season all-time RBI leaders are Hack Wilson 191, in 1930, and Lou Gehrig 184, in 1937.

Today's baseball wisdom:

"I would always sing it ('take me out to the ballgame') because it's the only song I know the words to."
Harry Caray

Baseball history this date:

1912 – The Phillies Sherry Magee steals home twice in one game.

Game: #95

Teams: Cubs @ Milwaukee
Date: Friday, July 22
Final: Cubs win 5 – 2
Record: 58 – 37

V – mail: "I witnessed most of the game. Solid pitching from the bullpen as the Cubs welcomed back Dexter Fowler who delivered three hits including a home run. Cubs win 5 – 2."

Recap:

It was interesting that Fowler should have a really nice game just off the disabled list for 27 days. When he get hurt, hamstring, and the Cubs started losing, a baseball writer had opined that they had lost the catalyst to their offense, namely Fowler. I think that's a very good observation as with Fowler leading off and getting on base early in the game the Cubs often get a lead that they never relinquish. No doubt he's an important guy to start the offense. He had a double, single, home run, and three RBIs enough to win the game. Hammel went five innings and allowed four hits and two runs. The relievers took over and allowed no runs as Edwards pitched one inning, Wood two thirds of an inning, Grimm one third of an inning, and Rondon one inning. Six pitchers total and five in the last four innings.

Lackey goes tomorrow and I hope he has a better outing; he is 0 – 3 with a 6.75 ERA over his last five starts.

Extra innings:

Gene went to the game and I called him to see how he enjoyed it. He called it the "game from hell." First, the bus lost its air-conditioning on the way up (almost 90° and extreme humidity) and when they got to Milwaukee they got caught in a terrible traffic jam. They didn't get to the ballpark until 8 PM and the Cubs were already ahead 4 – 0 (the game essentially over) because the game started at 7 PM. He said the stadium was terribly hot, but at least the air conditioner worked on the bus on the way home. He said the bus dropped him off at Rock City and it was so humid he had a terrible time seeing the road even with the windshield wipers on full speed plus the defroster. "It was a terrible night, and I got home at 1:30 AM completely drained."

However, he said he's going again on September 6, and maybe it will be a lot cooler then. Ha!

Today's baseball wisdom:

"It ain't the heat, it's the humility."
Yogi Berra

Baseball history this date:

1997 – Greg Maddux throws a complete game with just 76 pitches. The Braves were at the Cubs and won the game 4 – 1. Of the 76 pitches that Maddux threw, 63 were strikes, and the time of the game was 2:07.

Game: #96

Teams: Cubs @ Milwaukee
Date: Saturday, July 23
Final: Cubs lose 6 – 1
Record: 58 – 38

V – mail: "Pitching was all on the other side tonight as the final was 6 – 1 on a very hot night."

Recap:

So this guy named Kirk Nieuwenhuis who has been in an 0 – 18 slump hits two home runs, gets a season high four RBIs and the Cubs lose 6 – 1. Oh, also his batting average is a whopping .207! The Brewers pitcher Zach Davis took a shutout into the seventh inning before giving up a run. John Lackey lost again, now four straight losses, but pitched six innings allowing only three runs. Not a bad outing but enough to lose. The Cubs newest reliever, Mike Montgomery, came on in the eighth inning and promptly gave up a three-run homer. Wow, some trade the Cubs made, Montgomery for a minor leaguer named Dan Vogelbach. He was hitting .319 with 17 home runs and 66 RBIs – 24 years old. I hope Montgomery was worth the trade.

Extra innings:

Speaking of relievers, now old Joe Nathan, 41 years old, once a terrific reliever with the Twins will be joining the Cubs after a 30 day rehab assignment in the Cubs minor-league system. He's recovering from Tommy John surgery and hasn't pitched in the majors since April 2015 with Detroit. NEWS FLASH- Now Aroldis Chapman the 100 mph "flame throwing bad boy" from the Yankees is apparently on the radar. "Oh please save me."

Today's baseball wisdom:

"Nice guys finish last."
Leo Durocher

Baseball history this date:

1866 – The Cincinnati baseball club, the "red stockings," forms. It is the first all professional baseball team.

Game: #97

Teams: Cubs @ Milwaukee
Date: Sunday, July 24
Final: Cubs win 6 – 5
Record: 59 – 38

V – mail: "A bases-loaded base clearing double by Rizzo was the big blow in the game as the Cubs came from behind to beat the Brewers 6 – 5."

Recap:
"Oh no, not again! Lester gave up four runs in four innings; the Milwaukee pitcher Guerra gave up no earned runs in 6 1/3 innings and it's 4 – 1 "brew crew" going into the seventh. Then Rizzo hit's a three-run double and Zobrist knocks him in and the Cubs hang on to win the game 6 – 5. When I said they hung on I mean they really had to hang on. Rondon gave up a hit in the ninth, which troubles me, but Gene and I talked about it and he doesn't seem too concerned.

Extra innings:
Remember that yesterday I said old Joe Nathan had joined the team, well he won the game today! He came on in the sixth inning, and the Cubs score 5 in the seventh, so he's the pitcher of record. He gave up a triple to start, then a walk (two on with no outs) then he proceeded to strike out their number 2, 3, and 4 hitters who were Braun, Lucroy and Carter. They are all really good hitters and if old Harry Caray were still with us he would have exclaimed, "holy cow."

Today's baseball wisdom:

This game I'm dedicating to Vernelle Kohn, Marlys' sister who "loved" Joe Nathan when he was a great reliever for the Minnesota Twins from 2004 – 2011. Vernelle passed away in 2009. The Twins had many good years back then (unlike this year) and Vernelle was a very knowledgeable fan. We had many extended discussions about baseball strategy, managers' decisions, skills of individual players and especially "our teams."

Vernelle was 100% loyal to her Minnesota "Twinkies" and Nathan was her guy. Somehow I'm sure she is celebrating today.

Baseball history this date:

1958 – Ted Williams was fined $250 today for spitting at fans again.*

*(Are you kidding me, $250, today it would be a $25,000 or maybe $50,000 as it was his second offense)

Game: #98

Teams: Cubs @ White Sox
Date: Monday, July 25
Final: Cubs lose 5 – 4
Record: 59 – 39

V – mail: "The Cubs came from behind again in this game, but only to tie and then end up losing in the bottom of the ninth 5 – 4."

Recap:
I continue to bitch and moan about the Cubs relief pitching, and here we go again. The Cubs finally tied the score at 4 – 4 in the ninth after trailing 4 – 0 through six innings. Then Baez hit a two-run in the seventh and they added two more in the ninth. Unfortunately, Bryant was thrown out in the ninth trying to stretch a single into a double (so erase that run) and also Baez was thrown out at the plate in the third.

Well they bring in Mike Montgomery, the new lefty acquired last weekend from Seattle for a top-flight AAA minor leaguer and the guy gives up a hit, a sacrifice to second and then another hit and the game is over. My oh my.

Extra innings:
I just can't imagine what's gone wrong with the Cubs starting pitching. First lackey loses Saturday, then Lester yesterday and today, although he didn't lose, Arrieta was breezing along only down 1 – 0 and then he gives up a three-run homer to Todd Frazier – there's nothing more to say.

Today's baseball wisdom:

"When I was in baseball and you went into the clubhouse he didn't see any curling irons."
Red Barber

Baseball history this date:

1961 – Roger Maris hit home runs #37, #38, #39, and #40 in a doubleheader today.

Game: #99

Teams: Cubs @ White Sox
Date: Tuesday, July 26
Final: Cubs lose 3 – 0
Record: 59 – 40

V – mail: "Cubs could not get a clutch hit to save their soul on this night when they got a good night from their pitcher. Sox 3, Cubs 0."

Recap:

Bob Uecker once said while on the air, "We only got one God damn hit." Well today the Cubs only got four "God - - singles," and lost the game 3 – 0. The Cubs hitting was obviously abysmal. They got no extra-base hits, and Kris Bryant was 0 – 4 with three strikeouts. He has struck out 7 of his last 10 at-bats.

Once again Kyle Hendricks deserved a better fate. He pitched 5 2/3 innings giving up six hits, seven strikeouts and three earned runs. However, Travis Wood came in and walked three straight batters forcing in a run, which means Hendricks was only responsible for only two of the runs. Old Joe Nathan pitched a perfect seventh inning. Way to go Joe.

Extra innings:

The Cubs and Yankees did pull off the mega trade that has been rumored for several days. The Cubs landed arguably the top relief pitcher in the major leagues, Aroldis Chapman, the 28-year-old lefty with a career ERA of .183. They gave up a total of four young guys, some of them really top-notch prospects. A key guy was Gleyber Torres (what a name) a 19-year-old shortstop rated the 27th best prospect by Baseball America. They also sent Adam Warren, who they got from the Yankees in the Castro trade, Rashad Crawford, and Billy McKinney who has had some terrific years in the minors. It seems obvious to me that the Cubs made the trade to "win this year." Chapman, who will probably be a free agent at the end of the year, will command a huge, likely multiyear contract. So it boils down to selling a bit of the "future" to win now. Chapman does come with a little baggage, as he was suspended earlier in the year, 30 days for "domestic violence." Of course the Cubs ownership and management have fully embraced Chapman with all the expected platitudes. Baloney, whatever they think of the guy as a person, it boils down to they think he will help them win. Isn't the real issue behind professional sports these days the $?

Today's baseball wisdom:

"I became a good pitcher when I stopped trying to make them miss the balls and started trying to make them hit it."

Sandy Koufax

Baseball history this date:

1933 – Joe DiMaggio's 61 game hitting streak in the Pacific Coast league ended.

Game: #100

Teams: Cubs/White Sox
Date: Wednesday, July 27
Final: Cubs win 8 – 1
Record: 60 –40

V – mail: "A well pitched game on both sides. 1 – 1 in the seventh inning until Baez hit a two-run homer. In the eighth the Cubs put it away. 8 – 1 final with Hammel the winner."

Recap:
The Cubs did not get a hit until the sixth inning. Then Bryant hit a home run to tie the score at 1 – 1.

The announcer later said that his blast was the key to the game as everyone seemed to breathe a sigh of relief and "decided to win." In the seventh Baez hit a two-run homer and in the eighth Russell hit a grand slam and put the game away. Hammel has now won 10 games and I hope the other starters get back on track.

Extra innings:
Maddon brought in Chapman for the ninth inning, I think just to get his Cub debut over with. He had two strikeouts and a ground ball to third; that's what the Cub loyalists wanted to see. Several of his pitches hit 104 mph! "God, Marlys said, if he hit you with a pitch he would kill you. I think she's probably right especially, if he hit you in the "noggin."

Today's baseball wisdom:

"Just take the ball and throw it where you want to. Throw strikes, home plate don't move."
Satchel Paige

Baseball history this date:

1993 – The new York Mets pitcher Anthony Young won today, ending his losing streak at 27 games.

A Century-Long Journey to the Day of Redemption

Game: #101

Teams: Cubs/White Sox
Date: Thursday, July 28
Final: Cubs win 3 – 1
Record: 61 – 40

V – mail: "Lackey and the defense were great as the Cubs sneaked out a 3 – 1 win, with the help of the Cubs 'nasty boys 2'."

Recap:
I'm not sure what "nasty boys 2" means, I have to call Gene. Ha! John Lackey gave up one run in six innings and Aroldis Chapman out pitched the White Sox ace, Chris Sale to get his first save for the Cubs. His fastball consistently hit 102 mph, and they say you can hear a "sizzle" when the ball comes in. Sale had returned after a five day suspension for cutting up his and other team members "throwback", that is old-style jerseys. They didn't fit well so he shredded them. He said the team was putting "marketing" over baseball. I don't get that one.

The White Sox got a run in the first but nothing after that and the Cubs tied it in the first and then got single runs in the third and eighth innings.

Extra innings:
Jason Heyward, with a $184 million contract, is hitting .229 with four home runs and a .315 slugging percentage. Those are pretty terrible numbers, but Joe Maddon (I think he must be quite a good amateur psychologist) only says, "man I don't know that anybody could handle it better than the way he has. I really believe we're due for a nice run out of him shortly."Yes Joe, I said this many times before, as the Minnesotans say "you got that right." I sure hope so as he's really a great defensive outfielder.

Now, concerning the "nasty boys 2" from Gene, I went to the Internet and discovered the following. Nasty boys #1 were Rob Dibble, Norm Charlton, and Randy Myers of the 1990 Cincinnati Reds, who were "wire -to -wire" winners of the pennant. They swept the World Series from Oakland in four straight games. Their manager was none other than "Sweet" Lou Piniella. Barry Larkin said of the nasty boys (relievers) "those three guys I thought, were the most valuable piece of the 1990 team."

They weren't the "big red machine of the 70s that featured Johnny Bench, Pete Rose, Joe Morgan, Tony Perez, George Foster, Dave Concepcion, Ken Griffey Sr. and Cesar Geronimo (known as the great eight) but the 90s team had a number of stars, like Ken Griffey Jr. Eric Davis, Barry Larkin, and of course the "nasty boys."

But I've strayed from the point Of Gene's v-mail. He was suggesting that the "nasty boys #2" are now The Cub trio of Chapman, Hector Rondon and Pedro Strop.

Gosh, I'm impressed with Gene, he has a pretty good memory (especially for baseball) for an "old guy."

Today's baseball wisdom:

"Nolan Ryan is pitching much better now that he has his curve ball straightened out."

Joe Garagiola

Baseball history this date:

1991 – Dennis Martinez of the Phillies pitches the 13th perfect game in baseball history.

(Also, on the same date:)

1994 – Kenny Rogers pitches baseball's 14th perfect game.

Game: #102

Teams: Cubs/Seattle
Date: Friday, July 29
Final: Cubs win 12 – 1
Record: 62 – 40

V mail: "Cubs had a whole bunch of hits in this one while Jon Lester threw six shutout innings. Cubs win 12 – 1."

Recap:

Really nice pitching performance by Lester; six innings, no runs and seven strikeouts. The Cubs scored six runs in the sixth so Maddon took Lester out. Grimm pitched the seventh and gave up only a hit. Montgomery got through the eighth okay, but then gave up two hits and a walk in the ninth for Seattle's only run. Montgomery who came from Seattle in a trade had a 2.34 ERA, but in three appearances with the Cubs his ERA is over 11. I complained to Gene, who as usual said, "hey it's a new team, give him a chance to get adjusted." My response was "mumble, grumble, baloney I'm a bad loser, do it now, I mean get people out."

Obviously, lots of hitting. Baez had three hits and is now up to .293, Rizzo had three RBIs and has 79 which is tops in the National League, while "grandpa" Ross had a home run. Maddon said yesterday, that he was looking forward to good things from Heyward, and Heyward responded with a three-run shot.

Extra innings:

Tomorrow Arrieta is pitching for the Cubs. The last two games Lackey and Lester have really been good news as they appear to have regained some of their early season "magic." Let's hope Arrieta also has a good outing. Go Cubs!

Today's baseball wisdom:

As the Cubs had 14 hits today, they must have taken the advice of "Wee Willie" Keeler who said: "I keep my eyes clear and hit em where they ain't."
Willie Keeler

Baseball history this date:

1961 – Philadelphia Phillies lose the first of 23 straight games.

Game: #103

Teams: Cubs/Seattle
Date: Saturday, July 30
Final: Cubs lose 4 – 1
Record: 62 – 41

V – mail: "A really tough loss. Jake pitched good, but two walks in the eighth beat him. Cubs lose 4 -1."

Recap:

Gene's v-mail is right on, a tough one to lose. Arrieta pitched a great game and was leading 1 – 0 after seven innings. He walked two to start the eighth and Rondon came in. He got a sacrifice out, and got a runner out at the plate. Chapman comes in and promptly gives up a two-run double to Leonys Martin, a .250 hitter. Then Martin stole third and scored on a wild pitch by Chapman. Well, it's obvious Chapman is not invincible. It is really too bad that Arrieta gets a loss as he pitched a great game and it ends up going down the drain. However, Arrieta actually got out pitched by a former diamondback, Wade Miley, who took a no hit bid into the seventh inning with nine strikeouts. Bryant got a single and eventually scored on a ground out by Baez. Wow, what a difference a year can make as Arrieta is 0 – 3 with a 6.88 ERA during five starts in July. Last year he was almost untouchable after the All-Star break.

Extra innings:

Even though the Cubs lost, there was good news as the Cardinals lost, as did the Pirates. Maddon may not start Hendricks tomorrow giving him more rest. I hope that works out as Seattle is pitching "King" Hernandez who is really a tough guy to beat. We'll see what happens.

Today's baseball wisdom:

"I told the kids, somebody's gotta win, somebody's gotta lose. Just don't fight about it. Just try to get better.*
Yogi Berra
*(That's advice that I should listen to)

Baseball history this date:

1874 – Today the first baseball teams to play outside of the United States, Boston and Philadelphia, played in the British Isles.

Game: #104

Teams: Cubs/Seattle
Date: Sunday, July 31
Final: Cubs win 7 – 6 ((12 innings)
Record: 63 – 41

V mail: "A great team victory. My take is that this win is due to the Cubs bullpen as they threw nine innings of shutout baseball. Lots of heroes in this one. Cubs win 7 – 6 in 12 innings."

Recap:
Gene's v-mail sums up the game pretty succinctly. The heroes were, the bullpen (seven different guys), especially Wood who got out of a bases-loaded jam with no outs, Contreras legging out what looked like a game ending double play ball to shortstop, Heyward leading off the 12th with a double, and Jon Lester (hitting .075) getting down a two strike perfect squeeze bunt to win the game in the 12th. We also should not forget Joe Maddon whom the ESPN announcers called a "wizard" moving players around and having multiple pitchers in the game at one time. Finally having Lester pinch hit in the 12th was a classic Maddon move. Harry Caray would have said "holy, holy, holy cow!"

Maddon had given a AAA guy named Brian Matusz a start, to rest the other guys, and he gave up two-run homers in the first, second and third innings. Seattle 6, Cubs 0, game over? Nope, the bullpen was amazing. The Cubs scored three the ninth, the last on a wild pitch with two outs to tie the game. Seattle must be sick about this one.

Extra innings:
A couple of days back, Bradford Doolittle, a staff writer for ESPN wrote an article entitled "Joe Maddon must make the most of the Cubs new bullpen trifecta." He was speaking of Strop, Rondon and Chapman of course. He suggested that with those three they had the most powerful group of stoppers in the game. Hoyer and Epstein got the guys and now Doolittle said they have turned the game of flamethrowers over to the "mad scientist of bullpen management" Joe Maddon.

Maddon concluded that he had to figure out how to maximize their effectiveness, and added that he had to include in his strategy Travis Wood, CJ Edwards, Joe Nathan, and Grimm. His bullpen philosophy is considered the most progressive in baseball. He wants personalities with no egos, that is pitchers who "buy into" percentages, matchups and no pre-determined roles. Last year, Ned Yost, KC, won the series with a set system. Guy #1 in the seventh, guy #2 in the eighth, and guy #3 in the ninth, always the same. Not Maddon, he's the quintessential "anti-Yost", and who knows what he will do. Both managers have won at the highest levels, but as Doolittle said, "let's face it Maddon's way is more fun." Today's game certainly epitomized Joe's philosophy and it was not only fun, it was hilarious. Lester pinch-hitting and bunting with two strikes. Amazing!

Today's baseball wisdom:

"You don't save a pitcher for tomorrow, it might rain."
Leo Durocher

Baseball history this date:

1978 – Pete Rose ties the National League hitting streak at 44.*
*("Wee Willie" Keeler did it in 1897 when he hit .424 for the year.)

Game: #105

Teams: Cubs/Miami
Date: Monday, August 1
Final: Cubs win 5 – 0
Record: 64 – 41

V – mail: "Wow! The more I see Kyle Hendricks, the more I see Greg Maddux. A master at his job, he never overpowers just thinks his opponents. A complete game shutout. Cubs win 5 – 0."

Recap:
Hendricks is one of Gene's favorite guys, and apparently Hendricks is very well-liked. Maddon said, "he's a great team player and he's just a joy to be around." After the 12 inning game yesterday, in which the Cubs used 22 players and 8 pitchers, Hendricks throws a complete game, 123 pitches, and lowered his ERA to 2.22, third best in the majors. His effort gave the bullpen a much-needed rest, the second time he has "saved" the relievers. He pitched 6 2/3 innings at Cincinnati the day after a 15 inning game. Today the Cubs left 12 men on base. Addison Russell, the great fielding shortstop who is only hitting .240 has quietly driven in 65 runs just behind Rizzo with 79 and Bryant with 68. He's really a young star at only 22 years old.

Extra innings:
The Cubs traded for another relief pitcher, Joe Smith, from the Angels for a minor-league prospect. Smith, a right-handed pitcher has pitched well lately with a 1.93 ERA in his last 9.1 outings. To recap, recently they have acquired Mike Montgomery LHP, Aroldis Chapman LHP, Joe Smith RHP, and signed "old" Joe Nathan RHP. They should have enough relief pitching now.

Today's baseball wisdom:

"The reason I think I'm a good pitcher is that I locate my fastball and I change speeds. That's what you do to pitch. That's what pitchers have to do to win games."
Greg Maddux

Baseball history this date:

1957 – Gil Hodges hits his National League record 13th grand slam. (Last one in Brooklyn)
(Also, on the same date)*
*1977 – Willie McCovey, of the San Francisco Giants hits the now National League record 18th grand slam.

Game: #106

Teams: Cubs/Miami
Date: Tuesday, August 2
Final: Cubs win 3 – 2
Record: 65 – 41

V – mail: "Jason Hammel threw six innings of shutout baseball is a Cubs held on to win 3 – 2."

Recap:
Hammel won his 11th game (11 –5, 3.07 ERA) pitching six scoreless innings. He threw only 80 pitches, but typical of Maddon he had Montero pinch-hit for him with two on in the seventh. Maddon called his move a "National League moment." What the hell is that; I'll have to ask Gene. Dexter Fowler had three hits and scored two runs. I think that it is more than just coincidental that since his return Cubs are again winning. He is, in my view, the "engine" that starts the Cubs offense.

Extra innings:
The Cubs defeated the Marlins ace pitcher, Jose Fernandez. (I had noted earlier in one of the write ups of a game that he was killed in a boating accident later this year).

Strop got in trouble in the seventh inning, giving up two runs, but Travis Wood came in and got the final out as Coghlan made a diving catch of a line drive. Then in the eighth Rondon picked Dee Gordon off first. In the ninth inning Chapman struck out one guy and then Baez made two terrific plays at third. It seems that a number of Cub players are contributing to their winning ways.

Today's baseball wisdom:

Commenting on Fowler today made me think of another switch-hitting center fielder, one of my all-time heroes, the "Commerce Comet" Mickey Mantle, which led to today's wisdom thought. Frank Sullivan was asked how he pitched a Mickey Mantle: He replied "with tears in my eyes."

Baseball history this date:

1906 – The Chicago White Sox begin an American League record 19 game win streak.

Game: #107

Teams: Cubs/Miami
Date: Wednesday, August 3
Final: Cubs win 5 – 4
Record: 66 – 41

V – mail: "Great pitching to start the game. Cubs were behind but with the "fighting fish" help we pulled it out. Shades of Carlos Marmol! Final 5 – 4. Cubs now 25 games above .500."

Recap:
Merry Christmas in August! The Marlins reliever, Ramos, gave this one away. In the ninth-inning with the Marlins leading 4 – 2 the Cubs started a rally. Montero got a double, Baez a single and Szczur walked to load the bases. Fowler got a sacrifice fly and the score is now 4 – 3. Bryant struck out on a ball way outside, and now there's 2 out. Rizzo gets an and intentional walk and then Zobrist walks that forces in a run and ties the score at 4 – 4. Contreras comes to the plate and Ramos throws a wild pitch 4 – 5 feet beyond the catcher and the Cubs win 5 – 4. Oh my, oh my! However, unlike the Cubs former closer Carlos Marmol, this was only his second blown save in 33 chances.

John Lackey went seven innings, allowed two runs, no walks and had eight strikeouts.

Extra innings:
Speaking of Carlos Marmol, I wonder where he is today. At one time he was really a good closer for the Cubs and then began to have difficulties. He would walk people to lose games, throw home run balls to lose games, you name it, he lost it. Gene tried to stay loyal to him long after I was going ballistic yelling "trade him, sell him, release him, give him away, just don't let him come into the ballgame."

The Cubs finally did give up on him and he quickly slid into oblivion. I checked the Internet today and he's listed as a "free agent." He is only 33 years old and I noted that in the beginning of 2016 in spring training the Red Sox gave him a tryout. He issued seven walks in four innings they released him. It's really kind of a sad situation; it's hard to understand how his game left him so suddenly. When he was able to get the ball over the plate he was almost unhittable.

Today's baseball wisdom:

"It ain't over till it's over."
Yogi Berra

Baseball history this date:

1941 – Browns pitcher Johnny Niggling gets Joe DiMaggio out in four at-bats to stop DiMaggio's streak of reaching base in 74 straight games.*
*(His streak is second to Ted Williams mark of 84 games in 1949)

Game: #108

Teams: Cubs @ Oakland
Date: Friday, August 5
Final: Cubs win 7 – 2
Record: 67 – 41

V – mail: "Both Fowler and Soler got the game going in the first inning with home runs. Then they scored again in the third and went on to win 7 – 2. Lester, the winning pitcher allowed two runs in seven innings."

Recap:
Fowler's home run was leading off the first inning; Soler's a three run shot in the first, was his first at-bat since coming off the disabled list (two months) with a hamstring injury. Joe Maddon remarked that he thought Soler "might get a jolt after his long rehab by starting this game." The Associated Press writer covering this game said, "boy was he right." Along with scoring four runs in the first the Cubs added three in the third, good enough to win 7 – 2. Joe Smith and Carl Edwards finished the eighth and ninth with nothing across.

Extra innings:
The good news is that Soler is finally back, but the other side of the coin is that "old" Joe Nathan was DFA, that's baseball jargon for designated for assignment. I wonder if it essentially means that after his three appearances with the Cubs it may be the end of his career. He did get a win which means that his 2016 record will show that he never lost a game, ending the year at 1 – 0. I hope so as he was a good guy.

Today's baseball wisdom:

"Pitching is 80% of the game, the other half is hitting and fielding!"
Mickey Rivers

Baseball history this date:

1921 – The first major league baseball broadcast; Pirates 8 – Phillies 0. (KDKA Pittsburgh)

Game: #109

Teams: Cubs @ Oakland
Date: Saturday, August 6
Final: Cubs win 4 – 0
Record: 68 – 41

V – mail: "Jake managed to get through eight innings and the Cubs were able to get four runs. Final score was 4 – 0."

Recap:

Although Arrieta isn't quite satisfied that he's recovered his dominant stuff after a "so – so" July, the AP writer said, "he didn't look far off." Arrieta was 0 – 3 in five previous starts and 1 – 4 since ending a 20 decision winning streak on June 22. He struck out four and walked one on 108 pitches. Travis Wood pitched the ninth allowing one hit and one strikeout. Zobrist had a key two-out 2 run single in the third; Russell and Soler each knocked in a run the sixth, and that was "all she wrote."

Extra innings:

The Cubs have won six in a row and are 15 – 6 since the All-Star break. They were 6 – 15 before the break. Maddon had said before the All-Star break not to worry as all teams have slumps, but I kept thinking of the 69 Cubs who blew the pennant to the Mets and I couldn't escape the feeling of "oh no, not again." Along with Maddon, my wife and Gene were saying things to me like "oh you person of little faith" or "get a grip, why are you so negative, you're a lousy fan." And finally something about you must believe in your team. Okay, okay I give up, I'll try harder, honest I will.

Today's baseball wisdom:

"No one likes to hear it because it's dull, but the reason you win or lose is darn near always the same, pitching."
Earl Weaver
(LA Times June 16, 1978)

Baseball history this date:

1972 – Hank Aaron hits home runs #660 and #661 for the Atlanta Braves. A record playing for one team.

Game: #110

Teams: Cubs @ Oakland
Date: Sunday, August 7
Final: Cubs win 3 – 1
Record: 69 – 41

V – mail: "Kyle Hendricks was great once again as he allowed one run in 7.1 innings before he turned it over to the bullpen. The Cubs went on to win over Oakland 3 – 1."

Recap:

Yes, as the "voice of victory" (a.k.a. Gene) said Hendricks was again terrific as he retired 17 straight before Marcus Semien's one-out home run in the eighth inning. Hendricks' ERA is now 2.17, second only to perennial All-Star Clayton Kershaw of the Dodgers who is at 1.79. Kershaw has been on the disabled list for quite a spell. The Cubs didn't score until Bryant hit a long home run in the sixth. Then Jorge Soler hit his second home run in three days after his two month stint on the disabled list. The Cubs added a third and final run in the eighth. Strop finished the eighth and Chapman went 1, 2, 3 in the ninth. The Cubs have won 10 of their last 11 games and are 28 games over .500! Wow, they are really on a roll.

Extra innings:

Of course the "voice" called after the game, singing the praises of Hendricks. This young pitcher is one of Gene's favorite players as he pitches like Greg Maddux, the former Cub and eventual hall of fame pitcher of the Atlanta Braves. Neither of them ever did or do anything fancy they just get the job done. Hendricks, like Maddux has good control, changes speeds, can spot his pitches and simply "outsmarts" the hitters. That is essentially what Gene had to say and I would have to agree with him. Even though they won, Gene was a bit "ticked off" as the Cubs left 12 men on base. Twice they had the bases loaded with no outs but did not score. Gene said, "why is it when Hendricks pitches they never yet him any runs?" That's true, they have a terrible history of getting him only a few runs when he pitches. The Cubs now lead the Cardinals by 11 1/2 games and those red birds are cooperating having lost two to the last place Atlanta Braves. Yea!

Today's baseball wisdom:

"A pitcher needs two pitches, one they're looking for and one to cross them up."
Warren Spahn

Baseball history this date:

1907 – Walter Johnson wins the first of his 416 games, 7 – 2, over Cleveland.

Game: #111

Teams: Cubs/Los Angeles Angels
Date: Tuesday, August 9
Final: Cubs win 5 – 1
Record: 70 – 41

V – mail: "John Lackey looked as good as I have seen him as he threw eight innings of one run baseball. Contreras and Bryant got the scoring started with home runs as the Cubs won 5 – 1."

Recap:
Yes the "voice" had called last night after the game and left a message. I was at a church meeting and when I got home the message light on the telephone was blinking so I knew the Cubs were winners.

Gene's voice was almost euphoric with "the beat goes on, and on, and on; they did it again and now it's eight in a row." Indeed John Lackey pitched a really nice game. He gave up a home run on his third pitch but only two more hits through eight innings. He had six strikeouts and all were "looking."

ESPN described Lackey as "ornery and fired up." Maddon added that he (Lackey) can get upset with umpires, coaches, and team mates. He stated "that's why we have him on our team." That comment is the sentiment for today's baseball wisdom.

Extra innings:
The ESPN recap today also mentioned that Geovany Soto had been activated off the 15 day disabled list for the Angels. In 2008 he was the rookie of the year for the Cubs, hitting .285 with 23 home runs and 86 runs batted in. Gene and I talked about him as we both remembered his great rookie year and at that time we had concluded that he was probably the Cubs catcher for "years to come." Whoa there, in 2009 he slumped to .218 with 11 home runs and 47 runs batted in. He had tested positive for marijuana at the world baseball classic (2009) and although the MLB did not take any disciplinary action The International Baseball Federation banned him for two years. He never returned to the promise of his rookie year and the Cubs traded him to Texas in 2012. His 12 year batting average is .247. What happened to the guy, was it the "Mary Jane?"

Today's baseball wisdom:

"Pitching is the art of instilling fear."
Sandy Koufax

Baseball history this date:

1980 – The Cubs beat the Mets 6 – 4 in their first official night game at Wrigley Field.

Game: #112

Teams: Cubs/Los Angeles Angels
Date: Wednesday, August 10
Final: Cubs win 3 – 1
Record: 71 – 41

V – mail: "Jason Hammel went seven innings, allowing four hits. Cubs relief came through also. Final score Cubs 3 – Angels – 1."

Recap:
Hammel won his fifth straight start, walking two, striking out six and allowing four hits in seven scoreless innings. LA got a run in the eighth, as Strop slipped trying to field a bunt, twisted his knee and had to leave the game. Wood came in and gave up a double and now there were runners on second and third with no outs. Enter young Carl Edwards. He strikes out Mike Trout (a really dangerous hitter) and gets two ground outs allowing a run to score, but ending the inning. Edwards, a tall skinny young black kid has really been tough lately. Chapman came on in the ninth and struck out the side. The Cubs have now won nine straight games and begin a four-game set with those dastardly Cardinals tomorrow.

Extra innings:
Maddon had no update on infielder Tommy LaStella who refused to report to Triple-A Iowa after being sent down two weeks ago, to make room for Jorge Soler. The Cubs placed him on the inactive list as he said he was contemplating retirement. BS! He is only 27 years old and makes $500,000 a year. He won't make that much flipping burgers or selling vacuum cleaners door-to-door. He might make more selling "dope," but that's risky and could mean he didn't need any income at all as he would get free room and board from the state. Come on kid, get a life!

Today's baseball wisdom:
"I can see how Sandy Koufax won 25 games. What I don't understand is how he lost 5."
Yogi Berra

Baseball history this date:
1997 – The Atlanta Braves sign Greg Maddux to a record five year $57.5 million deal.

Game: #113

Teams: Cubs/St. Louis
Date: Thursday, August 11
Final: Cubs win 4 – 3
Record: 72 – 41

V – mail: "This was another team victory so many great plays on defense. It took extra innings but the Cubs win 4 – 3."

Recap:
After a game filled with great defense and bizarre happenings the Cubs won with a bases-loaded walk to Rizzo in the 11th. The Cubs have recently won games in their last at-bat on a wild pitch, a bunt (by the pitcher) and now on a walk. It certainly has been a "Cub year" so far.

Now for the "craziness." The Cubs were behind 2 – 0 in the sixth inning. They had like 17 men in scoring position but none had come in. In the bottom of the sixth inning with two on and two out, Coghlan, with a 3 – 2 count tries to call time; he doesn't get it so in desperation he swings at the pitch and gets a hit and the game is tied 2 – 2. Then old David Ross bunts, a run scores and the Cubs lead 3 – 2. Travis Wood comes on in the seventh and promptly gives up a pinch-hit home run to tie the score at 3 – 3. In the ninth inning Maddon brings in flame throwing Chapman. He throws three pitches and gets three outs; two line drives to Baez at third and ground ball to second. In the 11th inning the Cardinals load the bases, but Carpenter (a really good hitter) strikes out. Then in the bottom of the 11th the Cubs have the bases loaded with one out, but Bryant strikes out. However, Rizzo walks forcing in a run as the Cubs win 4 – 3.

Gene had mentioned defense in his note. Besides Baez' two snags in the ninth, the Cardinals really messed up in the seventh inning. The lead off man singled and Ross picked him off first base. Grichuk then homered and the game (now 3 – 3) would have been 4 – 3 Cardinals. The next batter singles and the following guy hits the ball to the ivy in left field. Coghlan throws the ball to shortstop, Russell, then makes a perfect throw to nail the runner at the plate. Thus the Cardinals have lost the opportunity to score 2 runs for a 5 – 3 lead. The game would have been over if they had scored those runs. But, as we all know that little two letter word "if" is in reality one of the biggest in the English language.

Extra innings:
This is sort of a potpourri: the Cubs have won 10 games in a row; Matt Halliday has fractured his thumb (hit by a pitch); Pedro Strop is out four –

six weeks with torn meniscus in his knee; I watched the entire game (a rarity for me) and didn't have to "change my shorts" even once.

Maddon's take on the game was "crazy stuff yes, entertaining yes." He also promised to take Chapman out for a steak dinner, no limit put on the size of the steak. Apparently a four pitch inning in the minor leagues gets a steak dinner. Maddon said a three pitch inning in the majors gets the same thing. Ha!

Today's baseball wisdom:

"A manager uses a relief pitcher like a six-shooter, he fires until empty then takes the gun and throws it at the villain."

Dan Quisenberry

Baseball history this date:

1951 – The New York Giants lose and go 13 ½ games behind the Brooklyn Dodgers. However they would go on to win the pennant in a dramatic three-game playoff.

Game: #114

Teams: Cubs/St. Louis
Date: Friday, August 12
Final: Cubs win 13 – 2
Record: 73 – 41

V – mail: "It looks like when we hit we really hit. Jake lasted into the sixth inning and allowed only one run. Lots of home runs in this one, all by kids. Final Cubs 13 – Cardinals 2."

Recap:
Wow, the Cubs hit five home runs all by young guys; Contreras, Baez, Soler and Szczur hit two. Wainwright, arguably the Cardinals top pitcher lasted only two innings and left behind 7 – 0. It tied his shortest outing in 245 starts. The regulars, Heyward and Fowler had the day off. I think Heyward the $180 million man should take a few more days off. I know he's great defensively, but he's hitting a measly .226 with five home runs and 32 runs batted in in 103 games. I'm still not convinced that Epstein, who rarely makes a mistake in his trades or acquisitions didn't miss on this one.

On another note, that's 11 wins in a row, and although I don't want to be greedy (well actually I do want to be a "hog") but it would sure be great to see the Cubs sweep the red birds.

Extra innings:
I had to laugh at Gene during our phone conversation (I called him in the ninth inning as I was getting ready to leave for a funeral). He of course didn't know about the funeral and said "can't you wait until the game is over to discuss the outcome." He was a bit apologetic, not necessary, as I would've said the same thing. He did say, gosh they scored all those runs today and Hendricks goes tomorrow, and they never get him any runs. I had the same feeling, when I saw the final score later. The Cubs really haven't given Hendricks much run support and I hope they do tomorrow.

Today's baseball wisdom:

"The key to winning baseball games is pitching, fundamentals, and three-run homers."
Earl Weaver

Baseball history this date:

1974 – The Yankees Mickey Mantle and Whitey Ford become the first teammates inducted into the Hall of Fame on the same day.

Game: #115

Teams: Cubs/St. Louis
Date: Saturday, August 13
Final: Cubs lose 8 – 4
Record: 73 – 42

V – mail: "As expected, only scored two runs for Hendricks. He allowed two runs in seven innings, but the game was lost by the bullpen. Cardinals 8 – Cubs 4."
Record:

After the Cubs Blasted the Cards 13 – 2 yesterday, Gene remarked, "well Hendricks goes tomorrow and I sure hope they get him some runs, but frankly I don't think they will." He was right as Hendricks went seven innings, allowed five hits, two runs, no walks and 12 strikeouts. In comes Carl Edwards who loads the bases with two outs, he strikes the guy out but the ball gets away from the catcher and a run scores. Cardinals 3 – 2. Then Edwards walks the next two guys and another run scores. They bring on Joe Smith and he gives up a grand slam. Whoever reads this, I think you can count, and the score is now 8 – 2 in favor of "the bad guys." Joe Maddon's comment after the game was, "that's an example of what the team looks like without Pedro or Hector." Two new bullpen guys, Montgomery and Smith have not been very good. However, after three shaky appearances Montgomery has pitched four scoreless innings with seven strikeouts. But Smith has been simply terrible! He's faced 17 batters with eight reaching base (six hits and two walks) including three home runs. Smith was quoted as saying, "I've never had a problem with home runs before." Well, maybe not, but he sure has a problem now. The Cubs scored two runs in the ninth, which makes me wonder if Rondon and Strop had been available for the eighth and ninth, maybe they would have won.

Extra innings:

Maddon's comments are a bit scary for me concerning Rondon and Strop in that if these other guys don't step it up the season could "go south in a hurry." The Cubs have added five relievers recently, but Pedro and Hector were critical keys as relievers. Grimm and Wood will be available soon but the other guys need to help out until Rondon and Strop get healthy again. If Gene and I were discussing this issue he'd ask me "are you worried?" I have a simple answer, "you damn right I am."

Today's baseball wisdom:

"People don't know this, but I helped the Cardinals win the pennant. I came down with hepatitis. The team trainer injected me with it."
Bob Uecker

Baseball history this date:

1948 – Satchel Paige at 42 pitches his first major-league complete-game.

Game: #116

Teams: Cubs/St. Louis
Date: Sunday, August 14
Final: Cubs lose 6 – 4
Record: 73 – 43

V – mail: "Jon Lackey great for seven innings. The bullpen not so much. Cubs lose 6 – 4."

Recap:

I think that I am a "jinx" for the Cubs, as every time I watch them on ESPN, especially Sunday night baseball, they lose. John Lackey allowed only an unearned run in seven innings and the Cubs were leading 3 – 1 going into the bottom of the seventh. They loaded the bases with nobody out in the seventh but didn't score. At the end of the inning I had a sinking feeling that those dastardly Cardinals would come back after the Cubs failed to score. They have a tendency to come back in the later innings and steal the game. Rondon enters in the eighth inning (he hadn't pitched in 12 days) gives up a single than a bunt single, and Piscotty hits a three-run shot to very deep center field. The next batter Moss also hits one and it's 5 – 3. Travis Wood comes in and gives up two more hits and another run. The game at that point was essentially over. Rizzo homered in the eighth to make the final score 6 – 4. Really a tough loss especially against those despicable Cardinals. Chapman pitched the ninth inning and got two strikeouts, but it was too late.

Extra innings:

The Cubs are off tomorrow and then play a doubleheader against the "Brew – Crew" on Tuesday. Cahill, just off the disabled, will pitch the first game and Jason Hammel goes in the second game. He (Hammel) has pitched extremely well his last 4 to 5 starts. Maybe the Cubs can win two tomorrow; wouldn't that be nice?

Today's baseball wisdom:

"It's like déjà vu all over again."
Yogi Berra

Baseball history this date:

1969 – The New York Mets fall 9 1/2 games behind the Cubs, but later win the pennant.*

*(Marlys and I had moved to Tucson to enroll at the University of Arizona for my doctoral program. A 350 pound or more New York fellow named

Salvatore Pitelli, an undergraduate student at the University, who lived behind us in a shack, would daily hang over our snow fence dog yard and chat. He was a Mets fan and when the Cubs started losing, or "choking" as he liked to say, I would protest and say don't worry they won't catch the Cubs. Then as the losing continued he'd stop by every day and say "the Mets are coming, the Mets are coming." Well, crap, we know what happened.

Game: #117

Teams: Cubs/Milwaukee
Date: Tuesday, August 16
Final: Cubs win 4 – 0 (game #1 of a doubleheader)
Record: 74 – 43

V – mail: "The bullpen did it all today winning the first game as they shut out the Brewers 4 – 0."

Recap:
Trevor Cahill pitched five strong innings allowing only two hits. He had been on the disabled list since July 9. He was just reactivated and got the start as John Lackey has a "gimpy" arm. He was followed by Montgomery, two innings, Rondon in the eighth and Joe Smith who walked two in the ninth, got jerked, and Chapman got the last two outs. There was nothing really outstanding on the hitting side; Cahill, Russell and Coghlan each had runs batted in. Russell has quietly driven in 72 runs this year, which is only one less than Kris Bryant. Besides being an outstanding defensive shortstop, he seems to have a knack for getting RBIs when he has the chance.

Extra innings:
My goodness, after the game there was no call from the "voice of victory". Matt, Marlys and I all wondered what could have happened. So I called and left a message, and then headed off for a church meeting. When I got home I had two calls from "the voice". He had been gone and when he returned he forget to call after the Cubs won game number one. The Cubs then won the second game of the doubleheader, so he called again. I didn't call back as it was after 11 o'clock in Illinois, instead I called the next day. Holy cow, we were like a couple teenagers calling, then recalling then calling again!

Today's baseball wisdom:

"I came up to bat with three men on and two outs in the ninth inning. I looked in the other team's dugout and they are already in street clothes."
Bob Uecker

Baseball history this date:

1927- The 1st HR hit out of Comiskey Park Chicago (NY Yankees Babe Ruth)

Game: #118

Teams: Cubs/Milwaukee
Date: Tuesday, August 16 (second game of the doubleheader)
Final: Cubs win 4 – 1
Record: 75 – 43

V – mail: "The second game was owned by Jason Hammel as he threw seven innings of two hit no run baseball. Final score 4 – 1. The Brewers only had eight hits all day."

Recap:
Great pitching job by Jason Hammel as he allowed no runs, two hits and had seven strikeouts to expand his scoreless innings streak to 22. The Cubs scored three runs in the sixth, highlighted by Javy Baez's two-run homer. They had gotten the other run on a single by Bryant in the third. The Brewers got their only run in the ninth inning with a home run off Travis Wood who has been struggling a bit lately. Wood then gave up a single and a walk that brought in Chapman who got the last out for his second save of the day with the Cubs. (A save in each game of the doubleheader).

Extra innings:
The highlight of the game was provided for the fans by Anthony Rizzo. He literally jumped on the wall down the first base line, leaned into the crowd to snag a pop foul off the bat of Keon Broxton. He snapped upright, jumped off the wall and landed perfectly. He evidently had watched the US women's gymnastics team that won the gold medal in Rio, as his landing, (like many of the gals) was according to Hammel "a great dismount and he stuck the landing." It was a great catch and I watched the video replay several times. He had raced to the wall, hopped up onto a huge rolled up tarp, nimbly skipped to the wall, leaned way over and caught it!

Today's baseball wisdom:

"I never threw an illegal pitch. The trouble is once in awhile I toss one that ain't never been seen by this generation."
Satchel Paige

Baseball history this date:

1920 – Ray Chapman of the Cleveland Indians is hit in the head by Yankees pitcher Carl Mays; he dies the next day in the major leagues only fatality.

Game: #119

Teams: Cubs/Milwaukee
Date: Wednesday, August 17
Final: Cubs win 6 – 1
Record: 76 – 43

V – mail: "Jon Lester was on his game for 6 2/3 innings giving up one run. Jorge Soler hit a three-run homer in the first and that was all that was needed as the Cubs win 6 – 1."

Recap:
Jon Lester got his fourth straight win giving up only one run and three hits in 6 2/3 innings. The Cubs scored five runs in the first and Lester said, "it kind of relaxes you and you don't have to grind as much." Jorge Soler whacked a three run homer in the first inning; since coming off the disabled list he has hit seven home runs in seven starts, hitting .379 in 10 games over that stretch. Edwards and Wood combined for 2 1/3 innings of scoreless relief.

Extra innings:
The recap of the game from the Associated Press wire stated "Lester and the rest of the Cubs starting pitchers have been magnificent, going 11 – 0 in August with Chicago's only two losses being hung on the relievers." On another note, Tommy La Stella who was optioned to Triple-A Iowa on July 29, but refused to report (he must have felt he was too good to be sent down) and was contemplating retirement agreed to report to double-A Tennessee. His salary is $513,000 and I guess at 27 years old, a graduate of Coastal Carolina, he decided there aren't a bunch of jobs out there where we can start at 500,000 dollars. Does anyone else (as I do) feel that today's professional athletes are both overpaid and overappreciated?

Today's baseball wisdom:

"All last year we tried to teach him (Fernando Valenzuela) English, the only word he learned was million."
Tommy Lasorda

Baseball history this date:

1957 – Richie Ashburn, Philadelphia Phillies, fouls off a ball and hits Alice Roth twice in the same time at bat; the first foul breaks her nose, and the second one hits her while she is on the stretcher.

Game: #120

Teams: Cubs/Milwaukee
Date: Thursday, August 18
Final: Cubs win 9 – 6
Record: 77 – 43

V – mail: "Jake was not sharp as he walked seven and allowed five runs on his way to his 15th win. Bryant had another five hit day with two home runs leading the Cubs to a 9 – 6 win."

Recap:

Arrieta was very wild and in addition to the seven walks he had 103 pitches in 5 2/3 innings. Patton came on and he walked three in two innings. Kris Bryant had a wonderful day, going 5 for 5, with two home runs, five RBIs, and four runs scored. An ESPN writer wrote on Bryant; among other accolades he mentioned that Bryant is only the second player ever to have two 5 hit, two home run games in one season. (Joe Carter of the 1986 Indians was the other). Going further back to 1913, he is only the 17th player, all-time, with two 5 hit, two home run games in their career. He added that now he has maybe 15 years to try and catch Willie Stargell and Bob Johnson as the only players with three 5 hit, two home run games in a career. The article was entitled, "Five things we learned Thursday; The Cubs are great and so is Kris Bryant." He concluded by suggesting that Bryant is among the top several in the race for the National League MVP.

Extra innings:

The Cubs play 18 of their next 25 games on the road. Also they put Lackey and Rondon on the disabled list with triceps and arm "issues." They called the moves "precautionary." In another move they recalled two young pitchers from Iowa, Felix Pena and Rob Zastryzny. Holy smokes, you thought Szczur was tough to spell and pronounce how about, Zastryzny? I still don't know how to say the name of the Rob guy!

Today's baseball wisdom:

"Trying to sneak a fastball past Hank Aaron is like trying to sneak a sunrise past a rooster."
Joe Adcock

Baseball history this date:

1982 – The longest baseball game at Wrigley Field ended after 21 innings. The LA Dodgers beat the Cubs 2 – 1.*

*(The game started on August 17, was suspended and completed on August 18)

Game: #121

Teams: Cubs @ Colorado
Date: Friday, August 19
Final: Cubs lose 7 – 6
Record: 77 – 44

V – mail: "Another good performance by Kyle Hendricks down the drain. We are now starting to feel the injury bug. I hope they can get through this as these losses are hard to take."

Recap:
As Al McCoy, the 44 year announcer for the Phoenix Suns would exclaim in anguish, "Heartbreak Hotel." Unfortunately I started to follow this game on my computer (game cast) as the Cubs were leading 5 – 4 going into the seventh. Hendricks had pitched six innings allowing four hits and only one run. An error had cost the Cubs a run in the seventh so the score was 5 – 2. Travis Wood comes in and gives up two hits and a walk in the eighth for three runs and the score is 5 – 5. Now I am really hacked off as these Cubs continue to "blow" games for Hendricks. The game goes to the 11th inning and the Cubs score for a 6 – 5 lead. Now I'm in bed watching the Diamondbacks also blow a great game by Zach Greinke (7 – 4 in 10 innings) and I see that the Cubs are ahead. I find out later that Chapman came in and gave it away allowing two runs for a 7 – 6 Rocky win. The last run scored on a wild throw. In defense of Chapman, he had been warming up for 3 – 4 inning sand when he finally got in the game he was tired (he even admitted it). Maddon subsequently gave him two days off because of fatigue.

Extra innings:
To completely ruin my day, those despicable Cardinals were trailing Philadelphia 3 – 1 in the ninth inning and wouldn't you know it that guy Groyko hit's a two-run homer to tie it, and they go on to win the game in the 11th inning 4 – 3. My depression was complete. I woke up several times during the night in a cold sweat, boy am I a poor loser. It makes me think of what one of my old friends Dick Rockey used to say to me, "you really are a sore ass." Meaning that I can't stand to lose and get mad about it. Ha!

Today's baseball wisdom:

"You can't sit on a lead and run a few plays into the line and just kill the clock. You've got to throw the ball over the damn plate and give the other man his chance. That's why baseball is the greatest game of them all."
Earl Weaver

Baseball history this date:

1917– A Sunday benefit baseball game at the Polo grounds resulted in John McGraw and Christy Mathewson being arrested for violating Blue laws.

Game: #122

Teams: Cubs @ Colorado
Date: Saturday, August 20
Final: Cubs win 9 – 2
Record: 78 – 44

V – mail: "Two relief pitchers and Kris Bryant about sum up the game as the Cubs win 9 – 2."

Recap:
Mike Montgomery pitched four innings giving up one hit, a home run, and had a 60 pitch count when Maddon took them out of the game. Gene was a bit disgusted because as he didn't pitch five innings he didn't get the win. Maddon said, "it's almost like spring training for him right now and we are just stretching him out." Montgomery had not started a game since July 17th with the Mariners. Montgomery noted, "as a competitor I wanted to stay in and I was a little pissed, but I understand the situation… and I respect his decision." Trevor Cahill pitched the final 4 2/3 innings for the win.

Kris Bryant, is playing and hitting like an MVP candidate. He blasted a 471 foot home run to dead center, drove in four runs and is now hitting .300. It's been quite a year for only his second go around in the majors.

Extra innings:
Gene's v-mail yesterday alluded to the "injury bug" concerning the relievers and commented that he hoped we could "weather the storm." It was really terrific how Montgomery and Cahill plugged the hole in the dike for this one. I should mention that Miguel Montero had three hits and three RBIs, a season high for him although he is only hitting .197!

Today's baseball wisdom:

"I don't make speeches. I just let my bat speak for me in the summertime."
Honus Wagner

Baseball history this date:

1958 – The Chicago Cubs use first baseman Dale Long as their first lefty catcher since 1906.

Game: #123

Teams: Cubs @ Colorado
Date: Sunday, August 21
Final: Cubs lose 11 – 4
Record: 78 – 45

V – mail: "Hammel's scoreless inning streak of 22 ended in the first inning, as the Rockies scored seven in the first inning. Game over."

Recap:

It's 5 PM mountain time in Tucson and today's Cubs – Rockies game is already becoming only a distant memory. No use to cry about this one as the best approach is to laugh and exclaim philosophically, "oh shit." It was one of those days. I turned on the game cast in the second inning and the score was already 7 – 0 as the Cubs committed three errors in the first inning that led to seven runs. The Rockies third baseman, Arenado broke out of a 1 for 16 slump with two three-run homers. He has 104 RBIs and 32 home runs one more than Bryant; he is only 25, and Bryant only 24, two young guys apparently destined for stardom. Hammel, who's scoreless streak ended had been 6 – 0 with an ERA of 0.95 since the All-Star break. The streak had to end sometime, so there's no use making excuses or having bad feelings. Speaking of young stars, the Cubs first two runs were two solo shots by 22-year-old Addison Russell. Although he's hitting only .250 he has 78 RBIs. He has a bright future don't you think?

Extra innings:

I decided to call the "voice" as one of the new minor-league pitchers just up, Rob Zastryny (you pronounce it if you can) threw 2.2 innings and gave up no runs and had five strikeouts. I wondered how Gene thought he looked. Gene had missed most of his turn pitching and was, understandably, a bit subdued in talking about the game. I don't blame him as this is really serious stuff, that is the Cubs of course. Ha!

Today's baseball wisdom:

"My first basemen is George "catfish" Metkovich from our 1952 Pittsburgh Pirates team which lost 112 games. After a terrible series against the New York Giants in which our center fielder made three throwing errors and let two balls get through his legs, manager Billy Meyer pleaded, "can somebody think of something to help us win a game."

"I'd like to make a suggestion," Metkovich said, "on any ball hit to center field, let's just let it roll to see if it might go foul."

Joe Garagiola

Baseball history this date:

1967 – Ken Harrelson becomes the first free agent in baseball.

Game: #124

Teams: Cubs @ San Diego
Date: Monday, August 22
Final: Cubs win 5 – 1
Record: 79 – 45

V – mail: "Good pitching by Jon Lester and home runs by Russell, Bryant and Heyward put this one away as the Cubs win 5 – 1."

Recap:
Lester improved to 14 – 4 with eight strikeouts, and two walks, as he won for the 10th time in his last 11 decisions. He is now 5 – 0 with six quality starts out of seven since the All-Star break. Bryant hit number 32 and is tied with Nolan Arenado of the Rockies. Russell hit his third home run in two days and even the struggling Heyward, recently benched to rest mentally, hit his first since July 29. Rizzo had four hits and is now hitting .301.

The Cubs beat Edwin Jackson, an ex-cub who drove Gene crazy with his slow, deliberate, fooling around style of pitching. Every time I hear his name I think of a young flame-throwing pitcher for the Arizona Diamondbacks that they traded away for Edwin Jackson. Jackson has been mostly a mediocre, current ERA of 5.71, if not a downright "dud" (as he was when he was with the Cubs) while the young pitcher of whom I speak is currently 13 – 7 with a 3.05 ERA. He threw two no-hitters in 2015 and has tied the National League record for a nine inning strikeouts with 20. Oh, his name is Max Scherzer. What a mistake the Diamondbacks made letting him go. Interestingly Jackson was born in New Ulm Germany, I guess he was an Army brat. Well enough pontificating – tomorrow Arrieta goes and I hope his control is better than his last outing when he walked seven.

Extra innings:
As the game ended at 10:30 PM Tucson time, 12:30 PM in Illinois, the "voice" did not call. As it was his birthday I decided to call him even at this late hour. The call woke him up and grudgingly he said "you missed my birthday by 30 minutes as it's now the 23rd." He didn't have much to say other than "what was the final score?" After I hung up, I thought maybe I should not have called so late. I'll call him tomorrow and apologize.

Today's baseball wisdom:

"Being with a woman all night never hurt no professional baseball player. It's staying up all night looking for a woman that does him in."
Casey Stengel

Baseball history this date:

2007 – The Texas Rangers routed the Baltimore Orioles 30 – 3, the most runs scored by team in modern MLB history.

Game: #125

Teams: Cubs @ San Diego
Date: Tuesday, August 23
Final: Cubs win 5 – 3
Record: 80 – 45

V – mail: "Jake was great tonight as he threw eight innings of shutout baseball. The bullpen had a hard time getting through one inning. The Cubs win 5 – 3, their 80th win of the year.

Recap:
The summary for this game boils down to three names; Arrieta, Bryant, and Russell. Arrieta was terrific allowing only a single in the second inning and a double in the eighth inning and that was all! Arrieta said he was "mad" at Maddon for taking him out, but said he understood the manager is trying to conserve his pitching staff's energy for September and October. Bryant and Russell are both on hitting "tears" lately; Bryant hit home run number 33 and has 86 RBIs while Russell hit home run number 19 and has 82 RBIs. Tomorrow Hendricks goes and he is now the major leagues leading ERA man at 2.14. Kershaw, who is on the disabled list, is no longer eligible. All I have to say is what terrific starting pitching the Cubs have had this year.

Extra innings:
Gene returned the favor (of my 12:30 AM call to him yesterday) by calling us after the game (12:15 AM Illinois time) and 10:15 PM Tucson time. Ha! He was of course happy with the win, but also displeased with the relievers giving up three runs in the ninth. When I had gone to bed the score was 5 – 0. He started off the phone call by saying "where is Carlos Marmol when you need him?" Marmol, a guy with" electric stuff" was wild, unpredictable and begin blowing games so often the Cubs dumped him. He was "bad mouthing" Chapman the 100 mph man. "He was wild as a March Hare, all over the plate, and although he wasn't charged with any runs, his two walks and wild pitch allowed the three runs. Pena, a new guy, had given up two hits and a walk and was charged with the runs.

Talking about wild Cub pitchers, the name "sad" Sam Jones came up. He was a Cub pitcher in 1955/56 and led the National League in strikeouts and walks three years 1955, 56, and 1958. Both Gene and I laughed recalling maybe his most "shining or bizarre game" or both as a Cub. On May 12, 1955 he pitched and won a 4 – 0 no-hitter at Wrigley against he Pirates. But the real story of the game was the ninth-inning. Leading 4 – 0, Sam walked three not very potent hitters Gene Freese, Preston Ward, and Tom Saffell with no outs. Obviously the bases were loaded. Then, almost unbelievably, he strikes out Dick Groat, Roberto Clemente, and Frank Thomas in succession, three outstanding hitters. He did win 21 games with the Giants in 1959, but we (Gene and I) still remember him for the three walks and then the three strikeouts to preserve the no-hitter. Really a weird sequence of pitching.

Today's baseball wisdom:

"I would not admire hitting against Ryne Duren, because if he ever hit you in the head you might be in the past tense."*

Casey Stengel

*(Duren wore very thick glasses and had a tendency to be extremely wild. Folklore suggested his vision was really poor and you took your life in your hands when you went up to bat against him. He would occasionally throw a ball completely out of the reach of the catcher during warm-up. Most believed it was just to intimidate the hitter).

Baseball history this date:

1883 – The Philadelphia Phillies make 27 errors against Providence (wild pitches, walks and passed balls counted as errors prior to 1888)

A Century-Long Journey to the Day of Redemption

Game: #126

Teams: Cubs @ San Diego
Date: Wednesday, August 24
Final: Cubs win 6 – 3
Record: 81 – 45

V mail: "Kyle Hendricks once again shows his importance to this team as he goes six innings allowing two runs with six strikeouts. The Cubs win 5 – 3.

Recap:

Very true, that Hendricks has become the "X factor" in their drive to the World Series. At the start of the year the Cubs recognized that their four starting pitchers were Lester, Arrieta, Hammel, and Lackey. (They were guys with long-standing records). Hendricks, I believe, was seen as their fifth guy. That isn't the case anymore as he leads the major leagues in ERA at 2.19 and has allowed no more than three earned runs over 17 straight starts with an ERA of 1.70 during that stretch. If he had gotten more run support he would probably be leading the majors in wins as he now has 12. Gene said earlier that he is a Greg Maddux style pitcher; changes speeds, has great control and out thinks the hitters. Trevor Cahill pitched the seventh and eighth innings and gave up one run. Chapman struck out the side in the ninth

Oh yes, the Cubs did score 6 runs; Contreras had a home run, Zobrist had two RBIs, and Russell and Soler each knocked in a run.

Extra innings:

In Gene's v-mail he stated that the Cubs won 5 – 3 and that Hendricks had six strikeouts. Actually, the Cubs won 6 – 3 and Hendricks had eight strikeouts. Gene is usually very precise and accurate in reporting on a game. I'd guess he's a bit distracted as he had spent most of the day at the Shippy family farm visiting with his younger brother Denny who has been fighting cancer for several years. He was just home from his fifth or sixth surgery to remove tumors. Gene said he looked "tough." Boy cancer is really a devastating disease; eliminate one tumor and another one pops up. It is really tough to deal with and also difficult for family to watch the struggle. It takes great courage to battle the disease on a daily basis.

Today's baseball wisdom:

This daily Journal not only has a focus on the game of baseball, but it also speaks to matters of friendship and loyalty. It seemed to me that a former Hall of Fame major-league pitcher summed up both sentiments well in a single sentence. He said:

"The two most important things in life are good friends and a strong bullpen."*

Bob Gibson

*(others have attributed the remark to Bob lemon)

Baseball history this date:

1989 – Pete Rose is suspended for life from baseball for gambling.

Game: #127

Teams: Cubs @ LA Dodgers
Date: Friday, August 26
Final: Cubs win 6 – 4
Record: 82 – 45

V – mail: "I saw only the first six innings. I was upset with the wildness I saw with Montgomery; however we were still in the game trailing 3 – 2. I did hear some of the game on my trusty radio, and I woke up to hear the final score and a few highlights, so I had a very peaceful sleep. Cubs win by way of Kris Bryant."

Recap:
Yes, Bryant was the story for the Cubs this night. The Cubs were down 4 – 2 going into the eighth (I followed this game on game cast) and went to bed assuming they would lose. Bryant hit a solo home run leading off the eighth and the Cubs tied it on a wild pitch in the ninth. Heyward, who's really had a tough year, had led off with a double and then scored on a wild pitch. Good for him. Then Bryant hit a two-run shot in the 10th, his National League leading 35th. He also leads the majors in runs scored with 107 and he's hitting .303. The Cubs really got this draft right, selecting him with the second pick.

Extra innings:
Gene doesn't like walks as his v-mail points out. His mantra is, "throw the ball over the plate, if they hit it they hit it." That almost sounds like a Yogi-ism!

Today's baseball wisdom:

"Four out of five doctors prescribe baseball for whatever ails you, the fifth guy is a quack."
Tom Swyers*
*(Swyers is the award-winning author of Saving Babe Ruth, 2014)

Baseball history this date:

1939 – The first major league baseball telecast was today as the Reds beat the Brooklyn Dodgers. (W2XBS, NY)

Game: #128

Teams: Cubs @ LA Dodgers
Date: Saturday, August 27
Final: Cubs lose 3 – 2
Record: 82 – 46

V – mail: "Well played game, Cubs lose 3 – 2."

Recap:

Where in Hades, or maybe how, do the Dodgers seem to come up with good young pitchers all the time? Today, a 20-year-old rookie from Culiacan, Mexico, Julio Urias, went six innings, allowed only one run, walked two and had eight strikeouts. The dodger relievers allowed only one more run. Hammel only went 2 1/3 innings giving up five hits and three runs before Maddon, who has a quick trigger, took him out. Hammel wasn't happy, but Maddon said "I didn't see things getting better so I made the move." A really bright spot for the Cubs was the young guy just up from the minors, Rob Zastryzny, who went 3.2 innings allowing only one hit, no walks and three strikeouts. There's not much more to say about the game.

Extra innings:

Cub fans will get a chance to hear the legendary Dodger announcer Vin Scully tomorrow, as Comcast Sportsnet Chicago, will carry the live audio of Scully's broadcast during the series finale. Scully, 88, in the booth for 67 years has truly been among the all-time greats calling the game. The article that I was reading said he is one of the greats like Red Barber, Dick Engberg, and Ernie Harwell. I'm okay with two of the three, but I think Engberg is just "so-so." Why not add Jack Buck, Mel Allen, Harry Caray, Bob Uecker, Russ Hodges and Joe Garagiola? Actually, my list would be: #1 – Vin Scully, #2 – Ernie Harwell (47 years with the Tigers), #3 – Red Barber, #4 Jack Buck (47 years with the Cardinals), #5 – Harry Caray, and I'd throw in the guy known for "how about that," Mel Allen. They really don't make announcers today like they did back then. Oh, there are some good ones but some I just can't tolerate. A good example is Joe Buck, Jack's son. For whatever reasons, although I suppose many like him, he strikes me as an egotistical, "pretty boy" riding on his father's coat tails. I literally will not listen to him broadcast and I turn off the sound. Sorry Joe, but you probably don't give a hoot about my views as you laugh all the way to the bank!

Today's baseball wisdom:

Speaking of great announcers, one of the members of my top six, once remarked during a game:

"Aw come on how could you lose the ball in the sun? He's from Mexico."*

Harry Caray

*(Harry was grousing about Jorge Orta missplaying a fly ball)

Baseball history this date:

1982 – Rickey Henderson steals base number 119, breaking Lou Brock's record.

Game: #129

Teams: Cubs @ LA Dodgers
Date Sunday, August 28
Final: Cubs lose 1 – 0
Record: 82 – 47

V – mail: "Great pitching on both sides. It would have been no score in the ninth, if the Cubs did not give it away in the eighth by committing errors. Dodgers win 1 –0."

Recap:

Harry Caray would have said "holy cow" several times. Lester went six innings, three hits, two walks and strikeouts and no runs, while Grimm had three strikeouts in seventh. In the eighth inning Cahill strikes out the first guy; then hits the next guy, then throws away a slow roller which puts runners on second and third. An intentional walk loads the bases. The next batter strikes out, the bases still loaded but now two out. Another slow roller is hit to third, but Baez casually tosses to second to a late arriving Zobrist, the runner is safe, the run scores, game over. Holy cow! Another rookie pitcher and four relievers held the Cubs to four hits; really a tough one to lose.

Extra innings:

Maddon said "we made a number of mistakes at second base and it cost us. Baez is a young player, but he has as much instinct for the game as anyone I've ever seen. I'm not going to beat up my guys." That's really a great attitude on Maddon's part. He really is a wily and cagey old dude.

Today's baseball wisdom:

"Losing feels worse than winning feels good."
Vin Scully

Baseball history this date:

1990 – The Cubs Ryne Sandberg is the first second baseman to hit 30 home runs in consecutive years.(30 in 1989 and 40 in 1990)

Game: #130

Teams: Cubs/Pittsburgh
Date: Monday, August 29
Final: Cubs win 8 – 7 (13 innings)
Record: 83 – 47

V – mail: "The luckiest guy in the ballpark last night was the home plate umpire. This was a team victory as everyone got involved to win this one in 13 innings. Final score 8 – 7 Cubs."

Recap:

The Cubs led 3 – 0, then 3 – 1 and then were behind 6 – 3. I turned on the game cast at 10 PM and it was 6 – 5 in the eighth inning. Contreras had hit a two-run homer and the Cubs had two men on and two out and Rizzo struck out. Crap, I went to bed. The next morning August 30, I got the above v-mail saying the Cubs won. I called Gene and asked him what had happened. "Well yes, the Cubs won" he said. Soler hit a home run in the bottom of the ninth to tie the game at 6-6. In the 10th inning the Cubs had the bases loaded and Rizzo grounds to first and Baez is out at the plate. In the 12th inning Baez is again thrown out at the plate by Marte, who has a reputation of having a great arm. Boy, if I had been listening to the game I would have had a stroke. But things got worse as the Pirates got a run in the top of the 13th. Then Fowler, Bryant and Rizzo all get singles to tie the score at 7 – 7. The Pirates walk Zobrist intentionally and Montero who has been sitting on the bench for five hours comes in (he's the last guy available) singles and the Cubs win 8 – 7!

Extra innings:

Gene was really "ticked" (his words) saying the game should have been over in nine innings. He said, "I was so mad I shut off TV and went to bed with my radio."

"What happened," I asked?

Well the story was in the sixth inning with one on and no outs and a 3 – 2 count on the hitter, Arrieta throws a perfect strike and Ross throws out the runner trying to steal second. So it's two out and no one on. Hold it, the umpire called the pitch ball four! Maddon and Arrieta argue ferociously, lose the argument of course, but don't get thrown out. Gene said, "the umpire knew he blew the call so he didn't toss them." Gene was still smoking this morning wondering how the umpire could miss such an obvious pitch. I think they should eliminate the home plate umpire in calling balls and strikes and just do it electronically. The home plate umpire would only call plays at the plate. Umpires have gotten so bad they literally can cost a team the game. Because the Cubs won, Gene said the umpire was lucky as if they had lost Cub fans would have lynched him. Interestingly, the umpire who made the terrible call, Trippe Gibson, once threw Mike Napoli out of the game or not picking up his bat after he struck out. Napoli told him, "that's why we have bat boys."

Today's baseball wisdom:

"I never questioned the integrity of an umpire. Their eyesight, yes"
Leo Durocher

Baseball history this date:

1977 – St. Louis Cardinal Lou Brock eclipses Ty Cobb's 49-year-old career stolen base record of 893.

Game: #131

Teams: Cubs/Pirates
Date: Tuesday, August 30
Final: Cubs win 3 – 0
Record: 84 – 47

V – mail: "Wow!!! Kyle Hendricks did not give up a hit until the fifth inning. He went seven innings and gave up three hits, one walk, four strikeouts and no runs. His ERA is now at 2.09, lowest in the league. Rizzo gave him all the scoring he needed with a home run in the first. Final was 3 – 0 Cubs."

Recap:
Hendricks started the year as the Cubs fifth starter and now he's on pace to be the major leagues ERA leader. Maddon, the manager, stated "he has to be in Cy Young contention." Hendricks allowed only three hits. Most amazing, in my view, is he has given up three or less runs in 18 straight starts. "That's not bad for a guy who doesn't often hit 90 mph with his fastball" said the AP reporter. It's obvious, at least I think so, that Hendricks is a very smart pitcher. Rizzo, his teammate, remarked "… He knows how to attack hitters as he went to Dartmouth and has a really good education, so he out-tricks guys." I agree he's really a smart guy, but I'm not sure a college degree has anything to do with one's native intelligence. Rizzo hit a two-run homer in the first which really amounted to the game being over.

Extra innings:
Hendricks is clearly one of Gene's favorite Cubbies. He "sings his praises" every time we speak. He has maintained throughout Hendricks career that he was a high-quality pitcher with a really good future. He was right on in his assessment of Hendricks. In contrast I originally saw him as a pretty good 5 – 7 inning guy, maybe even a long relief type. Well, the "voice" out-thought, out – analyzed or out – tricked me on this one. Ha!

Today's baseball wisdom:

"A guy who throws what he intends to throw, that's the definition of a good pitcher."
Sandy Koufax

Baseball history this date:

1965 – Casey Stengel announces his retirement after 55 years in baseball. Also:
1922 – Babe Ruth is thrown out of a game for the fifth time this year.

Game: #132

Teams: Cubs/ Pittsburgh
Date: Wednesday, August 31
Final: Cubs win 6 – 5
Record: 85 – 47

V – mail: "Oh those bases on balls! But with 31 pitches by Chapman we win. A very stressful game to watch. Final score 6 – 5."

Recap:

Kris Bryant not only hit homer, #36, in the first inning, but also made three solid defensive plays at third base. What a terrific young player. But hold on, the play of the game was made by arguably the best, or one of the best, shortstops in either league. With the bases loaded in the seventh inning, two outs and the score 5 – 2 Cubs, Gregory Polanco hits a "dying dove" down the third base line, and if it drops likely all three runs will score and tie the game. However, Russell races from his position, slides and makes a sensational catch. Pirate manager, Clint Hurdle called it a fantastic play and Bryant said "I had a front row seat and it was one of the best catches I have ever seen." Wow, another great young talent, he's 22 has 86 RBIs in only his second year. Hammel went six innings and left leading 5 – 1. Enter the relief corps. Cahill gets one out, but gives up two hits and a walk which leads to one run. Grimm comes in and gives up a walk but no runs.. Travis Wood gets one out, but gives up a walk and two hits which equals two runs. The Cubs score their sixth run in the bottom of the seventh. Finally Chapman comes in and 31 pitches later after a walk, two hits and three wild pitches a run is scored. The final score is 6 – 5.

Extra innings:

Stressful, that's an understatement. Marlys and I were watching the game, she's in bed, and I went to another room to get a phone in case the "voice" called after the Cubs win. I watched the ninth-inning as Chapman almost gave it away. Gene did call and he was really "bent" about all the walks. There were 14 in all and the game was over four hours long. "Lord preserve us from bases on balls."

Today's baseball wisdom:

"If I had my career to play over, one thing I'd do differently was swing more. Those 1200 walks I got, nobody remembers them."
Pee wee Reese

Baseball history this date:

1990 – Ken Griffey Senior and Junior are the first father and son play on the same team; both go 1 – 4.

Game: #133

Teams: Cubs/San Francisco
Date: Thursday, September 1
Final: Cubs win 5 – 4
Record: 86 – 47

V – mail: "The Cubs bullpen did the job as they held the Giants to no runs. Cubs pull off the victory 5 – 4."

Recap:
The Cubs bullpen did indeed do the job, going five perfect innings giving up no hits or walks. Zastryzny two innings, Smith two innings, and C.J. Edwards one inning. Montgomery, the starter gave up all four runs in three innings, but shut out the Giants in the fourth. The Giants, thus went six innings with no hits or walks. Zip! Addison Russell hit a two-run single with two outs in the seventh for the 5 – 4 win. I think I was raving about him yesterday, but as of today he has 88 RBIs; he is 8 – 18 with the bases-loaded driving in 23 runs. The AP commenting on him said, "on top of his great clutch hitting he is playing gold glove level defense."

Extra innings:
Gosh as a "Cub groupie" I'm not sure who my favorite player is today. Hendricks is such a crafty young guy, Bryant can do it all, Rizzo is really solid, Baez is a coming star as is Willson Contreras, but I'm beginning to think that the slick fielding Yogi Berra type clutch hitter, playing shortstop, is my current Cub "hero." At least today! On another note, Gene called and we had an extended BS session. He mentioned that he thought they might lose with the score 4 – 3 Giants in the seventh. He stated "you know I really wasn't very concerned if the Cubs did lose as the Giants are a non-division team and the "magic number" for the Cubs to clinch their division is now 15 or 16." We were both on the same wave length for this game.

As I hung up the phone it rang again almost immediately. It was my sister Carol Silva who said "hey, I've been trying to get you as I see the Cubs beat our Giants." Her friend Dolly is apparently worse than Gene when it comes to her loyalty for the Giants. She told Carol earlier in the day," I know my Giants will whip those Cubs." Well not today, maybe tomorrow.

Today's baseball wisdom:

"A team is where a boy can prove his courage on his own. A gang is where a coward goes to hide."
Mickey Mantle

A Century-Long Journey to the Day of Redemption

Baseball history this date:

1918 – The baseball season ends due to World War I. Also, the first time the Star-Spangled Banner was performed at a major league game.

Game: #134

Teams: Cubs/San Francisco
Date: Friday, September 2
Final: Cubs win 2 – 1
Record: 87 – 47

V – mail: "Forty games over .500. The last time the Cubs were 40 games over was in 1945, the last time they were in the World Series."

Recap:
It's difficult to come up with more or new accolades to describe the Cubs starting pitchers. Lester took a no-hitter into the seventh inning (6 2/3) and settled for a complete game 2 – 1 win. Kris Bryant and Dexter Fowler made sparkling defensive plays to keep the "no-no" intact through six innings. Lester did pitch a no-hitter with Boston in May 2008.

Extra innings:
It was interesting that Anthony Rizzo, who was celebrating his eighth year of being cancer free, had told Lester he thought he was going to pitch a no-hitter. He didn't, but he came close. Rizzo is a survivor of Hodgkin's lymphoma and Lester beat lymphoma a decade ago. Both have foundations and Rizzo's has raised over $2 million in support of families whose children have cancer and for cancer research. The day was further special for Rizzo and Lester as it was "kids strike out cancer day," the major leagues initiative that had players and umpires wearing gold sweat bands to raise awareness for childhood cancer. It was a special day for a couple of special Cubs and of course a special game. (As they won).

Today's baseball wisdom:

"Ain't no man can avoid being born average, but there ain't no man got to be common."
Satchel Paige

Baseball history this date:

1965 – Ernie Banks hits his 400th home run off Curt Simmons.

Game: #135

Teams: Cubs/San Francisco
Date Saturday, September 3
Final: Cubs lose 3 – 2
Record: 87 – 48

V – mail: "The score was 2 – 1 when I left so I do not know the particulars of the rest of the game. I know we lost 3 – 2."

Recap:
This was a tough one to lose. Bumgarner won and Arrieta lost although he only gave up three runs, two of them earned. Arrieta gave up a total of four hits while Bumgarner gave up five, however the Cubs couldn't capitalize when they got men on base. But talk about frustration with how the Giants got their runs; run #1, La Stella throws away a grounder with two outs in the first inning; run #2, in the fourth inning with a man on first a wild pitch than a passed ball puts him on third and a single scores the run; run #3, in the sixth inning with two outs Arrieta throws a wild pitch for the final run. Thus, three Cub mistakes account for all the Giant runs.

Extra innings:
I am a Cub fan and like old Earl Weaver (incendiary former manager of the Orioles) I am a "sore loser." The AP writeup stated "Bumgarner out pitched Arrieta with 10 strikeouts in six innings." Oh it did add later that the Giants had "pounced on rare Cub miscues in a 3 – 2 victory." The remark that Bumgarner out pitched our Arrieta is "baloney"! Who cares about the 10 strikeouts, Arrieta had seven strikeouts and gave up one less hit. The Giants just got lucky as Lily Tomlin would say, "and that's the truth."

Today's baseball wisdom:
"We make too many wrong mistakes."
Yogi Berra

Baseball history this date:
1928 – Ty Cobb gets his 4191 final career hit.

Game: #136

Teams: Cubs/Giants
Date: Sunday, September 4
Final: Cubs win 3 -2 (13 innings)
Record: 88 – 48

V – mail: "Pitching is the name of the game as both teams really showed how good they are, as it went 13 innings before it was over. The Cubs prevailed 3 – 2."

Recap:

Well not much to argue with Gene about, "pitching being the name of the game." John Lackey went five innings and gave up two runs and left trailing 2 – 1. Enter the Cubs relief corps, seven different guys, and they held the Giants scoreless for eight straight innings. They gave up only three hits, two bases on balls and had 11 strikeouts. Cahill eventually won it with a perfect 13 inning. But to again quote an old time radio broadcaster from the Midwest, Paul Harvey, who related a news story and then when you thought he had finished, he would intone, "and now for the rest of the story." And the rest of the story was really the crux of the matter in this game. I've detailed it in the next section, extra innings.

Extra innings:

A couple of games back in the aftermath of a Cub loss I was "ragging" to Gene about that $183 million "loser" Jason Heyward. "I wouldn't have him on the team, he's as bad as poor old Carlos Marmol, ex-Cub reliever who continually blew games." "Just get rid of the guy, he makes all that money, 8.8 million a year, and by contrast Hendricks the major league ERA leader makes $510,000! Well, after the game the "voice" called and I told Marlys that I suppose I had to answer the call. You see, Jason Heyward singled in run #1 in the fourth inning, then singled in run #2 in the ninth to send the game into extra innings; and then of course he singled in run #3 in the 13th inning to win the game. "And that's the rest of the story! Gene was pretty diplomatic about the whole matter, but he did chuckle, and I think I recall him saying "see I told you so." Well maybe he didn't say that, if not I'll claim memory lapse.

Today's baseball wisdom:

"Every day is a new opportunity. You can build on yesterday's success or put its failures behind and start over again. That's the way life is, with a new

game every day, and that's the way baseball is."
Bob Feller

Baseball history this date:

1991 – A panel of eight baseball experts vote to drop the asterisk next to Roger Maris home run record.*

*(Originally an asterisk was next to his 61 home runs as he had hit only 59 in 154 games. Ruth had hit 60 home runs in 154 games, the total games played then, but subsequently lengthened to 162 games)

Game: #137

Teams: Cubs @ Milwaukee
Date: Monday, September 5
Final: Cubs win 7 – 2
Record: 89 – 48

V – mail: "Kyle once again proved his value to the Cubs giving up one run in six innings as they win 7 – 2."

Recap:
The game was on the MLB, (major league baseball), and I turned it on about the sixth inning with the score 1 – 1. Jeepers I thought, Hendricks has gone six innings again, and the Cubs scored the one run in the sixth inning to tie the score. Then with two outs in the seventh, Montero doubled, Coghlan hits for Hendricks and singles in Montero. If he had made an out Hendricks would not have gotten a decision. La Stella also singles and the score is 3 – 1. The Cubs scored four more in the eighth with Soler, Russell, Baez, and Coghlan doing the damage. Felix Pena, a young rookie pitcher and Joe Smith really looked sharp pitching the seventh and eighth. Some guy named Jake Buchanan came on in the ninth and gave up a home run to the PED king, Braun, and two other "rockets," that were caught, as the Cubs won 7 – 2.

Extra innings:
I called the "voice" at 7:30 AM as I missed his call yesterday after the Cubs won. I thought he had gone to the game but instead he goes today 9/6/16. We had the usual BS session about the game, but then he said something that really made me feel good for him. He said "you know Kent I've decided that even if the Cubs don't win it all, this summer has been so wonderful (the way the Cubs have played) giving me, by the time it's over 162 games of pleasure." Amazing, Marlys, Matt and I had the same conversation this past week. The Cubs are by far the best team in baseball, but anything can happen in a short series in the division and league championships that are five and seven games. So, whatever happens it has been a great fun summer. It's too bad the game is all about money today; in the past when you finished first, you had won the pennant for your league and the next step was the World Series. Dare I say, "oh for the good old days."

Today's baseball wisdom:

"The riches of the game are in the thrills, not the money."
Ernie Banks

A Century-Long Journey to the Day of Redemption

Baseball history this date:

1995 – Cal Ripken Jr. ties Lou Gehrig's record of playing in 2130 straight games.

Game: #138

Teams: Cubs @ Milwaukee
Date: Tuesday, September 6
Final: Cubs lose 12-5
Record: 89 – 49

V – mail: "As an eyewitness to this game I can only say, wow, did we get one. Brewers 12 – Cubs 5. Rizzo did hit two home runs."

Recap:

Not only wow, but yikes, as the Cubs got bushwhacked for five runs in the first inning on the way to a "brew crew" rout. The first seven batters for the Brewers reached base off Jason Hammel who previously had not allowed a total of five runs in his 14 previous career starts against Milwaukee. He was 10 – 1 with an ERA of 2.50 against them. Maddon didn't bother to use his bullpen for a save, letting him go for 5 2/3 innings, giving up 13 hits and 9 runs. Maybe the only two good things to come out of this game were Rizzo hitting two home runs and maybe more importantly Hector Rondon coming off the disabled list. They really need him for the playoffs.

Extra innings:

As the "voice" noted, he was at the game and was a witness to the mayhem. Ha! On quite a different note, I have attached a letter from my aunt Esther, written to me on September 6, 1951. That's 65 years ago, and I still have the original. I was in a private rehab facility in Oshkosh Wisconsin, hoping to improve my walking, when I got the letter. The Milton Berry school, as it was called, was a beautiful estate on Lake Winnebago and was mostly a "dumping ground" for rich folks who wanted to rid themselves of an unwanted family member who had a disability, (many of them mild). My parents didn't know that, but with their efforts to do the best for me they decided to give it a try. After several months they realized that the program that was offered was nothing more than a series of daily exercises, fabrication of a cumbersome set of leg braces, and a "healthy" contribution of cash each month. The most memorable event during my stay there was listening to the radio and hearing the "shot heard round the world," that is Bobby Thomson's dramatic three-run home run off Ralph Branca of the Dodgers in the bottom of the ninth to give the New York Giants the National League pennant over the Brooklyn Dodgers.

Today's baseball wisdom:

"I know a baseball star who would not report the theft of his wife's credit

card because the thief spent less than she did."
Joe Garagiola

Baseball history this date:

1943 – Carl Scheib of the Philadelphia Athletics becomes the youngest pitcher in the American League, 16 years, 8 months.

HERBERT W. ANDERECK   TELEPHONE 34-D   MRS. NETTIE ANDERECK

ANDERECK CHEVROLET
HIGHWAYS 11 AND 81
JUDA, WISCONSIN

September 6, 1951

Dear Kent:

I wrote for tickets to Wrigley Field for the September 16 game. Asked for five. I think your mother will go, don't you? The game is with Brooklyn in case you haven't already found out. Should be a good game; everyone says a game with Brooklyn is always good.

Well, Elaine is going to school now and the second day she didn't want to go. I sent her with Audrey the first morning instead of going along myself because I thought that would be best, but evidently it was a mistake. I went with her the second day and she showed me her seat and just beamed when I talked to her teacher and I have been meeting her up on the corner at 11:30 every day when she comes home for lunch. She has been OK since. She's a little afraid of the boys. She says they play cops and robbers and it makes her so tired, they just play cops and robbers every recess and all the time and she wished there weren't any boys there because it makes her so tired to play cops and robbers all the time, etc., etc. I think she played cops and robbers all night last night if you ask me. She woke up at midnight and I took her to the bathroom and then she wanted me to sleep with her, but that single bed is too small for both of us so she crawled in with her daddy and I slept alone in her bed. An hour or so later Hub came over and said he just couldn't sleep with her, so I got out of her bed and went over and crawled in with her and Hub got in her bed. And I'm telling you she jumped all over me all night long. Do I feel beat up today!

I guess everything is going lovely for Audrey in High School anyway chatter, chatter, chatter. She thinks her Biology teacher is a dream boy, and that the new music teacher knows his stuff and won't put up with much kidding around. She took a lesson from Mrs. Collins last night. The first one since last May.

Janice and Patty Siedschlag (across the street) wander in and out of the house at all times of the day looking for xxxxxxx Elaine. I don't think their mother knows it. If Eddie doesn't plan to come home the weekend of the ball game, let us know and we'll come up for you Friday night or Saturday or whenever you want to come home. I didn't know I was down to the bottom of the page. Can't think of anything to fill this up with.

Love,

Aunt Esther

Game: #139

Teams: Cubs @ Milwaukee
Date: Wednesday, September 7
Final: Cubs lose 2 – 1
Record: 89 – 50

V – mail: "A well played game by both teams. All runs were scored by homers. Brewers win 2 – 1."

Recap:
Gene really is a fan; he can watch the game, not necessarily be happy with the Cubs losing, but he is able to unemotionally provide an objective viewpoint re: the quality of the game. By contrast, I was not happy with the Cubs loading the bases in inning number one with one out and not scoring. The game is 1 – 1 as Villar had homered for the "brew crew" and Rizzo for the Cubs. Then the bottom of the eighth Villar hits another one and the score is 2 – 1 Brewers. In ninth-inning Rizzo blasts one to the wall and it looks like it's going out, but a guy named Keon Broxton leaps up, times his jump perfectly and snags the ball over the fence. Crap! "Well played game", said the voice. Well I'm PO'D because they lost the game. Now I have to pout for several hours and have bad thoughts about that guy Keon! Gosh, maybe I'm a worse loser than old Earl Weaver (long time manager of Baltimore). Actually, "venting my spleen" gets it out of my system and I feel better. My wife had the audacity to call me a "crybaby."

Extra innings:
Today was my 53rd wedding anniversary, September 7, 1963. I wasn't watching the Cubs that day, I was getting ready to take "the plunge." So today I went to the internet to check on the Cubs for that date. I wasn't surprised as they were playing like the "lovable losers." They were leading 1 – 0 in the bottom of the ninth and Dick Ellsworth had gone all the way. I think you can guess what happened next. Two out in the bottom of the ninth and a two-run double beats them 2 – 1. Kind of ironic or coincidental the same score 53 years to the day. They lost to the Houston Colts, who's record was 52 – 91. In 1965 they became the Houston Astros. On a final note, my good buddy, the "voice" failed to show for my wedding in South branch Minnesota that fall. You see he was sitting in a fox hole somewhere in Korea at the time. I guess that's a reasonable excuse for not being present isn't it?

Today's baseball wisdom:

"Above anything else, I hate to lose."
Jackie Robinson

Baseball history this date:

1952 – Outfielder Don Grate (with the Chattanooga Lookouts) throws a baseball a record 445 feet, 1 inch.*

* I learned later that in 1957 Glen Gorbous (Omaha Cardinals) broke Grate's record with a throw of 445 feet 10 inches.(9 inches more)

Game:

No game today, Cubs are traveling.
Teams: None
Date: Thursday, September 8
Final: The Cubs did not lose
Record: Remains 89 – 50
Phone call:
The phone rang around 6:30 PM, it was the "voice."
"What I said, there wasn't a game today was there?"
"Well no," replied Gene, "but I was so tickled I had to call."
"Why," I inquired?
"Didn't you see that the "Brew Crew" whacked the Cardinals 12 – 5; so even though we didn't play we still essentially won." Gene was literally chortling that the red birds got beat. He's really enjoying the season, and why not, it's been a great run. Then the next morning (the ninth) I have a v-mail concerning yesterday's Cardinal loss that simply said: "The magic number is now 8, Yahoo!

Today's baseball wisdom:

"People ask me what I do in winter when there is no baseball. I'll tell you what I do. I stare out the window and wait for spring."
Rogers Hornsby
(I think the "voice" can relate to this one)

Baseball history this date:

1985 – Pete Rose ties Ty Cobb with 4191 hits.

Game: #140

Teams: Cubs @ Houston
Date: Friday, September 9
Final: Cubs win 2 – 0
Record: 90 – 50

V – mail: "Jon Lester threw seven innings of shutout baseball, allowing seven hits, no walks, and seven strikeouts. With a lot of help from David Ross and great plays by Baez and Heyward they won the game 2 – 0. Bryant hit a two-run homer for the only score."

Recap:
Lester won for the seventh straight time and hasn't lost since July 3. In three starts he hasn't allowed a run and in the other four he has allowed only one run. Now he, Hendricks, and maybe even Arrieta could all three be in the running for the Cy Young Award. Rondon pitched the eighth with two strikeouts, good to have him back. Chapman had a perfect ninth with one strikeout. The Cubs are now 90 – 50, giving them consecutive 90 win seasons since they last did it three straight years 1928 – 1930. ESPN recap did not mention Heyward or Baez concerning any defensive plays. I'll ask Gene when I talk to him.

Extra innings:
This was Kris Bryant's first career game against Houston, the team that passed over him with the first draft pick in 2013. Houston had selected Mark Appel who was traded to Philadelphia this off-season before ever playing in the majors. When Joe Maddon was asked about Houston's decision not to draft Bryant, his only response was "thank you." That's enough said.

Today's baseball wisdom:

"I won 28 games in 1935 and couldn't believe my eyes when the Cardinals sent a contract with a cut in salary. Mr. Ricky said I deserved to cut because I didn't win 30 games." (He was 30 – 7 in 1934)*
Dizzy Dean

*(I'd like to see that system today; sign for 10 million or more, have a terrible year, and then take a 20% salary cut. It will never happen)

Baseball history this date:

1965 – Sandy Koufax pitches his fourth no-hitter, a perfect game against the Cubs, winning 1 – 0.

Game: #141

Teams: Cubs @ Houston
Date: Saturday, September 10
Final: Cubs lose 2 – 1
Record: 90 – 51

V – mail: "Another good pitching, low-scoring game as the Cubs lost for the second time this week 2 – 1. The magic number is still at 7 with 21 games to play."

Recap:

I suppose everyone will think or say I'm being negative pointing out that the Cubs have scored only four runs in the last three games. What is that all about? They "whacked" Houston pitching for two big hits and only struck out 12 times! I know that the number today, even if the Cardinals win, will still be seven. However, I'm a worry wart and if they happen to take a nosedive at the end of the year in the playoffs, a five and seven game series, it could be curtains. This game is almost not worth reporting. It just ended, 1:30 PM Tucson time, so I'll wait for the v-mail tomorrow from the "voice" to see if I need to continue ranting or I should moderate my tone. So the v-mail (see above) arrives and it's totally benign. Nothing but the comment on good pitching and the score. Gene then called September 11 about 2 PM to inform me that the magic number had fallen to six, as the Brewers beat the Cardinals again. During our conversation I asked him, "aren't you concerned they only scored four runs in the last three games?"

He simply replied, "no."

Extra innings:

After the voice called I began thinking about the fact that I seem to be routinely getting "bent out of shape" about the Cubs. I thought about Mad Magazine, a ridiculously satirical rag that I used to read on a regular basis. It hadn't crossed my mind in years and I visualized the cover with the image of Alfred E. Neuman, the jug-eared, freckle-faced, missing a tooth, supposed simpleton. Versions of his "mug" have been around since at least 1894 in an advertisement for a stage play called New Boy. The point of this rambling is I think I need to adopt Alfred's signature phrase, "What Me Worry?"

I'm going to try.

Today's baseball wisdom:

"We picked the Red Sox because they lose. If you root for something that loses 86 years you're a pretty good fan. You don't have to win everything to

be a fan of something."
Jimmy Fallon

Baseball history this date:

1960 – New York Yankee Mickey Mantle hits 643 foot home run over the right field roof in Detroit.

Game: #142

Teams: Cubs @ Houston
Date: Sunday, September 11
Final: Cubs win 9 – 5
Record: 91 – 51

V – mail: "The Cubs scored quickly in this one as they took the early lead and never looked back winning 9 – 5. With a Cardinal loss the magic number is now 5."

Recap:
As usual, I was late turning on the game. The top of the third inning had just finished and the Cubs were ahead 7 – 0. Arrieta who has been mostly pitching well lately, cruised through five innings only allowing a solo home run. But in the sixth an RBI double and a wild pitch made the score 9 – 3. The Astros then loaded the bases, but Grimm got two pop-ups to end the threat. Trevor Cahill, who has been good, gave up back-to-back homers on two pitches for the 9 to 5 final. Travis Wood who got them 1, 2, 3 prompted Gene to point out in his usual post game call, "well what did you think of Woodie? You've been complaining about him lately so did his work tonight make you feel better?" Before I could answer he snickered, no more like guffawed. Okay, point taken old friend.

Extra innings:
I did see Russell really blast one, his 20th homer. He is only the second shortstop in Cubs history to have 20 home runs and 90 RBIs in a season. Of course all good Cubs fans know who the other shortstop was, "Mr. Cub" Ernie Banks, who had 117 RBIs in 1960; he had 41 home runs that year. I have said this before, but Russell is really an amazing young talent.

Today's baseball wisdom:

"I don't believe it. Lou Brock could never make that play again, even on instant replay."
Bill Virdon

Baseball history this date:

1918 – The Boston Red Sox beat the Chicago Cubs, four games to two to win the 15th World Series.

Game: #143

Teams: Cubs @ St. Louis
Date: Monday, September 12
Final: Cubs win 4 – 1
Record: 92 – 51

V – mail: "What a pleasure to watch Kyle Hendricks pitch. He threw eight innings of no-hit ball with two walks and seven strikeouts. A lead off homer in the ninth got him. A lot of great defensive plays behind him. Final was 4 – 1. The magic number is now 3."

Recap:

I didn't realize the game was on MLB network, but when I saw the "ticker" on TV that Hendricks had a no-hitter through seven innings I went to the channel and there it was. The eighth inning was okay, but with an 0 – 2 count on a guy named Hazelbaker, he hit it out of the park. Interestingly, one of the Cub announcers had mentioned earlier that if the Cardinals did get a hit it would probably be a home run. Chapman finished the game after Maddon lifted Hendricks following the home run. It was a great performance by Hendricks, who truly is a facsimile of the Hall of Famer Greg Maddux. As the "voice" stated, "what a pleasure to watch him pitch; his fastball is maybe 90, but he gets people out by out – thinking them. It's really refreshing to see a guy who doesn't have to get people out by simply overpowering the batter with velocity." Hendricks later said he was surprised he got so close, "as a guy who throws to contact and doesn't throw hard, you don't think about it."

In fact, Heyward, Russell and Bryant all made terrific defensive plays earlier to keep the no-hitter in play, especially Russell, who went deep to short on his knees and threw out the runner. Fowler and Zobrist homered for the Cubs.

Extra innings:

The "voice" called Post game, ecstatic with Hendricks performance (as he should be). But I also know that he is Gene's favorite Cub. Hey, what's not to like about the guy. We had quite a long animated BS session, and at one point he said well the magic number is now 3. He added "while I hate to lose to the Cardinals, if the Cubs sweep, the Cub fans at Wrigley won't be present to celebrate when they clinch." On a humorous note, Maddon got ejected in the ninth after the asinine home plate umpire said that the players visiting with Hendricks after the home run constituted a "visit" to the mound. You can only make two visits and that you must remove the pitcher. The more I watch home plate umpires the more I detest them. They're nothing more than obnoxious autocrats!

Today's baseball wisdom:

"He didn't sound like a baseball player. He said things like, nevertheless, and if in fact."

Dan Quisenberry on Ted Simmons

Baseball history this date:

1976 – Minnie Minoso, age 53, of the Chicago White Sox, becomes the oldest player in the major leagues to get a hit.

Game: #144

Teams: Cubs @ St. Louis
Date: Tuesday, September 13
Final: Cubs lose 4 – 2
Record: 92 – 52

V – mail: "The Cubs lost this game due to the inability to get hits when they had a chance, and there were plenty of them early in the game. Both teams had good relief pitching. Final score Cardinals 4, Cubs 2."

Recap:
The Cubs had the bases loaded in both the second and fourth innings and failed to get any of the runners in. The first Cardinal reliever, Reyes, walked six in four innings, but again the Cubs didn't capitalize. Of course the Cardinals scored four runs on two two- run homers. Jason Hammel didn't pitch all that bad, giving up four runs on six hits in 5 2/3 innings, striking out nine and walking two. Hammel, had been pitching well after the All-Star break, but now has lost three or four in a row. There is some speculation that he may miss the playoff roster.

Extra innings:
I have always felt that the Cardinals are a bunch of lucky "Son-of-a-guns". For example, Brandon Moss is on a 1 – 41 batting skid. So he watches tape of himself and presto hits the game winning home run today. Likewise, Diaz, who had been on the disabled list, returns to the starting lineup, and his first game back also hits a two-run homer. I'm not paranoid, but maybe they have a rabbits foot hidden in their jockstraps.

Today's baseball wisdom:

"I don't know if they were men or women fans running naked across the field. They all had bags over their heads."
Yogi Berra

Baseball history this date:

1909 – Ty Cobb clinches the American League home run title with his ninth home run. (All inside the park)

Game: #145

Teams: Cubs @ St. Louis
Date: Wednesday, September 14
Final: Cubs win 7 – 0
Record: 93 – 52

V – mail: "Another strong pitching performance by Jon Lester allowing no base runners past first, and allowing only three hits. He was supported by his catcher David Ross who picked off two base runners and belted a two-run homer. Anthony Rizzo hit two home runs."

Recap:

Right, Mr. "voice!" But I'd suggest his performance, Lester, was nothing short of spectacular. He improved to 7 – 0 in his last nine starts with an ERA of 1.02. It's interesting how well he and old David Ross (he's actually only 39) work together. He always catches Lester and it seems to help Lester rise to the occasion as he does the "extra things" in a baseball game that can make the difference between winning and losing. Today his contributions were more obvious, throwing out two base runners and also hitting a two-run homer. His numbers aren't very impressive, a .231 batting average, nine home runs and 31 runs batted in. But to those who understand and follow baseball closely, he is an invaluable member of the team; great leadership, great defensive catcher, and a terrific mentor for the young Cub team.

Extra innings:

Rizzo's two-run homer in the ninth gave him 31 home runs and 101 RBIs for the year. He's only the second left-handed hitter in Cubs franchise history to have multiple 30 home run and 100 RBI seasons. The great Cub left fielder, Billy Williams, did it in 1965, 1970, in 1972. As I am a betting man, I'd wager today that before he's finished Rizzo will surpass Williams in that respect.

Today's baseball wisdom:

"Not only was I not the best catcher in the major leagues, I wasn't even the best catcher on my street."*

Joe Garagiola

*(Garagiola was born in St. Louis on Elizabeth Ave., an Italian – American neighborhood, known as the hill. Across the street from his home lived a childhood friend and competitor a kid named Lawrence Peter Berra, better known to many as "Yogi." Professional scouts had originally rated Garagiola

a better prospect than Berra who had a magnificent career with the Yankees. Garagiola was a good and solid player but he never achieved the level of Berra).

Baseball history this date:

1994 – All 28 baseball owners vote to cancel the rest of the 1994 season. *
*(The players had gone on strike and in retaliation the owners cancel the rest of the season including the World Series)

Game: #146

Teams: Cubs/Milwaukee
Date: Thursday, September 15
Final: Cubs lose 5 – 4
Record: 93 – 53

V – mail: "The Cubs actually lost a game due to fielding errors, first time all year. Montgomery only gave up one earned run in six innings of work, but the score was tied at three. Cubs lose 5 – 4 as the bullpen gave up two runs in the seventh."

Recap:

The ESPN headlines were, "Brewers crash Cubs party with 5 – 4 win at Wrigley Field." With the loss the Cubs did not clinch the division, so the celebration had to be delayed. However the Cardinals decided to cooperate and lose 6 – 2 at San Francisco which gave the division to the Cubs. Yea!

As far as the game itself, Montgomery pitched well enough to win, but two unearned runs forced him to leave after six innings with the score tied 3 – 3. Russell threw the ball away in the third leading to two runs. Jorge Soler hit a two-run home run and Justin Grimm gave up a pinch-hit two-run double in the seventh to take the loss.

Extra innings:

While the Cubs have had a great regular season, literally running away from the competition, Theo Epstein, the architect of the team, stated "we've got a lot ahead of us." He further stated, "it kind of all boils down to how you perform in October." Of course I agree with young Theo except on one point. It's not "… kind of boils down," rather it totally boils down to October.

Today's baseball wisdom:

"You can sum up the game of baseball in one word. You never know."
Joaquin Andujar

Baseball history this date:

1977 – The Baltimore Orioles forfeit the game to the Blue Jays when manager Earl Weaver pulls his team off the field in the fifth inning citing hazardous conditions.*

*(He claimed the tarpaulin covering the pitcher's mound was too small.) Really Earl?

A Century-Long Journey to the Day of Redemption

Game: #147

Teams: Cubs/Milwaukee
Date: Friday, September 16
Final: Cubs win 5 – 4 (10 innings)
Record: 94 – 53

V – mail: "A game that looked like the Brewers were going to win with a 4 – 2 lead going into the last of the ninth; but the Cubs rallied to tie it up. Then Montero belted a home run to lead off the 10th to give the Cubs the win and help the Cubs celebrate their division championship. Now we wait."

Recap:
Yes, wait is the operative word, and I think it will be with some anxiety or nervousness waiting to see how the division and league series goes. In addition to the ninth-inning rally and Montero's home run I really enjoyed watching Chapman pitch the 10th. He started off throwing two balls, then I'm not sure, but I think he "whiffed" the next three guys with nine pitches, including "steroid head" Ryan Braun, which tickled the hell out of me! Today's game was the 65th anniversary of my first major league baseball game at Wrigley Field. Aunt Esther got the tickets for mom, dad, herself, uncle "Hub" and myself.

Extra innings:
Watching today's game I thought well, Cubs lost 65 years ago on September 16, 1951 and today it looks like a repeat. That game in 1951, with the Brooklyn Dodgers, featuring an all-star cast of players like Carl Furillo, Pee Wee Reese, Duke Snider, Jackie Robinson, Roy Campanella, Andy Pafko, Gil Hodges, and Billy Cox was a great team. The Dodgers won 6 – 1 behind a young guy named Clem Labine. By contrast the Cubs featured a group of mostly "unknowns" such as Eddie Mikis, Hal Jeffcoat, Frankie, Baumholtz, Bob Ramazzoti, Smokey Burgess and an aging Hank Sauer. There was however one guy on the Cubs, unknown at the time, playing first base, by the name of Chuck Connors. Yes, you might have guessed he was later to star in the movies and on television as "The Rifleman." Unlike stories I always hear people say when they saw Jackie Robinson play, (that he stole home), not this date, Robinson went 0 – 3, no stolen bases, and in baseball parlance his line was "nothing across."

However, just his presence in the ballpark that day provide an experience for me that has lasted a lifetime. I recall the moment like it was yesterday. I'm including an excerpt from a short article I wrote entitled "A Day At Wrigley", which was subsequently published in a memoir. The incident is as follows:

"As game time neared, the excitement and noise levels increased in anticipation. Then suddenly it was quiet for the national anthem. At the final note of the anthem 30,000+ fans erupted with a mighty roar. As the din subsided a strange hush fell over the entire stadium. Almost imperceptibly at first, a faint murmuring sound began. The still heavy air seemed electric, no, more like charged with a building force of energy. It became almost oppressive for me, I suddenly gasped for air. "Dad what's happening, can you feel it? "

"Yes," he replied gently as he looked at me.

I asked, "what is it?"

"It's Robinson I think, Jackie."

I stared at my father in amazement "what do you mean it's Jackie, what's he doing?" What was this silent, yet powerful crescendo, building and enveloping everyone!

The moment passed, the game began, but I sat wondering and confused by what had transpired. I was jolted by the sudden loud staccato voice from the P. A. system, "attention, attention please, now batting for the Brooklyn Dodgers, playing second base, Jackie Robinson." The crowd rose as one, another mighty roar came from thousands of throats, but unlike the enthusiastic cheering at the conclusion of the anthem, there was a strange dissonance of sounds; shrieks of joy, but also mournful sounds, his name spoken repeatedly, chords of adulation, as if supplications to a master or even a Messiah. It was as if it were a symphony of wailing, from deep within tortured souls, seeking spiritual release. Everyone, it seemed was standing and gently swaying, and I sat, unable to stand, fully engulfed in this unknown force and energy. However, when Robinson reached first on error in the second inning, the stadium was suddenly transformed into a gleeful, raucous, baseball crowd; familiar and joyous sounds of the ballpark the "Cubbies" and "Da Bums" playing America's game. The Cubs lost and it sent their season record to 58 – 85 good for last place. Clem Labine, a Dodger rookie, beat Bob Kelly, a journeyman pitcher. Oh well, maybe next year I thought. Riding home, exhausted, stuffed with hot dogs, candy, Peanuts, and soda pop, snug in the back seat of Hub's new Chevy, I dozed dreamily, thinking about the day. I thought about that strange overwhelming moment, unable to comprehend its meaning. What was clear was the overpowering energy that swirled around us for a brief time and seemed to gently envelop the man, Jackie.

That day, now over 65 years ago, remains indelibly etched in my memory. I'm not certain I'll ever fully understand or appreciate what happened that day at Wrigley Field. What I do know is that Jackie Robinson was much more than just the Dodgers second baseman. And today, as I reflect on his lonely pilgrimage I think of another gentle, yet fiercely determined soul, Mohandas

Gandhi, "the Mahatma," who, as Jackie changed a nation.

Today's baseball wisdom:

"Baseball, it is said, is only a game. True, and the Grand Canyon is only a hole in Arizona."

George Will

Baseball history this date:

1940 – Leo Durocher was suspended from Ebbets Field for "inciting a riot."

Game: #148

Teams: Cubs/Milwaukee
Date: Saturday, September 17
Final: Cubs lose 11 – 3
Record: 94 – 54

V – mail: "Shades of the past. I cannot remember being blown out this bad this year as the Cubs lost 11 – 3."

Recap:

Arrieta went six innings and gave up three earned runs, four hits and four walks. He is now 3 – 2 in his last six starts with an ERA of 4.58 and 21 walks in those starts. Lately, he seems to be okay for 5 to 6 to innings, but then loses it. Through five innings today he was ahead 3 – 1, then in the sixth two walks, a double and a home run and the score is 4 – 3 Milwaukee. Arrieta is out of the game. In the seventh inning Carl Edwards gives up two home runs and the score is 7 – 3. In the eighth inning this "dude" named Patton (no relation to General George I don't think) walks two, then hits a batter, and then gives up a grand slam. I've never thought Patton was worth too much. His ERA in 2016 is 5.75 and his career ERA is 6.37. I'm not sure he's a "keeper." This was kind of a weird game as the first three Cub hitters got a single, triple, and a home run for a 3 – 0 lead to start the game. But that was it, as the rest of the game the Cubs went into a complete hitting "funk."

Extra innings:

Maybe the entire team got "bombed" yesterday celebrating the division win. After the first inning outburst they had four puny singles and a double. They did play five or six bench guys rather than regulars, but what a flat unenthusiastic effort. Oh well, we'll see what tomorrow brings.

Today's baseball wisdom:

"I hit a grand slam off Ron Herbel and when his manager, Herman Franks, came out to get him, he was bringing Herbel's suitcase."
Bob Uecker

Baseball history this date:

1912 – Casey Stengel, center fielder, broke in with Brooklyn and had four singles.

Game: #149

Teams: Cubs/Milwaukee
Date: Sunday, September 18
Final: Cubs lose 3 – 1
Record: 94 – 55

V – mail: "If Kyle wants to win he has to throw a shutout as his teammates once again only scored one run for him. The Cubs left seven runners on base in three innings. The final was 3 – 1. Kyle threw six innings with no walks and nine strikeouts."

Recap:
Neither the "voice"or I have a clue as to why the Cub bats go silent whenever Hendricks pitches. Once again he had a terrific outing giving up only six hits, no walks and nine strikeouts. But it seems that when he pitches the hitters "make sure" they don't score any runs so he will lose. (Is that paranoia or what?) They get men on base, but leave seven stranded. Maddon's take on the game was that Milwaukee's defense and the wind blowing in (although they hit the ball well) stymied the Cubs. Okay Joe, but with two on and one out in the ninth inning, both Rizzo and Bryant strike out, which doesn't help the cause either. The Cubs have lost four of their last six and are 0 – 10 with runners in scoring position. The only positive I can see at this point is, if the Cubs are going to slump after winning the division it's better that they do it now and get it out of their system before the playoffs begin.

Extra innings:
Hendricks, has really blossomed into a quality pitcher. Last year he was 8 – 7 with an ERA of 3.95. Today his ERA rose to 2.06 as he lost for the first time since July 26 at the White Sox. Hendricks hasn't allowed more than two earned runs in a home start since April 15 against Colorado. Furthermore, in his last 21 starts he has allowed three or fewer earned runs. How's that for some minutia? That's why baseball is still a great game, as you can come up with all kinds of statistics. It's one thing to break down or analyze Hendricks performance, but then one can continue the monologue or dialogue with seemingly endless machinations of the data. We real (or rabid) baseball fans (that my son says need to get a life) love these kind of discussions. It's really sort of a form of self-validation that we are really experts in this child's game that "real man" play.

Today's baseball wisdom:

"The charm of baseball is that, dull as it may be on the field, it is endlessly fascinating as a rehash."
Jim Murray

Football history this date:

1938 – The Chicago Bears beat the Green Bay Packers 2 – 0.*

*(Obviously this is not baseball history this date, but I enjoyed reading the above so much I had to include it here)

A Century-Long Journey to the Day of Redemption

Game: #150

Teams: Cubs/Cincinnati
Date: Monday, September 19
Final: Cubs win 5 – 2
Record: 95 – 55

V – mail: "A good outing by Jason Hammel and three home runs by Russell, Contreras, and Heyward wrapped this one up. Cubs win 5 – 2"

Recap:

Hammel allowed two runs and four hits, his best outing in a month. He had gone 1 – 4 with an ERA of 8.61 in his previous five starts. The Cubs now have four 15 game winning starting pitchers. Even though Hammel is one of the four he may be in "limbo" with the playoffs looming as Lester, Arrieta and Hendricks appear to be "locks" to pitch along with Lackey. The Cubs trailed 2 – 0 going into the seventh and I was thinking they're going to lose their fourth in five games. But then Russell and Contreras homered (Contreras' going completely out of Wrigley) and Fowler later singled to make it 3 – 2. Heyward then hit a two-run shot in the eighth for the final score of 5 – 2. Rondon and Chapman pitched the eighth and ninth, with Rondon giving up two hits and Chapman a walk. They gave up no runs and had three strikeouts between them.

Extra innings:

The Washington Nationals lost, giving the Cubs a seven-game lead over the Nationals for the best record in the National League. The Cubs magic number to secure home field advantage throughout the playoffs is now five. The season has only 12 more games, and the summer has "flown away." Many of the older generations I have known would say that "as one gets older time seems to accelerate." Now I think I understand what they meant.

Today's baseball wisdom:

"Now I know why they boo Richie all the time. When he hits a home run there is no souvenir."*
Willie Stargell

*(Willie commenting on a home run that cleared two decks in Connie Mack Stadium. Allen, a terrific power hitter was also unpopular with the fans)

Baseball history this date:

1947 – Jackie Robinson was named National League "rookie of the year."

Game: #151

Teams: Cubs/Cincinnati
Date: Tuesday, September 20
Final: Cubs win 6 – 1
Record: 96 – 55

V – mail: "The tone was set early in this game when David Ross got a base hit and Jon Lester doubled him home for the first run of the game. After that it was all Lester as he give up one run all night. Cubs win 6 – 1."

Recap:

Jon Lester took another step in his journey that could lead him to the 2016 National League Cy Young award winner. He was again dominant as his scoreless innings streak reached 21 before an RBI triple in the fifth ended the long string of zeros. He is 9 – 0 since the All-Star break, and although I'm probably biased, I think his competition for the award is teammate Kyle Hendricks with an ERA of 2.06. Lester's ERA is 2.36 and as of today, he's leading the league in wins with 18. He's having quite a year.

Rizzo had three RBIs giving him 104 for the year. Bryant is right behind with 97. Addison Russell has an outside chance of reaching 100 RBIs as he has 93 with four games left in the regular schedule.

Extra innings:

Now, with the Cubs an amazing 41 games over .500 and 96 wins, they will match last year's total with a win tomorrow. My conversations with the "voice" are now relaxed and easily stray from the Cubs and baseball in general. The focus of our baseball rehashes now focus on such things as; #1 will they win 100 games? (almost a certainty); #2 who will be the Cubs opponent in the division playoff series? (Cardinals, Mets, or Giants); #3 who will be the starting pitchers for the Cubs, that is in what order? Gene thinks it will be Lester, Hendricks, and Arrieta. I think it's a good guess, but I wonder who will go fourth?

Today's baseball wisdom:

"I couldn't have done it without my players."*
Casey Stengel
*(Casey's comments on winning the 1958 World Series)

Baseball history this date:

1968 – Mickey Mantle hit his final home run, #536, off Jim Lonborg of the Red Sox)

Game: #152

Teams: Cubs/Cincinnati
Date Wednesday, September 21
Final: Cubs win 9 – 2
Record: 97 – 52

V – mail: "Two runs, five hits, one walk, and four strikeouts in seven innings by John Lackey sums up the game as the Cubs offense exploded for nine runs to win their 97th game."

Recap:

Not only did John Lackey have a strong outing to win his 10th game, (the Cubs now have five starting pitchers with double-digit wins) but every starter in the lineup except Lackey had hits. Montero, who's beginning to hit better lately, Baez and Zobrist each had three hits. Bryant hit his 38th home run, the first in September. The score was 3 – 2 in the fourth inning and then the Cubs scored in the fifth, sixth, seventh, and eighth. Maddon, the manager, is a crafty old guy as he used three relievers after Lackey exited in the seventh. He's apparently wanting to get his large group of relievers (there are 11 guys in the bullpen) innings to pitch to keep them sharp. One guy got two outs, another guy got one out, and the last guy got three outs. It's always good when the Cubs win, but it was really kind of a "ho-hum" affair. When Gene reads this he'll say, "what the devil kind of fan are you anyway?"

Extra innings:

Gene called after the game and we only talked baseball briefly. Somehow we got on the subject of old movies. I had watched "It's A Mad Mad Mad World" which is one of my favorite movies. Johnny Winters, another of my all time favorites, has a scene where he wrecks a gas station. The two garage owners are played by Arnold Stang and Marvin Kaplan, who recently passed away at the age of 89. Gene recalled that Kaplan had played an aspiring poet on the 1952 – 56 TV sitcom "Meet Millie." His name on that show was Alfred Prinzmetal. He was Millie's (played by Elena Verdugo) next door neighbor and would frequently drop in unannounced to recite some new verse he had composed. It was usually pretty bad and if Millie and her mother didn't act or show appropriate enthusiasm, he would immediately frown, start to pout, do an about-face and storm out of the apartment shouting "you hate me" as he slammed the door. I used to watch the show all the time just to see Alfred "blow his cool." I guess Gene and I needed a change of pace in our discussions as we had had enough talk about baseball.

Today's baseball wisdom:

"We have deep depth."*
Yogi bear
*(As the Cubs have a large number of relief pitchers, I recalled this gem by Berra)

Baseball history this date:

1981 – Steve Carlton strikes out a National League record 3118th batter. (Andre Dawson of the Cubs)

Game: #153

Teams: Cubs/St. Louis
Date: Friday, September 23
Final: Cubs win 5 – 0
Record: 98 – 55

V – mail: "The Cubs struck quick in this one scoring four runs in the first inning and ended up winning over the Cardinals 5 – 0. Jake was great at this one as he shut them out through seven innings allowing zero runs, five hits, one walk, and 10 strikeouts. It was also the return of Strop off the disabled list."

Recap:
Arrieta was dominant and Maddon commented that he looked "familiar" when he struck out the side in the first inning on only 11 pitches. Strop, Edwards, and Wood finished the shutout. Rizzo had three hits, Zobrist had two RBIs and Coghlan one. The Cardinals, uncharacteristically, had a number of gaffes in the game. Leake, the pitcher, allowed a run on two wild pitches, Wong at second base, fell flat on his face chasing Rizzo's double and Matt Adams got picked off first base in the fourth inning by "Miggy" Montero. Ha!

Extra innings:
The Cubs won their 98 game, the most since they played in the 1945 World Series. Here's a bit of trivia. Jake Arrieta and the Cardinals Matt Carpenter were college teammates at TCU. Arrieta was Carpenter's wedding groomsman, yet Carpenter can't solve his friend's pitching. He went 0 – 3 with two strikeouts leaving him with 0 – 24 in the regular season against Arrieta. Gosh Jake that's not very nice to treat the guy you stood up for at his wedding!

Today's baseball wisdom:

"Barry bonds? I'll tell you what, if he hit a home run off Bob Gibson (or Don Drysdale) and stood and admired it, they would knock that earring out of his ear the next time up."*
Doug Harvey
*(National League umpire Doug Harvey commenting on Bob Gibson)

Baseball history this date:

1935 The Chicago Cubs win their 21st consecutive game to clinch the National League pennant.

Game: #154

Teams: Cubs/St. Louis
Date: Saturday, September 24
Final: Cubs lose 10 –4
Record: 98 – 56

V – mail: "Turn about is fair play as the Cardinals jumped on the Cubs with four runs in the first inning and won 10 – 4."

Recap:
Well, the "voice" is a whole lot more charitable than I am when it comes to those despicable St. Louis "Peckers." (Oh sorry, I meant to say red birds!) It is apparent that I don't like them, and I don't want to see them the playoffs, they're just too damn lucky, or is it good. In any event, it was "bombs away" beginning in the first inning. Hammel got the first two guys out, then a base on ball, a hit, hit batsman, a double, and the Cardinals have three runs. Then another single and it's 4 – 0. The Cubs did get two runs in the first inning but could never catch up. Rondon got banged around in a seventh inning for three runs. Hammel likely lost (or really damaged) his chances for a starting spot in the playoff rotation. At 15 – 10, he's had a pretty good year, but his ERA has risen to 3.83, having "blown up" to 8.71 in September. I hope the "bird legs," sorry I mean the red birds, got their hitting out of their systems as they face Lester tomorrow.

Extra innings:
I will admit to being pretty negative when it comes to the Cardinals. But if I'm honest, the real issue is, shall I say, "they scare the holy B – Jesus out of me." They have a really good organization and a long history and tradition of winning. They also remind me of the football Green Bay Packers(were they named for sausage packers) as one of the luckiest teams in baseball. I mean both the Cardinals and the Packers; they are really lucky. I have said this before, according to Lily Tomlin, "and that's the truth!"

Today's baseball wisdom:

"You want proof that baseball players are smarter than football players? How often do you see a baseball team penalized for having too many men on the field?"
Jim Bouton

Baseball history this date:

1957 – The Brooklyn Dodgers played their last game in Ebbets Field, and defeat the Pirates 2 – 0.

Game: #155

Teams: Cubs/St. Louis
Date: Sunday, September 25
Final: Cubs win 3 – 1
Record: 99 – 56

V – mail: "It was Jon Lester and David Ross night as they were both above everybody else this evening. Jon was great again as he gave up no runs, two hits, one walk and had eight strikeouts in 6 2/3 innings. David received a standing ovation every time he came up in the game, as it was his last regular-season game at Wrigley. He responded with a home run putting the Cubs up 1 – 0. The Cubs ended up winning 3 – 1 giving them 57 home victories this year, and a winning edge over the Cardinals."

Recap:
The v-mail from Gene pretty well sums up the game. The Cardinals did not go away easy as they had men on base, once with two on and no outs in the sixth and didn't score, two on in the seventh and didn't score, but two hits and a walk in the eighth got them one run. They also had a one-out double in the second. They are a bunch of "pesky polecats" and frankly, as I said before, I hope they don't make the playoffs.

Extra innings:
It was quite an emotional night at Wrigley Field with David Ross's (affectionately known as "Gramps") last home game. When Gene called after the game he began with "wow what a storybook ending for Ross this night." When Maddon came out in the seventh, Ross thought it was to lift Lester, but Lester and Maddon had a different plan. Ross started to protest Maddon lifting Lester, but Maddon asked him "have you ever been a part of the game where the catcher gets taken out of the game before that pitcher?" With a look of disbelief (Ross) slammed his mask back on muttering, "I love you guys, I love you guys." It was really a class move by Maddon. Later the camera swung into the Cubs dugout showing Ross unable to keep from shedding a few tears. Ross later said, "it was an amazing night."

Today's baseball wisdom:

"Age is a case of mind over matter. If you don't mind, it don't matter."
Satchel Paige

Baseball history this date:

1908 – the Cubs Ed Reuibach becomes the only pitcher to throw a doubleheader shutout beating Brooklyn 5 – 0 and 3 – 0.

Game: #156

Teams: Cubs @ Pittsburgh
Date Monday, September 26
Final: Cubs win 12 – 2
Record: 100 – 56

V – mail: "Kyle Hendricks did it again; six innings, no runs, seven hits, no walks and five strikeouts to lower his ERA to 1.99. Baez hit a grand slam and Bryant a two-run homer to help the Cubs win their 100th ballgame of the season, 12 – 2 over Pittsburgh. Lackey will pitch today."
(recall that Gene's v-mails always come the morning after the game)

Recap:
The Cubs have now won 100 games for the first time since 1935. As the "voice" stated, Hendricks was again outstanding, with his ERA dropping below 2.00. In his call after the game, that was the first statistic Gene mentioned. As anyone who will read this document knows by now, Gene is a great fan of Hendricks, as well he should be of this great young talent. The Cubs offense really unloaded against the Pirates with Baez driving in six runs; Bryant hit a two-run homer, Almora Jr. had three hits, and the team got a total of 18 hits. The score was 5 – 0 going into the sixth and the Cubs scored six more to put it away.

Extra innings:
Hooray, the Cardinals "cooperated" by getting blown out (at home) by Cincinnati, 15 – 2. It was a good day all around as Marlys' Diamondbacks also blasted the Nationals 14 – 4. They (D – backs) have plenty of punch in their lineup, but their pitching, especially the starters have not been consistent and their relief pitching is an abomination! Old Tony La Russa (ex-Cardinal manager), now with the Diamondbacks, better get his "S – – –") together and get some pitching or he'll be job hunting very shortly.

Today's baseball wisdom:

"Anybody's who's ever had the privilege of seeing me play knows that I am the greatest pitcher in the world."
Dizzy Dean

Baseball history this date:

1960 – Roger Maris hit home run #60 tying Babe Ruth for the most home runs in a season.*
*(He hit it off Jack Fisher)

A Century-Long Journey to the Day of Redemption

Game: #157

Teams: Cubs @ Pittsburgh
Date: Tuesday, September 27
Final: Cubs win 6 – 4
Record: 101 – 56

V – mail: "A really long unexciting game as the Cubs won out over Pittsburgh 6 – 4. John Lackey got his 11th win and the Cubs won their 101st game of the year."

Recap:
Lackey went five innings giving up five hits, one run, three bases on balls and he had three strikeouts. He finished his 14th season in the major leagues with an 11 – 8 record and a 3.35 ERA. He has pitched well since a stint on the disabled list to rest his right shoulder. He is 2 – 1 with a 3.00 ERA since coming off the disabled list earlier this month. Maddon said the rest was good for him and he will go into the postseason well rested. Wood, Cahill, Montgomery, and Edwards pitched well into the ninth. Then enter Justin Grimm, and things got "grim" as he got smacked around for three hits, two walks and three runs. Pena came in and walked a guy, but got the last two outs, with the bases loaded, to salvage the game. Per the v-mail, "the voice" didn't particularly enjoy the game. In fact after the game was over and the phone rang he started ragging about the game being four hours long, with much of the time doing everything but playing baseball.

Extra innings:
The Cardinals and Giants both won, so the race for the second wild-card spot is going to go down to the wire. I really have mixed feelings about who I would like to see win the second wild-card. Sometimes I think the Cubs could beat the Giants easier then again I'm not sure. I'll just have to wait and see who wins and believe the Cubs can beat either of them.

Today's baseball wisdom:

"On hearing that Reggie Jackson was reported to have an IQ of 165, Yankee teammate Mickey Rivers replied, "out of what – – – a 1000?"
Mickey Rivers

Baseball history this date:

1881 – The Cubs beat Troy before a record small "crowd" of 12.

Game: #158

Teams: Cubs @ Pittsburgh
Date: Wednesday, September 28
Final: Cubs lose 8 – 4
Record: 101 – 57

V – mail: "Jake did not have it in this one as Pittsburgh hit him hard and went on to win 8 – 4."

Recap:

Wow, this game is worrisome for me as Arrieta was excellent at the start, but once again he lost it and he got "bombed." I hope he gets it figured out before the playoffs. He went only five innings and gave up 10 hits, two bases on balls and allow seven earned runs. His earned run average is now 3.00, which is good, but the second half of the season, he has done a 180 about face over last year's second-half when he was almost unhittable. He began this year continuing his dominance of last year, including another no-hitter, but then began to struggle at times. When he was with Baltimore he had terrific "stuff", but had control problems. Then with the trade to the Cubs he blossomed. Odd, how a pitcher can be so overpowering and then it leaves them. I wonder if it's a matter of mechanics or is it mental. Small changes can make a huge difference, like the case of Dizzy Dean, who took a line drive off his foot in the 1937 All-Star game. Told that his big toe was fractured, Dean replied, "fractured Hell, the damn things broken." He came back too soon, changed his pitching motion to avoid landing hard on the toe. The change was enough to affect his mechanics and he lost his great fastball.

Extra innings:

A .260 hitter, John Jaso, hit for the cycle for the Pirates; that is a single, double, triple, and home run. He was the first player to hit for the cycle in the 16 year history of PNC Financial Services Park.

Today's baseball wisdom:

"I made a game effort to argue, but two things were against me; the umpires and the rules."
Leo Durocher

Baseball history this date:

1960 – Ted Williams hits his final home run, # 521 off Jack Fisher.

Game: #159

Teams: Cubs @ Pittsburgh
Date: Thursday, September 29
Final Cubs/Pittsburgh – tie – 1 – 1
Record: 101 – 57 – 1

V – mail: "Rookie Pitcher "2" was good as he did not give up an earned run in 3 2/3 innings. Travis Wood did not give up any runs either. Then the rain came. Game ended 1 – 1 all tied in the fifth. On to Cincy."

Recap:
The game was called in the top of the sixth after a rain delay of one hour and 23 minutes. The tie was the first in the majors since 2005 (Houston and Cincinnati). As the game has no effect on the playoffs and the two teams are not scheduled to play again, the statistics and the game count, that is it's not listed as suspended. The Cubs rookie Rob Zastryzny pitched in his first major league start and did a credible job

Extra innings:
Are the St. Louis Cardinals a bunch of lucky "A – holes?" They won 4 – 3 in the bottom of the ninth on a double that bounced into the stands, which meant the winning run had to stop at third. However Cincinnati didn't ask for a review of the call "quick enough" and the umpires charged off the field. So the game is over and everyone knew that Cincinnati got "hosed." What a screw job, especially that eventually it could mean the Cardinals get into the playoffs. How many games back was I ranting about how lucky the Cardinals and the Packers are? This game, the outcome, was unbelievable, given the fact that potentially it would let the Cardinals into the playoffs. Boy, talk about paranoia, I sat there wondering how much the umpires got paid for arguably one of the most egregious, asinine, unconscionable, ridiculous, decisions I have ever witnessed. In my state of paranoia I conclude that Major League baseball wanted the Cardinals in the playoffs because of money, as they could foresee a Cub/Cardinal battle.

I think I need to see a psychiatrist!

Today's baseball wisdom:

"If you don't know how to cheat, start now."*
Earl Weaver
*(Speaking to pitcher Ross Grimsley who was on the mound)

Baseball history this date:

2005 – The Chicago White Sox clinch their first division title since 2000 and become just the 10th team in the history of baseball to be in first place every day of the season.

Game: #160

Teams: Cubs @ Cincinnati
Date: Friday, September 30
Final: Cubs win 7 – 3
Record: 102 – 57 – 1

V – mail: "Jake Buchanan proved to be a worthy fill-in as he threw five innings of shutout baseball. Final was Cubs 7, Reds 3."

Recap:
It's tough to get excited about Cub games these last few days as the division had been wrapped up for some time. Also they have clinched home field advantage for the playoffs with the best record in baseball. The "voice" was a bit subdued in his mandatory phone call (after a Cub win), but he did point out that Buchanan pitched very well in his first start since 2014 with Houston, as he allowed only two hits.

Ben Zobrist, "Might he rounding into postseason form", so said the Associated Press recap of the game, as he had two home runs and three runs batted in. He is 11 – 22 with eight RBIs in his last seven games. He stated that he is feeling more rested than he felt in June, July, and August. He also added, "hopefully that translates into October."

Extra innings:
The final wild-card slot in the National League, either the Giants or the Cardinals is about the only interesting thing happening at this point. Both the Giants and Cardinals won last night, and I'm writing this with the Giants holding a one-game lead over the Cardinals. Let's hope the red birds "lay an egg" tonight and the Giants win. If that happens the Cardinals will be singing the "St. Louis Blues." Then I'll have to decide what kind of alcoholic toast I should have. Ha!

Today's baseball wisdom:
"Hell, I could have hit .600 myself, but I was paid to hit home runs." Babe Ruth to Ty Cobb

Baseball history this date:
1927 – Babe Ruth hits his record setting 60th home run (off Tom Zachary)

Game: #161

Date: Saturday, October 1
Teams: Cubs @ Cincinnati
Final: Cubs lose 7 – 4
Record: 102 – 58 – 1

V – mail: "Jon Lester was not on his game as the Reds powered over him 7 – 4."

Recap:
With an uncharacteristic poor performance, Lester let his chance for a 20 win season get away. It was the first time since mid-July that he has struggled. He had not allowed five runs since July 9, almost 2 months back. In fact, since the All-Star break he had won 10 straight decisions. In September he allowed only two runs (that's total) in winning five games. Later Lester said he was probably rushing his delivery and that he was more "bummed" about that than not getting his 20th win. Notwithstanding this glitch in this performance, Lester is likely the starting pitcher for the first playoff game.

Extra innings:
Interestingly, the overwhelming majority of the 30,970 fans in attendance for the game, were wearing blue for the Cubs, and cheering for Lester, even though the game was at Cincinnati's home-field. The only other news of note, in my opinion, was that Ben Zobrist hit his third home run in the last two games.

Today's baseball wisdom:

"It took me 17 years to get 3000 hits in baseball. It took me one afternoon on the golf course."
Hank Aaron

Baseball history this date:

1938 – The Chicago Cubs clinch the National League pennant.

A Century-Long Journey to the Day of Redemption

Game: #162

Date: Sunday, October 2
Teams: Cubs @ Cincinnati's
Final: Cubs win 7 – 4
Record: 103 – 58 – 1 (End of the regular season and the Cubs are Central division champions)

V – mail: "Kyle Hendricks was not good today, but he was not bad either. He gave up four runs in five innings but ended up not losing the game. The Cubs decided that they wanted to win this one and not give him the loss. With two out and nobody on base, they managed to score 4 runs and win the game 7 – 4. Justin Grimm threw one pitch and won the game. A great way to end the regular season.. Now it's time for some serious baseball."

Recap:
That v-mail was probably one of the longest that the "voice" sent all year. He called after the game and was "ticked off" that the umpire called two balls, that he thought should have been called strikes. The result was a walk that forced in a run, and then a two-run two-out single that cost Hendricks three runs. "Boy I was really irritated with the umpire; Kendrick should have been out of the inning with no runs against him! He still won the ERA title, (2.13) but if he had only been charged with one earned run he would have finished the season with an ERA below 2.00.

Extra innings:
As I have noted repeatedly in this journal, can there be any doubt about who is Gene's favorite Cub pitcher? More likely, Hendricks, is his favorite Cub player. Reading his v-mail I had to chuckle to myself as an image of an "old mother hen" protecting her chicks flashed through my mind. Ha! I do have to agree that Hendricks has really been underappreciated by the media and sports analysts, in addition to the Cubs never getting him any runs. But, never fear, the "voice" remains as Mr. Hendricks advocate and "ad man." Hendricks may in fact become the next Greg Maddux.

Today's baseball wisdom:

"The way I figured it, I was even with baseball and baseball with me. The game had done much for me and I had done much for it."
Jackie Robinson

Baseball history this date:

1968 – Bob Gibson of the St. Louis Cardinals sets a World Series record of 17 strikeouts against the Detroit Tigers. It broke Sandy Koufax's record of 15 strikeouts against the Yankees in 1963.

A Century-Long Journey to the Day of Redemption

Game: #163

Game: #1 – NLDS
Date: Friday, October 7
Teams: Cubs/Giants
Final: Cubs win 1 – 0
Record: 104 – 58 – 1
NLDS record: 1 – 0

V – mail: "And so it begins. What a game as both teams had excellent pitching. Both pitchers threw eight innings. Baez's home run in the bottom of the eighth was the winner with Chapman closing it out for a 1 – 0 victory."

Recap:

Jon Lester outpitched Johnny Cueto (sort of) giving up no runs and only six hits in eight innings. Cueto allowed only three hits in eight innings, but gave up a solo home run to Baez in the eighth inning, that landed in the left-field basket attached to the wall. In other words, it barely went out. Chapman, in relief, did give up a two-out double to Buster Posey, (who is now 6 – 11 against Chapman) but Baez made a sparkling play at second to throw out Hunter Pence. Both teams played excellent defense, and the Giants second baseman, Tomlinson saved a run for San Francisco with a terrific stop on a ground ball headed to right field by Ben Zobrist.

Extra innings:

Wrigley Field had a great crowd of 42,000+ including celebrities like Mike Ditka, Butler and Wade of the Chicago Bulls, Blackhawk defense man Brent Seabrook, and who else but Bill Murray wearing a shirt that read "I ain't afraid of no goat."

Today's baseball wisdom:

"Whenever I hit a home run I had a habit of running the bases with my head down. I figured the pitcher already felt bad enough without me showing him up rounding the bases."
Mickey Mantle

Baseball history this date:

1882 – In the first World Series, game two, the Chicago White Stockings of the National League, beat the Cincinnati Red Stockings of the American Association 2 – 0.

Game: #164

Game: #2 – NLDS
Date: Saturday, October 8
Teams: Cubs/Giants
Final: Cubs win 5 – 2
Record: 105– 58 – 1
NLDS record: 2 – 0

V – mail: "I finally got to watch the second game yesterday. Great pitching and hitting by the Cub pitchers as they drove in three of the five runs in a 5 – 2 victory. Kyle Hendricks was knocked out of the game by a line drive that hit him in his throwing arm. Cubs go up two games in the playoffs. Need nine more wins to keep us fans happy," *

*(Gene sent his v-mail on 10/10 as he had taped the second game)

Recap:
Travis Wood took over for Hendricks in the top of the fourth after he got hit on the forearm of his right arm. Wood retired the only man he faced and then in the bottom of the fourth he smacked a ball halfway up into the left field bleachers. The only other relief pitcher to homer in the postseason was the New York Giants reliever Rosy Ryan in game three of the 1924 World Series. Wood pitched a hitless fifth and four more relievers completed the game. They were Carl Edwards, Mike Montgomery, Hector Rondon, and Aroldis Chapman; they gave up a total of six hits and no runs in 5 2/3 innings. Earlier Hendricks had a two-run single, and with Wood's homer, the pitchers drove in three of the five runs. There was no scoring in the game after the fourth inning.

Extra innings:
Former great Cub reliever Lee Smith threw out the ceremonial first pitch. My father, Dale, always liked Lee as a reliever. He admired his slow almost nonchalant way he trudged to the mound to pitch. When he saved a game my dad would remark," by golly he did it again." Bill Murray was again in the audience, not wearing his, "I ain't afraid of no goat" shirt, but was animated and goofy as always.

Today's baseball wisdom:

"Casey knew baseball. He only made it look like he was fooling around. He knew every move that was ever invented and some we haven't caught on to yet."
Sparky Anderson*

*(Speaking of Casey Stengel)

Baseball history this date:

1909 – The Chicago Cubs beat the New York Giants 4 – 2 in a playoff to win the National League pennant.

Game: #165

Game: #3 – NLDS
Date: Monday, October 10
Teams: Cubs @ Giants
Final: Cubs lose 6 – 5 (13 innings)
Record: 105 – 59 – 1
NLDS record: 2 – 1

V – mail: "It took over five hours and 13 innings to beat the Cubs 6 – 5. My personal feeling is that Joe made a mistake in the eighth inning as he went for a victory right there. I think he should have allowed the former (Rondon vs Chapman) to stay in the game. I am not second-guessing, I said it out loud when he did it. Sorry no witnesses. I just hope the move does not hurt the team in the remaining games."

Recap:
Really a tough loss. Arrieta hits a three-run homer off Bumgarner in the second, but the Cubs blow several chances to score and the Giants get to 3 – 2 in the eighth inning. In the bottom of the eighth Wood gives up a hit so Maddon takes him out and brings in Rondon who walks a guy. Then Maddon brings in Chapman who strikes out Hunter Pence but then gives up a two-run triple to Gillespie and the Giants lead 4 – 3. Another single makes the score 5 – 3. In the ninth-inning Bryant hits a two-run homer to tie the game at 5. In the 13th inning Crawford and Panik both double and the Cubs lose 6 – 5.

Extra innings:
When the Cubs did not add on runs when they had three or four chances, I started "crying the blues," saying" they're going to lose, they're going to lose, and if they lose tomorrow, the playoffs will be tied two games apiece." My concern was that the series would then go back to Chicago and they would have to face Johnny Cueto. I wasn't sure they could beat him a second time. So now I'm in a snit and what does my family (Marlys and Matt) do? Rather than empathize with me they said" get a life it's only a game!"

Chapman had only given up 10 doubles to a left-handed hitter in his career, and this was the first triple off of him in his career. In his six-year career in the majors (383 games and 377 innings or 42 nine inning games) he also had never given up consecutive doubles to left-handed hitters. Ah yes, baseball statistics, there are millions of firsts, that is it never happened before! Don't we all love them?

Today's baseball wisdom:

#1) "There are lies, damned lies, and statistics."
Mark Twain
#2) "Statistics are to baseball what a flaky crust is to mom's apple pie."
Harry Reasoner

Baseball history this date:

1920 – The Cleveland Indian's Bill Wambsganss makes the only unassisted triple play in World Series history.

Game: #166

Game: #4 – NLDS
Date: Tuesday, October 11
Teams: Cubs @ Giants
Final: Cubs win 6 – 5
Record: 106 – 59 – 1
NLDS record: 3 – 1 (Cubs win NLDS)

V – mail: "I believe in all the years I have watched baseball this was the first time the Cubs gave me such a thrill in winning. For cub fans this game could only be beaten with a World Series win. The Giants pitcher had only given up two hits in eight innings yet he was taken out of the game. What a mistake, as I am sure the Giant fans are ready to fire the manager. The Cubs score 4 runs in the top of the ninth to win the game as Chapman struck out all three batters in the bottom of the ninth. Wow!!!!!!!!!!! Cubs win!!!!!!!!!!"

Recap:

The v-mail says it all, and every one of those exclamation points were there! The Giants pitcher, Matt Moore, had held the Cubs to two hits, with 10 strikeouts, and the Giants manager elected to take him out of the game in the ninth with the Cubs trailing 5 – 2. Then the roof fell in or maybe lightning struck. Law was pitching for the Giants and Bryant singled; Lopez relieves law and Rizzo walks; Romo relieves Lopez and Zobrist doubles in a run, to make the score 5 – 3; Coghlan hits for Russell; Smith relieves Romo; Contreras hits for Coghlan and singles to score Rizzo and Zobrist to tie the game at 5; Heyward fails to bunt and Contreras is out at second, but a wild throw sends him to second; Strickland relieves Smith; Baez singles to center and it's 6 – 5 Cubs! Ross hits into a double play. In the bottom of the ninth Chapman comes in for Rondon and Hernandez, Spahn, and Belt all strike out swinging. The Cubs win the NLDS and move on to the National League championship series.

Extra innings:

I must to admit to being "Chicken" as I turned the game off in the sixth or seventh inning figuring the game is over. I thought, now we have to go back to Chicago and face that weird, but very good pitcher, Johnny Cueto, who is likely to beat the Cubs. I turned on the computer to see the final score, as I couldn't bear to see it on TV after a loss, and holy cow it's in the bottom of the ninth and the Cubs are leading 6 – 5. I couldn't believe it! Then the phone rang, it was the "voice" who was ecstatic to say the least. ESPN called the ninth inning, "A Ferocious Rally by the Cubs."

Today's baseball wisdom:

"It's hard to beat a person who never gives up."
Babe Ruth

Baseball history this date:

1911 – Ty Cobb, American League, and Frank Schulte, National League, are the first MVP's in their leagues and each get an automobile.

Game: #167

Game: #1 – NLCS
Date: Saturday, October 15
Teams: Cubs/Dodgers
Final: Cubs win 8 – 4
Record: 107 – 59 – 1
NLCS record: 1 – 0

V – mail: "I hope the excitement continues. These late innings heroics are hard on the old heart. Again I believe the opposing manager made a mistake by walking Coghlan to get to Miguel. He made them pay with the grand slam. Great start as the Cubs win over the Dodgers 8 – 4."

Recap:

Miguel Montero blasted a pinch-hit home run with two outs in the bottom of the eighth inning to break a 3 – 3 tie. Then Fowler followed with a solo shot for the final score of 8 – 4. Jon Lester pitched six effective innings giving up only a home run to pinch-hitter Andre Either in the fifth inning. Wood, Edwards, and Montgomery blanked the Dodgers in the seventh. Strop entered in the eighth and gave up a single, a walk, and other infield single, to load the bases with no outs. He was relieved by Chapman who struck out two, but Gonzalez singled to tie the score at 3. In the bottom of the eighth Montero homered with a bases-loaded followed by Fowler's solo shot. Rondon closed out the game in the ninth.

Extra innings:

Javier Baez has been the bright spot for the Cubs in the post season. He was 2 – 4 with an RBI double in the second, then when Lester failed to get a bunt down (with Baez on third) he broke towards the plate and the dodger catcher threw to third; Baez continued on and stole home. He joined Jimmy Slagle as the second Cub to steal home in the postseason as Slagle did it in game #4 of the 1907 World Series. Montero's drive was the first go ahead grand slam by pinch-hitter in postseason history.

Today's baseball wisdom:

"The game of baseball is better when the Dodgers are playing well; just like when the Yankees are playing well, or the Cubs, the Phillies, the big-name teams."
Pete Rose

A Century-Long Journey to the Day of Redemption

Baseball history this date:

1969 – Baltimore Orioles manager Earl Weaver becomes the first manager ejected in a World Series.

Game: #168

Game: #2 – NLCS
Date: Sunday, October 16
Teams: Cubs/Dodgers
Final: Cubs lose 1 – 0
Record: 107– 60 – 1
NLCS record: 1 – 1

V – mail: "If you like pitching then this was your game. A total of five hits in the whole game with the Dodgers scoring the only run via a home run. Baseball as it was meant to be played. Just too bad the Cubs lost 1 – 0."

Recap:
The game can be summarized as follows; 1) too much Kershaw 2), one bad pitch to Adrian Gonzalez, and 3) what happened to the Cubs hitting? Clayton Kershaw gave up only two hits in seven innings, and Gonzalez hit a two-out home run in the first off Hendricks. In general the Cubs were pretty bad at the plate today. Rizzo, now 1 – 24, had a long drive to right that went foul, and Baez hit one to deep dead center with a man on in the seventh, but it was also caught. Had he pulled it to left it would have gone out. Baez and Contreras had back-to-back singles in the fifth, but old unreliable Heyward popped out. In my view he has been a real liability in the lineup for the entire year. Pitching was also excellent for the Cubs as Hendricks went 5 2/3 innings allowing one run; then Edwards, Montgomery, Strop, and Chapman threw 3 2/3 innings allowing no runs.

Extra innings:
Arrieta goes next Tuesday and I hope he has a good game. What a difference a year can make as he was almost untouchable last year at the All-Star break and started out the first half of this year pitching really well, including a no-hitter. But the last half of this year he has been "up and down" and his pitching as the third starter will be critical if they hope to win it all.

Today's baseball wisdom:

"I knew Sandy Koufax's weakness. He couldn't hit."
Whitey Ford

Baseball history this date:

1969 – The 100 – 1 shot New York Mets beat the Baltimore Orioles 5 – 3 and win the 66th World Series in five games.

Game: #169

Game: #3 – NLCS
Teams: Cubs @ Dodgers
Final: Cubs lose 6 – 0
Record: 107 – 61 – 1
NLCS record: 1 – 2

V – mail: "The last two games have seemed strangely familiar; let's hope not. It will be a test on the old guys these next two days, however if the Cubs don't hit, what difference does it make?"

Recap:
From the 1962 film, Music Man, we heard the song lyrics sung by Robert Preston,"Ya Trouble right here in River city, and that's trouble with a capital T and that rhymes with P and that stands for pool." Well in this case it's not River city, it's Chicago city and the T that rhymes with P stands for pitching not pool! Once again the Dodger starting pitcher, Rich Hill, (originally a Cub) pitched six scoreless innings allowing two hits, no walks and he had six strikeouts. Dodger pitching has been good, maybe outstanding, or has it been a matter of the Cubs offense being abysmal. They have been shut out in the last two games and outside of Montero's heroics in game one they're hitting has been pretty awful the entire series. The Cubs were shutout consecutive games for the first time since May 2014, getting just six hits, five of them singles. The 18 straight scoreless innings are the longest in their post season history. Against left-handed pitching the Cubs are hitting .152 in the post season and .106 in the NLCS. The number three, four, and five Cub hitters are 2 – 32 in three games with 0 RBIs. Individually Rizzo and Russell are 3 – 50; Russell 1 – 24 and Rizzo 2 – 26. Of course "old reliable" Heyward is 2 – 19, which I suppose is to be expected. I can't think of anything worse to say!

Extra innings:
I wrote this game up on 10/19 and today is game number four with the Dodgers pitching 20-year-old Julio Urias. He is a lefty from Mexico and is the youngest starting pitcher in postseason history. I'd submit to all of us Cub loyalists, that for any chance to win the NLCS (and get back to Wrigley) they have to win today.

Today's baseball wisdom:

"Hitting is timing. Pitching is upsetting timing."
Warren Spahn

Baseball history this date:

1950 – Connie Mack retires as manager of the Philadelphia Athletics after 50 years; the longest serving manager in baseball history.

Game:# 170

Game: #4 – NCLS
Date: Wednesday, October 19
Teams: Cubs @ Dodgers
Final: Cubs win 10 – 2
Record: 108 – 61 – 1
NLCS record: 2 – 2

V – mail: "How does one write a book when he is not watching the game? Finally, a game you could relax while viewing. Home runs by Russell and Rizzo took us to a 10 – 2, victory. Cub relievers were strong again."

Recap:
When Gene called after the Cubs win, I had to admit that I didn't turn the game on until the top of the sixth. I first looked at the score on the computer and the Cubs were ahead 6 – 2, and before I got to the television it was 10 – 2. I'm just "chicken-hearted" as after two straight shutouts and Rizzo and company essentially hitting zilch, I just couldn't watch. So today the North Siders get 13 hits, Rizzo is 3 – 5 with three RBIs and a home run. Russell is also 3 – 5 with three RBIs and a two-run homer. Fowler and Zobrist each had two hits. Lackey went four innings giving up three hits and two earned runs. Then Montgomery, Wood, Strop and Rondon shut the Dodger "Blue" out for the last five innings. The series is now tied at two games apiece.

Extra innings:
Now the series will return to Chicago even if Cubs lose tomorrow. I'm still a "wreck" as if they lose they are down 2 – 3 and will face Kershaw in Chicago for game #6. Even if they win tomorrow and go up 3 – 2 it's still Kershaw and Hill for games six and seven if necessary. I still have vivid memories of 2003, and sometimes I probably have nightmares. In 2003 the Cubs are up 3 games to 2 going back to Chicago with Kerry Wood and Mark prior, their one-two punch, to close it out. In game #6, the Cubs were leading 3 – 0 in the eighth inning. Alou goes for a foul ball down the left-field line and several fans reach for the ball and a guy named Steve Bartman apparently deflects what the Cubs thought would be out number two. I'm still not convinced that Alou would have made the catch. Poor Steve Bartman was maligned by the Cubs, the fans, the announcers, everyone. But the real key to the loss, that no one will talk about, was Alex Gonzalez, the Cub shortstop booting a ground ball with one out that would have ended the inning with the score 3 – 1 Cubs. After the error, the Marlins exploded scoring eight runs. If González turns the double play the Cubs only need three outs in the ninth

to go to the series. In the seventh game the Cubs led 5 – 3 heading into the fifth but they fell apart and lost 9 – 6.

Today's baseball wisdom:

"The greatest accomplishment is not in never failing, but in rising again after the fall."
Vince Lombardi"

Baseball history this date:

1919 – The Cincinnati Reds beat the Chicago White Sox 5 games to 3 to win the 16th World Series, known as the" Black Sox Scandal" because eight White Sox players threw the series.

Game: #171

Game: #5 – NLCS
Date: Thursday, October 20
Teams: Cubs @ Dodgers
Final: Cubs win 8 – 4
Record: 109 – 61 – 1
NLCS record: 3 – 2

V – mail: "The last two games the Cubs are starting to look like the team we have been watching all year. Great pitching by Jon Lester, hitting by Russell and Baez and defense by Baez helped the Cubs win this one 8 – 4."

Recap:
The Associated Press began their recap with "One win away, two chances at home, seven decades of waiting." Of course they also hearkened back to 2003 detailing what they termed, "one of its most excruciating failures." However, the hitting has returned and once again Jon Lester was excellent, going seven innings, allowing five hits and one earned run. Strop and Chapman finished, both a bit shaky, as Strop allowed two hits and a run, and Chapman two hits, a walk and two runs for the final 8 – 4. The Cubs led only 3 – 1 in the seventh, when Adrian Gonzalez bunted, and Baez playing a very deep second base stormed in and made a sensational pickup and throw for the first out. Two batters later Pederson singled to right and without Baez's brilliant play there are two on and only one out. The Cubs scored five in the eighth to "put it away" with a score of 8 – 1. As always, there were multiple heroes for the Cubs; Russell had two hits including a two-run homer, and Rizzo, Fowler, and Bryant each had two hits.

Extra innings:
Now it's back to Chicago with Kershaw for the Dodgers and Hendricks for the Cubs. I thought a lot about the game, and frankly I have concluded that the Cubs can and will in fact beat Kershaw. Despite all the "hype" by the so-called baseball experts, I think they sell Hendricks short. He's really a tough very smart pitcher, and I am going to watch the entire game, as I'm confident the Cubs will win. No more "wimpy" behavior on my part.

Today's baseball wisdom:

"If you ask me anything I don't know, I'm not going to answer."
Yogi Berra

Baseball history this date:

1924 – The first Negro League World Series was held this date. The Kansas City Monarchs, of the Negro National League shut out the Hilldales 5 – 0, of the Eastern Colored League in game #10 to win the series 5 – 4 – 1. The Hilldales club from Darby, Pennsylvania were previously known as the Darby Daisies.

Game: #172

Game: #6 – NLCS
Date Saturday, October 22
Teams: Cubs/Dodgers
Final: Cubs win 5 – 0
Record: 110 – 61 – 1
NLCS record: 4 – 2 – "ON TO THE WORLD SERIES!"

V – mail: "Kyle, Kyle, Kyle! It was all about Kyle in this game as he gave up two hits in 7 1/3 innings to help the Cubs finally win the pennant after 71 years of being a loser.. Between Hendricks and Chapman the Cubs only faced 27 Dodger batters. Lots of wild and happy fans in Chicago to help celebrate the 5 – 0 victory. On to Cleveland to go for it all. The Cubs activated Kyle Schwarber and he is playing in the Arizona fall league on Saturday as they are trying to win it all."

Recap:
Yes on to the World Series! The "voice" called after the game and was ecstatic as was I. We didn't talk for very long as Gene wanted to hear all the interviews with the players, managers, and anyone else who had something to say. He did call the next day, Sunday, and we talked for 30 – 45 minutes just reveling in the Cubs victory. We both concluded that win or lose in the series it's been a great year. Hendricks was amazing. The Dodgers got a lead off single, but a terrific double-play Baez to Rizzo ended the inning. The Cubs got two runs in the first on a double by Fowler, single by Bryant for one run, and then the Dodgers center fielder dropped a fly ball by Rizzo which led to a sacrifice fly and a 2 – 0 lead.

Baez made an error in the second but Hendricks picked the guy off first. It was an omen, as two big mistakes by the Dodgers in two innings and that was the ball game. The Cubs added a run in the second (3 – 0 lead) and then Contreras and Rizzo hit solo home runs in the fourth and fifth innings for the final score of 5 – 0. The Dodgers got a second hit in the eighth, but Chapman came in and got a double play. Wonderful game by Hendricks.

Extra innings:
I really get jaundiced by all of the "know-it-all" baseball, commentators and announcers. Joe Buck is a good example of the type. He's a slick talking, always running his mouth about the great Clayton Kershaw, who really is good. He referred to Kershaw as the Dodger "Ace," the stopper, the go-to-guy, and other platitudes ad nauseum! If one swallowed Buck's line of reasoning, it was a foregone conclusion that the Cubs were going to lose. Gene has

often remarked "I don't listen to those guys anyway, bottom line we know is much as they do, probably more." I don't want to be one of those guys who says "see I told you so," but for some reason, as I stated in Thursdays game write up, I fully expected the Cubs to beat him, Kershaw that is. In the first place, Hendricks continues to be underrated and secondly in game one the Cubs hit Kershaw pretty hard, but always right at someone. Furthermore Baez and Rizzo both just missed home runs. I'm usually not right on my hunches, but I was almost 100% sure they would get to him. They did, and now it's on to the World Series.

Today's baseball wisdom:

"What does a mama bear on the pill have in common with the World Series? No Cubs.
Harry Carey

Baseball history this date:

1997 – The coldest game in World Series history – Marlins versus Cleveland, 38°F.

Game: #173

Game: #1 – World Series
Date: Tuesday, October 25
Teams: Cubs @ Cleveland
Final: Cubs lose 6 – 0
Record: 110 – 62 – 1
World Series record: 0 – 1

V – mail: "The first game was a real downer for all of the Cub fans as they were soundly beaten by the Indians 6 – 0. We can only hope that they react like they did in the NLCS and come roaring back. Let's hope so."

Recap:
Was it "stage fright" or simply too much Corey Kluber? I think it was a bit of both, as Kluber fanned eight of the first nine batters he faced. Of course it didn't help matters later when Andrew Miller, Indians ace closer, escaped a bases-loaded no outs jam in the seventh. He also stranded runners at the corners in the eighth with the game still 3 – 0 at that point. Then Rondon gave up a three-run homer in the bottom of the eighth for the 6 – 0 win. The first-inning was a killer for Lester; with two outs and no one on he gave up a single and then two walks. (Oh those bases on balls!) A "dribbler" to third scored a run and to complete the disastrous inning, Lester plunked a guy that made it 2 – 0. Lester pitched well afterwards, going 4 2/3 innings allowing four hits, one run, a base on balls, six strikeouts, but it was too late.

Extra innings:
There really isn't much to say concerning the rest of the game. Of course the writers carried on and on about Cleveland; blah, blah, blah. They focused on Terry Francona, who is a good manager, and he is now 9 – 0 in World Series appearances. Yes, that's pretty impressive, but they made it appear as if he was again going to win four straight. I will admit, as a fan who's team had just lost I quickly had my fill of all the "guys who know it all."

It's kind of incredible to think that the Cubs had not played in a World Series game since five weeks after Japan signed the instruments of surrender in 1945. Furthermore, these two teams, Cubs and Indians had combined for 174 seasons of futility. I'm not sure where the comment came from, but the statement was "America's biggest droughts since the Great Plains dust bowl of the 1930s…." That further irritated me, and I said to myself silently "no shit Sherlock." It's hard to communicate how glad I was that the above "really relevant and critical" information was shared! For Christ sakes, I'm really "honked off" about the game and I don't want to hear any of that crap!

Today's baseball wisdom:

"Some day the Cubs are going to be in the World Series."
Harry Caray

Baseball history this date:

1887 – The Detroit Wolverines of National League defeat the St. Louis Browns, of the American Association 10 games to 5 in the World Series.*
*(The modern World Series began in 1903)

Game: #174

Game: #2 – World Series
Date: Wednesday, October 26
Teams: Cubs/Cleveland
Final: Cubs win 5 – 1
World Series record: 1 – 1

V – mail: "Great pitching by Jake and the relievers as the Cubs win 5 – 1. Multiple hits by Zobrist, Rizzo and Schwarber led the Cubs to a victory. Now on to Chicago!!!"

Recap:
The key players of the game, in my opinion, were Arrieta and Schwarber. Although Arrieta was scary wild in the first inning as he walked two and threw pitches way high, way low, way inside, and way outside, he was still very dominant carrying a no-hitter into the sixth inning. A double, a ground out and a wild pitch scored Cleveland's only run. With the score 1 – 0 in the third and two out Schwarber singled in a run for a 2 – 0 lead. In my view, again only my opinion, it was a key point in the game, not only because of the run, but it really demonstrated Maddon's confidence and baseball wisdom to insert Schwarber into the lineup. Then again the fifth he singled in the fourth run. Every run is critical of course, but with Schwarber literally missing the entire year (from April 7th I believe) for him to knock in two runs was a huge psychological boost for the Cubs. Mike Montgomery was terrific for Arrieta as he pitched two innings, allowed two hits, one walk and had four strikeouts. Chapman did his thing in 1 1/3 innings, striking out two, but also issuing a walk, I think just to make it interesting. Ha!

Extra innings:
Today the sports writers had little to say about the Indians. I suppose that's how they do their job, "glom onto the highlights" for us peons so we really understand what happened. Do I sound a little hostile here? Well I think I am, as I just can't stand "hot shot" Joe Buck on TV so I have to turn the sound off. Thus the broadcast is silent for me, like I am deaf. Surprisingly, I find it rather enjoyable, no interference from those yokels in the "peanut gallery."

Today's baseball wisdom:
"You just don't accidentally show up in the World Series."
Derek Jeter

Baseball history this date:

1924 – The White Sox beat the New York Giants in Dublin, Ireland with less than 20 fans in attendance.*

*(Owner Charles Comiskey had taken his "pals", that is players, managers, and the media on a world junket.

The group was known as the "Woodland Bards," as they fished, hunted, and caroused out of a cabin in Wisconsin)

Game: #175

Game: #3 – World Series
Date: Friday, October 28
Teams: Cubs @ Cleveland
Final: Cubs lose 1 – 0
Record: 111 – 63 – 1
World Series record: 1 – 2

V – mail: "The name of this game was pitching and defense, as the Indians prevailed 1 – 0. The Cubs had their chances as they had runners in scoring position on at least three occasions, but could not get the big hit when needed. Now we are down to four games and have to win three of them, just like the NLCS."

Recap:
37 year old Coco Crisp had a pinch-hit single in the seventh inning off of Carl Edwards for the only run, the winning run of the game as the Cubs fell 1 – 0. It was a tough loss as the Cubs had runners in scoring position in the second, fifth, seventh and ninth innings and were unable to get a hit to score a run. In fact they had runners on second and third with two outs in the ninth inning. Javier Baez made the last out in the second, fifth and ninth innings. He has been absolutely terrible in his at-bats this series, swinging wildly at pitches, (some in the dirt, others a foot outside) that aren't anywhere near the strike zone. He had played so well in the postseason up to now, but he has seemed to revert back to his early problems in his career, swinging at every pitch thrown no matter where it was. No one else is hitting, but his at-bats are becoming an automatic out.

Extra innings:
I am really concerned about the Cubs hitting, especially the young guys, Baez, Russell, Contreras, Soler, and even Bryant. Bob Brenly, announcer for the Diamondbacks, and former major league manager, stated before the playoffs had begun that a real potential weakness for the Cubs was their lineup of "easy outs." He said if pitchers miss their spots the Cubs will make them pay; however if they hit their spots, there are many easy outs in the lineup. I hope he is not totally prophetic.

Today' baseball wisdom:

"A baseball game is simply a nervous breakdown divided into nine innings."
Earl Wilson

Baseball history this date:

2015 – The longest ever first baseball game of a World Series, five hours and 9 minutes, between the Kansas City Royals and the New York Mets. Kansas City won 5 – 4 in 14 innings.*

*(Actually the game started on the 27th, but ended at 1:18 AM the 28th)

Game: #176

Game: #4 – World Series
Date: Saturday, October 29
Teams: Cubs @ Cleveland
Final: Cubs lose 7 – 2
Record: 111 – 64 – 01
World Series record: 1 – 3

V – mail: "The Cubs played a sloppy game as they allowed runs on errors early in the game and could not rebound. They seemed to be frustrated as they could not get any hits to mount any kind of rally. They lost 7 – 2 and now have to win the next three games. They have done that before."

Recap:
The Cubs are now literally between that proverbial "rock and a hard place." Although they scored first (first inning) and the broadcasters immediately reminded us with the statistic that the team that scored first was 11 – 0 in the playoffs, that fact went out the window in the second inning. A home run and two errors by Kris Bryant and the score was 2 – 1 in favor of the "bad guys." Cleveland added a run in the third, another run in the fifth, and then the "killer," a three-run blast in the seventh that put the game out of reach. Lackey wasn't too bad, giving up two earned runs in five innings, but Montgomery, Wood, and Grimm gave up four more. Once again the Cubs young guns were only 1 – 16. That simply won't work if they are to have any chance of winning the series.

Extra innings:
I couldn't watch the game after the score was 4 – 1 as the Cubs hitting was abysmal! So I turned on the University of Arizona football homecoming game against Stanford and watched an equally pathetic offensive performance by the Wildcats, getting blown out 34 – 10. The Wildcats, once noted for their vaunted passing attack completed 5, yes I said 5, passes the entire damn game. But back to the issue more relevant for this tirade, the Cubs and Indians, I began to think about "booze" to deaden the pain. I can't drink alcohol like it used to when I was younger (my mother used to say my misspent youth) but if I could, I'd probably try to polish off a fifth of single malt scotch whisky. Glenmorangie would be an excellent choice to obliterate the pain.

Today's baseball wisdom:

"Baseball gives you every chance to be great. Then it puts every pressure on you prove that you haven't got what it takes."
Joe Garagiola

Baseball history this date:

1889 – The New York Giants, (National League), beat the Brooklyn Bridegrooms, (American Association) 6 – 3 games in the World Series. The game had a seventh inning stretch after someone yelled, "stretch for luck."

A Century-Long Journey to the Day of Redemption

Game: #177

Game: #5 – World Series
Date: Sunday, October 30
Teams: Cubs @ Cleveland
Final: Cubs win 3 – 2
Record: 112 – 64 – 1
World Series record: 2 – 3

V – mail: "Another great pitching job by Jon Lester and Chapman took the Cubs to a 3 – 2 victory in the fifth game. Actually it was David Ross who drove in the winning run. It was his last game at Wrigley Field."

Recap:
Well it was, "do or die" and the Cubs were (barely) able to "do!" Chapman came on in the seventh inning and got an 8 – out save, the first of his major league career. (Eight outs that is). Cleveland got a home run in the second inning for a 1 – 0 lead and I thought oh no! However the Cubs scored three in the fourth. Bryant hit a home run, Rizzo added a double, Russell singled, and old David Ross got the game-winning sacrifice fly with a bases-loaded and one out. But that was it for the Cubs, as they got one lousy hit after the three run fourth inning. The Cubs struck out 14 times with Baez and Heyward whiffing three times each. All of a sudden, Baez looks horrible at the plate. What a change, when he was really the star of NLCS against the Dodgers, not only with his exceptional fielding but also his timely hitting. It's hard to believe he has gone into such a "funk." Lester pitched well, going six innings allowing four hits and two earned runs. Carl Edwards got one out and Chapman was super.

Extra innings:
One sportswriter said, "the Cubs have now gained the road field advantage." There are teams that have won games 6 and 7 on the road to win the series. The 1985 Kansas City Royals did it, beating the St. Louis Cardinals, and in 1979 the Pirates did it, beating the Baltimore Orioles. Now it's about time for another team to win games 6 and 7 in Cleveland for the title! I've decided that I'm going to assume that they are going to win it all, no matter what I say after this statement.

Today's baseball wisdom:

"All ballplayers want to end up their career with the Cubs, Giants or the Yankees. They just can't help it."
Dizzy Dean

Baseball history this date:

1945 – Branch Rickey signs Jackie Robinson to a Montreal Royals contract. (The Brooklyn Dodgers farm club)

Game: #178

Game: #6 – World Series
Date: Tuesday, November 1
Teams: Cubs @ Cleveland
Final: Cubs win 9 – 3
Record: 113 – 64 – 1
World Series record: 3 – 3

V – mail: "We can only hope the Cubs bats stay as strong tonight as they were yesterday. (Gene's v-mail arrived 11/2/16). They banged out three home runs and went on to win 9 – 3. By scoring three runs in the first inning they gave Jake enough of a lead and he got the win. So now here we are down to the final game of the year. Anything can happen in baseball, but if the Cubs play the way they have all year we could be happy one more time. Let's hope so."

Recap:
Yes, the Cubs scored three in the first inning and four more in the third as Addison Russell hit a bases-loaded home run. Cleveland scored single runs in the fourth, fifth, and ninth innings, but Rizzo belted a two-run shot in the ninth for a 9 – 2 lead, with the final score being 9 – 3. Russell became the second youngest player in major league history at age 22 to hit a grand slam in the World Series. The youngest (while I remember) was my all-time baseball hero, a fellow named Mickey Charles Mantle, who at age 21 hit a slam against the Brooklyn Dodgers in 1953 World Series. Overall the Cubs had 13 hits; Bryant had 4, and Rizzo, Russell, and Zobrist 2 each. The final game is tonight as I'm writing this on November 2.

Extra innings:
I was really curious and a bit perturbed about a decision that Maddon made in bringing Chapman into the game with two outs in the seventh inning. The Cubs are leading 7 – 2 and have guys like Grimm and especially Rondon in the bullpen. Instead, he goes to Aroldis, a move that neither Gene or I could understand and frankly didn't like. Chapman closed the game on Sunday, but he threw 42 pitches, and then for game six he threw 20 more for a total of 62. That's a lot of pitches for a guy throwing 100 miles an hour or faster. Oh well, Maddon is the manager, but Rondon's absence is puzzling.

Today's baseball wisdom:
"A manager has his cards dealt to him and he must play them."
Miller Huggins

Baseball history this date:

1951 – The Brooklyn Dodger catcher Roy Campanella wins the first of his three national league MVP's.

Game: #179

Game: #7 – World Series
Date: Wednesday, November 2
Teams: Cubs @ Cleveland
Final: Cubs win 8 – 7 – (10 innings) World Series Champions!
Record: 114 – 64 – 1
World Series record: 4 – 3 Again, World Series Champions!

V – mail: "The Cubs are the World Series Champions! Technically it was a sloppy played game that was really miss-managed, as was the game before. I can put up with 2 out of 114 and I am just glad they pulled it out. I am not sure if I really have grabbed the significance of this yet, as 63 years of frustration is hard to lose. There were a lot of heroes on this team, a very humble group who really deserved to be world champions. 8 -7 in 10 innings was the final score, with eight different guys driving in a run. Chapman was the winning pitcher, with Montgomery getting the save, and Zobrist the MVP. A night to remember for all Cubs fans."

Recap:
Wow, Dexter Fowler led off the game with a home run, the first player ever to lead off with a home run in the "winner-take-all" game. The Indians tied it 1 – 1 in the third, but the Cubs scored two in the fourth and two in the fifth for a 5 – 1 lead. I was so nervous about the game I didn't start watching until Lester relieved Hendricks in the fifth with two on. Lester promptly threw a wild pitch allowing both runners to score and it's now 5 – 3. Then a great old guy, David Ross homered in the sixth for a 6 – 3 Cub lead. Little did any Cub fan realize at the time, including myself, that if Ross had not hit the home run the Cubs would have lost the game in the eighth inning. Holy cow! With two out in the Indians' eighth Maddon brought in Chapman. I thought it was a bad move. Well, a double made it 6-4 and then Chapman threw a "gopher ball" to Rajai Davis and I yelled " well I'll be a son of a bitch," as the game was tied 6 – 6. My heart sank, oh so close, and I hadn't watched it earlier because I thought I was a jinx for them. And now this happens, will they blow it again, and I think, maybe I am a jinx. Chapman got through the ninth. So now it's going to be extra innings. But before the 10th inning begins rain starts to fall, and the umpires call the game for about a 20 minute delay. I'm a wreck! In the Cubs clubhouse Jason Heyward gathers the team and essentially communicates to them that we've come this far, let's finish it! They must have gotten the message. In the Cubs 10th (in my mind a real hero of the series, maybe his presence even more

important than Zobrist winning the MVP), Schwarber singles to start off the inning. Bryant hits a deep drive to center and Albert Almora running for Schwarber takes second. The Indians walk Rizzo, but Zobrist doubles and it's 7 – 6 Cubs. Then hallelujah "miggy" Montero singles in run number eight. The Cubs did give up a run in the 10th but held on for their first title in 100 years. The rain; sometimes I fantasize that the good Lord must be a Cub fan, as he sent a brief shower to allow the Cubs to relax and gather themselves. It could be true, don't you think.

Extra innings:

For all of you loyal Cub fans and anyone else who loves baseball now you can see that Gene and I were correct second-guessing Maddon for bringing Chapman in game six leading 7 – 2. Chapman was obviously "pooped" and gave up three hits and two runs. Gene and I both wondered and discussed where were Rondon and Strop, two guys that Maddon relied on heavily during the season. Maddon had been terrific all season in managing the team and shuffling players in and out, but in my opinion, he really "dodged a bullet" twice in this game. First by pulling Hendricks in the fifth inning and pulling Lester in the eighth. But they won, so all is forgiven. Had they lost I would had been beside myself for the whole damn year! Maybe even sent Maddon an obscene e-mail. Just kidding, but I would have been "torqued."

On the matter of forgiveness, anyone who reads this work will observe how critical I have been of Jason Heyward, (at times darn right mean and nasty) in his struggles with hitting. Obviously it isn't the only key to winning as defense, pitching, and a quality called leadership must also be in the mixture. Jason gathering his teammates together during the rain delay clearly exemplified this latter ingredient in the formula for winning. In proofing the document it occurred to me that (per Jay Leno) I was "really out of line" with all my "ragging" on the guy. So this is to say, "I apologize Jason, I hope you can forgive me."

Today's baseball wisdom:

"The best possible thing in baseball is winning the World Series. The second best thing is losing the World Series."
Tommy Lasorda

Baseball history this date:

2016 – The Chicago Cubs defeat the Cleveland Indians 8 – 7 in seven games and are the World Series Champions!

Epilogue

Paul Harvey, long time radio broadcaster from Chicago, with a very distinctive style of giving us the news, invariably included a story that we listeners often felt we knew how the story would end. Not so, for seemingly at the conclusion of the piece, he would pause and then say, "and now for the rest of the story." Well, friends, comrades, and all you enlightened followers of the Cubs, "this is the rest of the story!"

Epilogue: Webster says it's a short speech or poem at the end of a play, or a concluding statement of a novel to complete the plan. For this journal I intended it to mean, "there ain't no more!" Whatever, it seemed "cool" to end this endeavor with a section entitled Epilogue!

People who I think are good writers, (of course those that I read) like James Lee Burke, David McCullough, Eric Metaxis, Ken Follett, Doris Kearns Goodwin, Daniel Silva, the late Stephen Ambrose and others have a penchant (maybe an obligation) to acknowledge, thank and give credit to almost everyone except their next-door neighbor and the tax man. I suppose it's an accepted standard of the industry for those we consider "Masters of the pen." Not being a member of that elite fraternity, I don't have to follow suit, nor do I feel inclined to do so. However, there are a few kudos I would offer.

#1) Thanks to the Chicago Cubs for making it happen after 108 years. The "Voice" (a.k.a. Gene Shippy) and I started on Monday, April 4, 2016 with high hopes and great expectations and were rewarded with a World Series Championship on Wednesday, November 2, 2016. Hallelujah!

#2) Thanks To the "Voice," whom you all now know, for his steadfast support, the V – mails that he never missed, and his defense of struggling Cubbies when I railed against their failings. We had our disagreements on strategies of the game and although we most often resolved our differences, privately, we probably both thought we were right, at least 50% of the time. We had endless BS sessions often after each win, as he phoned after every win!

#3) To my son Matthew, not a huge baseball fan, who usually had something to say after a Cub win. After Gene called I would often begin raving on about things like, wow the lead is now seven, eleven, or even fifteen games. After tolerating my stream of platitudes about how wonderful the Cubs were doing, he would smile (or maybe it was a smirk), exit the room or even leave the house proclaiming rather loudly (rather insincerely I thought) "yes, yes, this is the year, it's going to happen, they're going all the way!" Well, now I can forgive him for his sarcasm, as I can now respond "you're damn right they did go all the way." So there!

I know that deep down in his heart he was really pulling for the Cubs.

He had one more wisecrack, I guess I'd call it a "zinger" for me. I was writing this section in late November and was also was trying to come up with a title for the document. Over morning coffee, he said "hey I have a good title for you." "Really," I said, "what do you think?" He gave me sort of a Machiavellian grin and replied, "just keep it simple, how about Holy Crap it Was the Year." I cleaned up the wording a bit and declined his suggestion.

#4) Marlys, my wife, a devout Diamondback fan who suffered through a tough year for the snakes, was a great sport, staying faithful to her team, but also pulling for the Cubs. She even had the courage to almost remain neutral when the Cubs and the Diamondbacks played. She also gave me "lots of grief" for being so negative when things didn't go well for the Cubs. "Why aren't you a positive, loyal fan like Gene?" Well maybe there was a modicum of truth in her perception (just a little though).

#5) I'd like to give thanks to the good Lord for my 78th year in 2016 that allowed me to witness, as us Cub fans say "an historic event." I've had many blessings, and a few rough spots along the way, but thankfully I was still around, when throughout the land we heard it exclaimed, "the Chicago Cubs are the 2016 World Champions of Baseball."

It has been said that life is like a baseball game, and we never know how long we will play; what day and what inning we will make our last out. Just remember my friends, through the lens of a baseball aficionado, that mother nature always gets the final at-bat.

A Final Thought

I love humor and I firmly believe that stories, sayings, events and incidents that bring laughter and merriment into our lives can be a key to living a more healthful, stress-free life.

This past year our Monday morning bagel group, euphemistically called, "the Monday Morning Irregulars" lost a friend, Ron Swanson, who was in my opinion, one of, if not at the top of the list in telling humorous stories. He was a master of the craft. One morning over coffee he told this anecdote. I think it is appropriate to include it here for all lovers of baseball and in the memory of Ron Swanson. He was, as my father would say about someone he admired, "well, he was really quite a guy." Thanks for your memory Ron.

-Baseball In Heaven-

Two great friends, one named Jim and the other named Jon loved baseball. They grew up together playing T- ball, little league, high school, college and even "old-timers" ball. One day after they had reached their 80s, Jim said to Jon, "you know one of these days one of us is going to pass on, maybe soon. Can we make a pact that whoever goes first (and hopefully gets to heaven) will somehow get a message back if there is baseball in heaven?"

"Sounds great to me," said Jon.

Not long after, Jim did pass away. Jon waited patiently and sure enough one day, as if in a dream, Jim spoke to him.

"Jon, Jon, it's true and wonderful, there is baseball in heaven, and we play every day. It's always Sunny and bright and we have great crowds; but I have good news and bad news for you."

Jon said, "but if there's baseball every day in heaven what could be the bad news?"

Jim replied, "well Jon, we are playing a doubleheader tomorrow, and you are the starting pitcher for the second game!"

Baseball Wisdom
– Contributors –

Game # Name:

1. Gene Shippy
2. Bob Uecker
3. Joe Garagiola
4. Rocky Bridges
5. Satchel Paige
6. Babe Ruth
7. Yogi Berra
8. Joe Garagiola
9. Gil Hodges
10. Lou Gehrig
11. Dizzy Dean
12. Casey Stengel
13. Branch Rickey
14. Vin Scully
15. Yogi Berra
16. Bobo Newsom
17. Bob Uecker
18. Dominican baseball players
19. Yogi Berra
20. Casey Stengel
21. Bob Uecker
22. Pete Rose
23. Pepper Martin
24. Ty Cobb
25. Satchel Paige
26. Yogi Berra
27. Casey Stengel
28. Gabby Hartnett
29. Pete Rose
30. David letterman
31. Joe McCarthy
32. Ernie Banks
33. Yogi Berra
34. Matt Kloepping
35. Dizzy Dean
36. Satchel Paige
37. Casey Stengel
38. Joe Garagiola
39. Bob Uecker
40. Tim McCarver
41. Mickey Mantle
42. Kent Kloepping
43. Alan Bannister

Game # Name:

44. Lefty Gomez
45. Yogi Berra
46. Casey Stengel
47. Tommy Lasorda
48. Harvey Haddix
49. Warren Spahn
50. Bob Uecker
51. Tommy Lasorda
52. Satchel Paige
53. Unknown
54. Yogi Berra
55. Sparky Anderson
56. Bob Uecker
57. Casey Stengel
58. Alvin Dark
59. Mickey Mantle
60. Babe Ruth
61. Catfish Hunter
62. Casey Stengel
63. Frankie Frisch
64. Joe Garagiola
65. Vince Lombardi
66. Jim Murray
67. Bob Uecker
68. Bob Gibson
69. Ernie Banks
70. Casey Stengel
71. Joe Garagiola
72. Unknown
73. Ted Lyons
74. Yogi Berra
75. Babe Ruth
76. Bob Uecker
77. Casey Stengel
78. Don Meredith
79. Letter to the manager of Washington Senators
80. Andy Van Slyke
81. Unknown
82. Jackie Robinson
83. Bob Feller
84. Whitey Herzog
85. Vince Lombardi

Game # Name:

86. George Brett
87. Gene Mauch
88. Casey Stengel
89. Billy Crystal
90. Harry Caray
91. Dizzy Dean
92. Casey Stengel
93. Lon Simmons
94. Harry Caray
95. Yogi Berra
96. Leo Durocher
97. Dedicated to Vernelle Kohn
98. Red Barber
99. Sandy Koufax
100. Satchel Paige
101. Joe Garagiola
102. Willie Keeler
103. Yogi Berra
104. Leo Durocher
105. Greg Maddux
106. Frank Sullivan
107. Yogi Berra
108. Mickey Rivers
109. Earl Weaver
110. Warren Spahn
111. Sandy Koufax
112. Yogi Berra
113. Dan Quisenberry
114. Earl Weaver
115. Bob Uecker
116. Yogi Berra
117. Bob Uecker
118. Satchel Paige
119. Tommy Lasorda
120. Joe Adcock
121. Earl Weaver
122. Honus Wagner
123. Joe Garagiola
124. Casey Stengel
125. Casey Stengel
126. Bob Gibson or Bob lemon
127. Thomas Swyers

Game# Name:

128. Harry Caray
129. Vin Scully
130. Leo Durocher
131. Sandy Koufax
132. Pee Wee Reese
133. Mickey mantle
134. Satchel Paige
135. Yogi Berra
136. Bob Feller
137. Ernie Banks
138. Joe Garagiola
Sept. 8 (no game) Rogers Hornsby
139. Jackie Robinson
140. Dizzy Dean
141. Jimmy Fallon
142. Bill Virdon
143. Dan Quisenberry
144. Yogi Berra
145. Joe Garagiola
146. Joaquin Andujar
147. George will
148. Bob Uecker
149. Jim Murray
150. Willie Stargell
151. Casey Stengel
152. Yogi Berra
153. Doug Harvey
154. Jim Bouton
155. Satchell Paige
156. Dizzy Dean
157. Mickey Rivers
158. Leo Durocher
159. Earl Weaver
160. Babe Ruth
161. Hank Aaron
162. Jackie Robinson
163. Mickey Mantle
164. Sparky Anderson
165. Harry Reasoner
166. Babe Ruth
167. Pete Rose
168. Whitey Ford
169. Warren Spahn

A Century-Long Journey to the Day of Redemption

Game #	Name:
169.	Warren Spahn
170.	Vince Lombardi
171.	Yogi Berra
172.	Harry Caray
173.	Harry Caray
174.	Derek Jeter
175.	Earl Wilson
176.	Joe Garagiola
177.	Dizzy Dean
178.	Miller Huggins
179.	Tommy Lasorda

www.ingramcontent.com/pod-product-compliance
Lightning Source LLC
Chambersburg PA
CBHW071858290426
44110CB00013B/1192